27 Hours

Gerald C. Anderson Publishing – August 28, 2012, July 8, 2014

Jaurin
Thank you for supporting my ministry
God Bless!

I would like to take a minute to thank the below listed contributors to 27 Hours. Without their assistance this book would not have been possible.

27 Hours Contributors:

Beryl Brackett
Anthony Radford
Jacqueline Ross
Shalana Reeves

Cover designed by Mad House Designs Inc. Email: madhousedesignsinc@gmail.com

Cover photography by Eye Dream Studio Email: eyedreamstudio@hotmail.com

Cover model: Shenese Caldwell Email: Shenese.caldwell@gmail.com Twitter: @shenesecaldwell

27 Hours is

Dedicated to

Mattie B. Jones

January 19, 1937 to June 12, 2011

We love you Aunt Mattie!

XXVII

I am writing this note to anyone who might find it, but the reality is no one will survive the asteroid strike. I guess I'm just kidding myself; hoping that my letter could float in space until someone finds it. If they do they won't even understand English. Oh well, if they do find it and can read it, then and only then will they know what happened to Earth.

Today is December 20, 2012 and we have 38 hours until the end of the world. I am sitting behind my desk in the Oval Office contemplating what we are doing to prevent this catastrophe from happening. Earth's greatest minds are making one last attempt to stop this asteroid from hitting us; but I fear it will be to no avail.

What am I going to say to the American people?

Our final attempt at destroying the asteroid was going as planned, but none of the world leaders had much hope that it would succeed. Every attempt to avert this catastrophe has failed. In fact, one attempt even hastened its approach.

For a year the world leaders deceived our people about the asteroid. Surprisingly, we managed to keep it a secret. But now the people needed to be told. They had to be told. I felt they needed the opportunity to say their final goodbyes. After all, the leaders of the world had been given that chance; so the people should get a chance as well.

My thoughts were interrupted when, my Chairman of the Joint Chiefs of Staff, Paul Wissenhut, and my vice president, Joe Simpson, entered. They were here to break the news that I already suspected. I put down my pen as both men walked to the front of my desk and stopped.

Vice President Simpson spoke…his voice was a deep, solemn tone and all he said was, "It didn't work." The sadness in his voice riveted around the office. I looked down at my desk and gathered my thoughts. I told them to find out what time the world leaders would meet. I knew it was time Earth's people found out what we already knew.

As they left the room I sat up in my chair, placed my head in my hands, and put my elbows on top of the desk. All I could do was pray.

XXVI

It was 36 hours to the end of the world. Earth's leaders had gathered to discuss the plan. They were meeting at the United Nations building in New York City. President Murphy enjoyed meeting in New York City. He preferred it over any other place.

As President Murphy walked into the building the level of security impressed him. He was glad there was no press involvement. He went into the briefing room and stood. He looked around at his contemporaries from around the world and then glanced down at his watch. The time was drawing near.

The UN Secretary General, Alan Paige, stood up and moved towards the podium. President Murphy watched intently as he gathered himself in preparation to speak.

He began, "As you all know, we now have 36 hours until the deadline. In one hour we will set forth our final action plan, freezing prices around the world. Our cover story will be that the countries of the G8 have gone broke. Each country represented—the United States, the United Kingdom, France, Italy, Germany, Russia, Canada, and Japan—will make this announcement to their respective citizens.

"Next, and approximately one hour later, you will

announce that all transportation outlets are closed. Airplanes will be grounded, no trains will be allowed to move, and entrances into and out of all major cities will be blocked to the best of our ability.

"Last, and with 33 hours remaining, we will institute martial law throughout our major cities. The military will move in and control any looting that may take place once the announcements have been made. Instituting martial law at the 33-hour point will give us 6 hours to gain control of our cities and the situation overall.

"At 3:00 Eastern Standard Time, we will make the Extinction Level Event announcement from here to the world." Then he paused for a moment. President Murphy knew he was "letting" the room take it all in. No one appeared to be surprised by these announcements. President Murphy knew his worries would begin when the people of the United States found out what the leaders already knew.

The secretary general continued, "These measures need to be in place prior to informing the world of the devastation it faces. With these measures in place, law enforcement officials should have an easier time maintaining control over their cities."

"I cannot stress enough the importance of maintaining order in these last hours. Remember, we have had a year to absorb the fact that the world could, and now will, end. The rest of the world will have just over a day to do the same."

"People will act totally out of character. Some will question their beliefs. Some will feel they can do anything they wish, while others may even take their own lives."

"Absolute control may be impossible, but we must do our best. I encourage all of you to stick to the cover story and not release any information until it is scheduled to be released. You all have a great responsibility, and there is no one better suited for the job than you.
Your people elected you to lead them and make decisions that are in their best interests. You have done that, and you should never question that you did your best."

"My prayers go out to each of you and your people. God bless all of you." He stepped away from the podium and returned to his seat. A man who Murphy did not recognize announced, "If there are any questions we can entertain them now."

President Murphy looked around the room. No one had any questions. He suspected that, like him, they all had known that this plan would come since the last effort to save Earth failed.

President Murphy rose, and his entourage of aides and Secret Service quickly followed after. They needed to get back to Washington DC to prepare to make the announcements specified by the secretary general.

XXV

Reverend C. Wilson Collins was a fearless leader of God. He believed that God was real and alive and that his son, Jesus, had died for his sins. No one could tell him otherwise. He led his church with a passion for Christ and was commonly referred to as "being on fire for the Lord." He was also known as an honorable man who was above reproach.

As he usually does, Reverend Collins was up early in the morning. He had just returned home from a five-mile run, and now his wife, Martha, was in the kitchen making breakfast for him.

"Good morning, dear. How was your run," she asked?

Reverend Collins replied, "It was great as usual. The morning air was invigorating. Praise the Lord!"

She responded, "Praise Him, Pastor!"

Reverend Collins tried to hug his wife, but she pushed him away. She said, "Don't put your sweaty body on me. I love you, but there are some boundaries. Go shower, old man."

He couldn't help but laugh when he saw the smile on her face. He laughed with her. Then he said with emphasis, "Who you calling *old*?" Reverend Collins went upstairs

6

and prepared to shower. He turned on the television as he gathered his clothes together. A news report caught his attention. "It is believed that the world leaders are withholding a major story from the press and the people…"

Reverend Collins asked rhetorically, "So what else is new?"

***

William "Bill" Walker was driving to work as normal. He was a federal government employee who was most admired for his strong Christian beliefs. Many of his friends and colleagues came to him for spiritual advice because they knew they would get a Biblical answer instead of a worldly response.

Bill's friends were always conscious not to curse in front of him because they respected his Christianity. His closest friend, Teddy, worked at the job with him. They often talked about world events and sports, but they rarely talked about religion.

Bill knew Teddy had gone to church in the past, but he had strayed away with no intention of returning. The difference in religious beliefs didn't stop them from being the best of friends. Bill and Teddy respected each other's beliefs and had maintained their friendship throughout the years. Teddy tried to get Bill to go to clubs with him, and Bill always resisted. Bill tried to get Teddy to go to church, and Teddy just laughed.

Today, Bill was deep in thought, anticipating the day's events. He found himself doing what he usually did, praying to God for another good day. A song came on the radio, causing Bill to praise the name of the Lord.

He shouted, "Praise the Lord!" Then he looked at the other cars around him and laughed to himself. He knew the other drivers on the road were probably wondering what was wrong with him. This seemed to happen to Bill every day when he drove to work. But he loved bringing his friend Jesus to work with him.

***

Contrary to how she felt the day before, Lisa woke up bright and early, happy for the first time in a long while. The news that she was HIV positive had caused her spirits to sink to their lowest level in her life. But last night that had all changed after her meeting at her new church.

Now she felt like a new person. At the encouragement of a friend and coworker, Lisa had gone to see Reverend Collins at the Living Word Ministries Church. It had been the most moving meeting she'd ever attended. She had talked to Reverend Collins and given her life to Christ. Now she felt her slate was clean and that she could start all over again.

She stood in the middle of her apartment and shouted out

loud, "God so loved me…that He gave His only begotten son, Jesus!" She smiled and continued getting herself together for work. As she was getting ready she reminisced about her childhood. Growing up, she knew nothing of Jesus.

At age 15, she started having sex but it wasn't enough. She then started experimenting with drugs and alcohol. She remembered how the drugs made it easier for her to say 'yes' to a boy she didn't even love.
He had the drugs and that's all that mattered to her at the time. The drugs made her feel that all of her problems went away. Now she knew it was only a temporary fix but back then she
thought it was all she needed. She hated her home. Her parents weren't saved.

When she was a child her mother used to take her to a strange man's house and make her watch television while they were upstairs. At the time she didn't know what they were doing. Later she realized that her mother was carrying on an affair.

When she realized it, she was sickened by the discovery. She asked her what was going on and her mother told her to mind her own business. She remembered the year she started high school. She finally got up the nerve to tell her father about her mother. She remembered skipping her last class and going home early one day.

As she was walking home she thought about how she was

going to tell her father. She decided to come straight out and tell him. She rushed into the house and yelled, *"Daddy! Daddy!"*
Lisa heard nothing in reply. She searched around downstairs and didn't see her father. His truck was in the driveway so he had to be around. He wasn't in the back yard either. She remembered yelling again and again, *"Daddy, where are you?"*

She ran upstairs and heard some sounds mixed with music coming from her parent's bedroom. She went upstairs and slowly opened the door. Lisa remembered that awful feeling in the gut of her stomach as she saw her father in bed with her mother's best friend. She ran down the stairs and out of the house.

Lisa couldn't remember how far she ran but she ran until she couldn't run anymore. When she stopped she wanted to run out into traffic and end her life. Now she was glad she didn't.
As a teenager, the behavior of her parents confused Lisa. When she returned her parents were arguing. Shortly after that day her father left. She'd only seen him once since that day. Lisa decided that sex was just for fun and amusement. She believed that everyone had sex whenever they wanted, with whomever they wanted.

It was nothing special. To Lisa love didn't equate with sex. To her sex was nothing but a tool for fun and amusement. Deep inside she knew it wasn't true. When she couldn't bring herself to have sex freely she turned to drugs to ease her inhabitations. Lisa started with marijuana then graduated to crack. The drugs made her feel like she was away from it all.

At 20 she noticed a rash on her body and she started feeling feverish and tired. She went to her doctor and her doctor ran some tests. The look on her doctor's face said it all. Lisa knew the news was not going to be good. Her doctor told her that the results showed that she was positive for HIV.

The news devastated Lisa. She left the office distraught, again wanting to kill herself. Her co-worker and friend at work told her to go see Reverend Collins. She decided she had nothing to lose by talking to him, so she did. It was the best decision she'd ever made. Now she was happier than she had ever been in her life.

***

Roger and Samantha Stevens had been married for ten years. Their marriage had seen some ups and downs but they continued to trust in the Lord to lead them and guide them. Roger had become a strong man of God and he was determined to never give in to the ways of the world again. He was determined not give up on his marriage. Roger believed that if he did he would be giving up on God.

He sat in his home office thinking about the mistake he made that almost cost him his wife. He was thankful that he was married to a woman who was wise to consult God in her decisions. She could have left him but she didn't.

Instead she decided to consult Reverend Collins at the Living Word Ministries church. Now it was up to him to make things right. He took this day off so he could spend some quality time with Samantha and their two children. Roger planned to take his family to the park and then head down South to visit Samantha's parents.

After Roger finished praying he saw the news on the television. He turned up the volume. The reporter was saying the country was broke. *The end of times must be near. I'm glad we are true believers.*

His wife, Samantha broke his concentration, "Hi honey, about last night…"

Roger quickly interrupted, "Not a problem my love. I could never equal the forgiveness you handed out to me."

Samantha responded, "That doesn't make it right. I'm sorry for acting like a jerk."

Roger walked over to her as she was standing in the doorway. He took her into his arms. She eased into his arms as if she belonged nowhere else. Roger said softly, "Baby, let's just forget it."

She replied equally as soft, "Okay."

Roger asked, "Are the kids ready?"

Samantha answered peacefully, "Not quite. Give us about an hour."

Roger replied, "Okay, I know that means two."

She pushed away laughing.

He smiled and said, "You know it's true!"

She said emphasis, "Whatever!"

***

Vanessa James' marriage was one of deception. She went to church with her husband every Sunday and Bible study every Wednesday, but she no longer loved him and she believed he felt the same.

Vanessa became a professional at pretending to be happily married. She had become adept at fooling her fellow church members. Every Sunday Vanessa made it a point to shout and praise the Lord with such enthusiasm that it fooled most people into believing she was a true Christian.

Her husband, Johnny did the same. Every Sunday when she looks at him in the pulpit, she feels utter hatred for him. She still can't believe he cheated on her. She purposely dropped hints of her affairs. She knew it made her husband furious but it gave her satisfaction to see him angry.

Vanessa is the head usher on Reverend Collins' staff. Her husband, Johnny is a minister on Reverend Collins' staff. She remember how they fell out of love when Johnny was caught cheating. After she found out, Vanessa cried for days. Her friends encouraged her to get revenge by cheating on him.

At first, she couldn't bring herself to do it. But after several months, and constant encouraging from her friends, she did. Vanessa was so nervous the first time, but it felt good to her. She didn't love the man at all. She focused solely on revenge, and never looked back.

She often wondered about her neighbor, Samantha. Samantha told her about her husband cheating on her. Vanessa encouraged her to cheat on him, as she had done when her husband cheated.. She thought Samantha was stupid for trying to work out her marriage.

That morning Vanessa laid in her bed thinking about her life. They always slept in separate rooms. Johnny had told her that he had to leave early because he had a project at work that he needed to complete.

She didn't say anything because that gave her a window of opportunity she so desired. Vanessa was on the phone with her man, Calvin, who was the choir director at church.

Calvin asked, "Hey, why are you calling me so early? What will dude say?"

Vanessa answered seductively, "He's gone.. He left at three this morning. I'm all alone and feeling vulnerable." She felt Calvin's smile through the phone. He said, "I'll be right over."
Vanessa continued her seductive voice, "The door is open." She moaned and added, "Just come on in and up to my room, sweetheart."

***

Johnny rolled over and kissed Katrina on the lips. He left his house at three that morning, after telling Vanessa he had to finish an important project at work. Johnny whispered in Katrina's ear, "This is the best project I've ever worked on." They both laughed at their deception of Vanessa.

Katrina responded, "I couldn't keep my eyes off of you at church yesterday. You looked so fine in that nicely tailored blue suit." Johnny excitedly replied, "And you in that dress! You were kicking it baby.. I had to contain myself up there. All I could think about was three in the morning."

***

President Murphy was in his office waiting to be lead to the briefing room where he would make the first

15

announcement. He picked up the phone to make a call. He dialed the number and waited for someone to answer. He hoped someone would answer.

After three rings a voice answered softly, "Hello."

President Murphy cautiously replied, "Hi sweetheart. How are you?"

The voice responded, "Hi dad. I'm fine."

After a slight paused she continued, "Is this the day?"

President Murphy said, "Right to the point I see."

Marcie brazenly said, "Well, I haven't heard from you in months."

Pausing momentarily then she asked, "What did you expect from me?"

President Murphy answered, "You're right. I should have called long before this but there were a lot of things said the last time we spoke. Regardless, you should always know that I love you and your brother."

Marcie replied, "I never doubted your love for us dad, but I do feel the people had a right to know long before now."

President Murphy said, "Trust me, I do know that."
Marcie asked, "Have you called Tommy?"

President Murphy answered, "I tried a month ago but he didn't answer. I guess he doesn't want to talk to me."

Marcie said, "Let me try…"

The President's aid came in and said, "Sir, it's time."

President Murphy interrupted Marcie, "I can't right now sweetheart. I have to make the first announcement. I'll try you back later."

Marcie sighed and hung up the phone.

President Murphy was disappointed that she didn't understand. Sometimes his job required him to leave quickly and his two oldest children never came to terms with that. He rose and followed his aid out of the office.

XXIV

I was minutes away from stepping to the podium to tell the citizens of the United States that their country was broke. News had already leaked but I would have to confirm the rumor was true. It wasn't a lie; we were in fact broke from all the expenditures made to try and destroy the asteroid. However, knowing the whole truth and not telling them right away pained me deeply.

I stepped up to the podium with all eyes and ears focused on me. It was so early in the morning and I knew that most Americans were not going to watch the announcement. Most of them didn't even know about it.

I took a deep breath, and let out slowly. I looked over the room and the eyes of the news reporters were piercing.

I started, "Due to the continuing problems with our economy, we are forced to take some drastic actions in the hope of minimizing the damage and to help us begin on a path to recovery."

I paused for a second and continued, "The rumors you have heard over the past hour that the government of the United States is broke are true. We are in fact broke."

"Over the past year we have had some unexpected drains on our funds.. Efforts to decrease our spending have

18

failed.. To prevent us from divulging into a state of total poverty as a nation, I am instituting the Hampton Act effectively freezing all prices at their current amounts.. The freeze will take effect immediately and will last indefinitely."

I could feel the camera flashes across my face as the reporters began to rapidly take pictures and ask me questions. I raised my hand to calm the room.

I continued, "I do not have any answers to give you now. Please be patient and if you know how to pray, please do so for our country.. Thank you and God bless all of you." I turned and headed out of the room without taking any questions, but that didn't stop reporters from firing them at me until I was out of sight.

What will they say when they find out the rest of the story?

***

Johnny was sitting up in the bed.. He heard the news report that the United States was broke. Being a federal government employee, the news angered him. Katrina walked in and slid across the sheets to him.

She said, "Hey babe, what's got you so upset? It can't be me after what I just put on you!"
Johnny replied, "The President just said we're broke!"
Katrina shouted, "What? He gonna pay me!"

Johnny responded, "I know that's right. Hey, I better get

to the bank before my ball and chain. I need to get the money out of our joint account before she does."

Katrina gleeful said, "Yeah, get it. Then you can buy me something sweet with it."
Johnny responded, "Amen, sister!" Katrina shouted, "Hallelujah!"

***

Brittney Washington was an 18 year old college student at Central State University and a strong Christian woman. She stayed the course in her beliefs and did not give into peer pressure.
Brittney was on her way to class when her roommate, Mia Sanchez, stopped her at the door.

Mia shouted, "Brittney, come check this out."

Brittney put her books down and darted back to the living room. She asked, "What? I'm gonna be late."

Mia responded, "The President just froze all prices and said we're broke."

Brittney replied with disbelief, "You're kidding." Mia responded, "I wish."

They continued watching the news when the anchor woman interrupted.

She announced, "We're receiving reports from all over the world that all the countries of the G8 are freezing their prices. This is stacking up to be a bigger story than anything this world has ever experienced. It is believed that not only America is broke…the world is broke!"

"Wait," she continued, "Italy has just announced that in conjunction with the price freeze all commercial transportation has been frozen. Mark, this has got to be about more than our economy, wouldn't you agree?"

Mark answered, "Yes Janel, there has to be more to this than just the American economy or the world's economy for that matter. The President has a lot of questions to answer but none seem to be forthcoming. The White House is amazingly quiet today."

Janel interrupted, "Excuse me Mark, but we're getting a report from the White House. Let's go to our reporter on the scene. Alvin…what's developing?"

Brittney decided to sit down at this point. She was becoming increasingly concerned with each report. She had a nervous feeling inside of her that more was going on than expected.
Mia had started biting her fingernails. Brittney knew her roommate was equally nervous.

Al answered, "Well Janel we are minutes away from the Secretary of Transportation taking the podium. We can only imagine that he is going to do the same as the

Italians. Everyone here feels that with these synchronized announcements; something much bigger must be going on today."

Janel stated, "Al has anyone tried to ask…"

Al interrupted, "Wait Janel, the Secretary is taking the podium."

Secretary of Transportation Jim Border began his announcement, "As you may have already heard the Italian government has suspended all air and ground transportation within its borders. At this moment several other countries are doing the same and we will be one of those countries."

"Effective immediately all air and ground transportation is suspended. We are putting these measures in place to protect our citizens. With the state of the economy in the shape it is, we do not want people rushing to airports, train stations, or bus stations. The more we stay in place, the less confusion will be in the streets."

"Order is our priority, and to maintain order, we must keep people in one place. As with the President, I will not entertain any questions at this time. Thank you."

Brittney watched as reporters continued to try and ask questions anyway as the Secretary walked away. He did not make any moves to turn back. Brittney looked at Mia in disbelief.

Her new roommate was just as concerned. She didn't know much about Mia, since they hadn't roomed together long, but that look would have been noticeable on anyone's face.

Brittney broke the ice, "Instead of class, I'm going to church.

My parents will know what to do and they should be at church by now." Mia responded as she was getting her purse, "I'm going with you!"

She looked back and added, "I got nowhere else to go."

XXIII

Reverend Collins watched the news reports concerning the nation's economy and the suspension of transportation blaring across the television. He was particularly concerned by the report of people raiding grocery stores all over the world and stocking up on food. People feared the state of the world's economy would force them to starve. Reverend Collins suspected it was not the economy that was their problem.

He said under his breath, *There's more going on here than meets the eye!*

Reverend Collins was meeting with some of the members of his church who had come to their church seeking hope in what was shaping up as utter devastation for the world.

Martha asked Reverend Collins, "Rev, what are we gonna do? The whole world is broke."

Reverend Collins answered, "Sweetheart, we must keep our focus on God. He will protect us in all times.. The country may be broke but God isn't and that's where our help cometh from."

"Psalms one twenty-one and one says, '*I will lift up mine eyes unto the hills, from whence cometh my help. My help cometh from the Lord, which made Heaven and Earth.*'"

24

One of the members came up as Reverend Collins was speaking and asked, "Rev, we don't have the finances to help everyone. What about the church expenses?"

Reverend Collins answered, "Brother Richards, we are here to help others. God will see to our expenses. We can't concern ourselves with that kind of stuff. The needs of the people must and will come first.. These are the times where the tithes and offerings from the people will help the people."

Brother Richards replied, "I don't know Rev."

Reverend Collins responded, "Don't trust me brother, but do trust God."

Brother Richards said, "Amen Rev. You always know what to do."

Another member, Desirae, asked, "Do you think this is actually the truth or is there more to this than we're being told?"

Dave, an usher in the church, answered, "I think we'll hear more in the next few hours. There's something rotten in Denmark."
A voice from the other room shouted, "Hey, y'all come listen to this.. They're getting ready to make another announcement."

They all went into the other room where the television was showing the Chairman of the Joint Chief of Staff as he was starting his announcement.

He started, "My fellow Americans, these times are devastating for us all.. Our economy is in total disarray. There's just no other way to put it. Our problems are not ours alone. Other countries are suffering as well.

"In these times we must reach out and help each other. We cannot attack our brother to feed our sister. There have been several skirmishes throughout our nation and law enforcement officers are stretched thin."

"Effective immediately and for an indefinite time we are instituting martial law in our nation's biggest cities. All National Guard and Reserve units are to report to duty and then to your assigned locations."

"Active duty military members are to report to their commanders for further instructions. We realize that these men and women can't be with their families at this time but it is paramount that our citizens are protected from harm and danger. This measure is designed to do just that; protect our citizens."

"We are not instituting this measure to control you; we are trying to protect you from those who would try to harm others in this time. As with previous announcements made today, there will be no question and answer session. Thank you and I pray that whatever God you serve, bless you."

Reverend Collins looked at everyone at the church. They
were all just looking at each other. Everyone was stunned
by yet another press conference. With martial law
enacted and military force was being used to restrain
American citizens, Reverend Collins knew he had to
gather his
people and console them.

XXII

Tommy and Marcie were sitting in a restaurant waiting for the final announcement to be made. Being the son and daughter of the President of the United States had given them inside information as to what was to come. Both of them had fallen out with their father. They both believed that he should have told the American people months ago.

Tommy couldn't stop thinking about how the relationship with his father had soured. The saddest day of their lives was the day Tommy's mother passed away.. The three of them were depressed but they always stuck together as a family.

Then President Murphy found Elizabeth. She made him happy and Tommy and Marcie shared in his happiness. They appeared to be a happy family again. That is until the day of the wedding.

Tommy felt Elizabeth changed. The look on her face that day stuck with him. It made him feel as though she had succeeded in whatever she meant to do.

After the wedding he asked her, "So, now that you are a part of the family, how does it feel?"
He thought her response was cold.

She replied, "Nothing will stop us from getting to the

White House.. Not even you and Marcie."

Tommy didn't know what that meant but it couldn't be good. A few months later Tommy came home. His father and stepmother were celebrating something.

He asked his father, "What's going on dad?" He responded, "You're going to be a brother." Tommy replied, "I'm already a brother."

He walked off and didn't look back.. Later that evening, Elizabeth came to his room.

She said, "I know you don't like the idea of my being pregnant, but you're going to have to live with it, or leave. I prefer you leave myself."

She walked out, and Tommy moved a week later.

When President Murphy told Tommy and Marcie of the asteroid, it further destroyed their relationship. Both Tommy and his sister felt the American people needed to know then, but the President and his constituents felt otherwise. They had not seen their father since the day they left home.

Tommy asked Marcie, "What do you think dad will say to the people?"

Marcie answered, "Don't know and frankly, I don't care."

Tommy said, "Come on Marcie, we need go see him. Tomorrow's the last day. We should go see our dad and even our evil stepmother."

Marcie laughed and replied, "She's not evil. We just don't see eye to eye."

Tommy responded, "I know, but just the same, we should go see them."

Marcie reared back in her chair and said, "Okay, let's go."

Tommy replied, "Not right now. Let's wait until tomorrow morning; I want to spend some time at our church. First thing in the morning we can head out to the Living Word."

Marcie asked, "How do you know they'll be there?"

Tommy answered, "His secretary told me."

Marcie replied, "Always the sneaky one."

***

I was sitting in the Oval Office and not looking forward to my
next trip to the podium. I knew I had done everything I could have done to save my country from annihilation.

Now, I would have to reveal to the American people that

their lives were hours away from ending. When I took office four years ago I never thought I would have to deal with this kind of situation. I knew there would be issues but none quite like this. I was so deep in thought I didn't see my wife walk into the room.

She said, "Are you okay? All things considered, I mean."

I responded, "I guess I'm doing as good as can be expected, given the situation."
Elizabeth replied, "You did the best you could. Keeping this from the people until the last moment was the best move. Imagine if the world knew they had a year to live. There would be such lawlessness and everything. Honey, you did right. I mean look at them now and you haven't even release the worst news yet."

I responded, "Still, it doesn't feel good that everyone is going to die and I couldn't save them. Do you know what it feels like to be the last President of the United States, ever?"

Elizabeth replied, "Stop feeling guilty and decide where we will spend our last hours."

I answered, "The only place we should, church."

Elizabeth responded, "You got it man!"

I watched as she sashayed out of the office passing Vice President Simpson on the way out. I tried to hide my facial expression when I noticed that Joe saw me looking at her, but I know he saw me. I'm glad he didn't say anything.

Elizabeth said happily waving her hand as she walked out, "Hi Joe."

He responded, "Hi Elizabeth."

He then turned to me and said, "Sir, we should head to the briefing room. The United Nations is almost ready to make the final announcement."

I quietly responded, "Okay Joe, let's go."

Vice President Simpson said, "Sir, as soon as the UN has finished, we will cut you in with an address to the American people and to answer any questions reporters might have."

I tried to lighten the mood and asked, "What are your plans for the final hours?"

Vice President Simpson answered, "We're going to spend it in the mountains. I had my family taken up there already. After the announcement, I plan to join them; if that's okay with you."

I replied, "Sure, we won't have anything else to do here." Vice President Simpson asked, "How about your plans?"

I smiled and answered, "My cousin has a church. I've never been there but I know he's doing great things. We're going over there."

I noticed the look on his face.

He asked, "You still have faith in God after all this? I mean, the Bible doesn't address alienation by an asteroid, right?"

I responded, "No, Joe, it doesn't. But, I'd rather spend my last hours serving God than anything else."

Vice President Simpson said, "I won't try and dissuade you." I replied, "Thanks."

Vice President Simpson asked, "Are the kids joining you? The two from the first marriage I mean."

Sadness covered me as I answered, "I know what you meant Joe and they won't even talk to me. I don't understand it. We gave them everything and they just shut us out over this."

Vice President Simpson asked, "Maybe once the news is released they will contact you."

President Murphy replied, "Maybe. I spoke to my daughter earlier and that didn't end well. I just pray they're safe."

***

Lisa made it to work where she ran into her friend, Carla, who had referred her to Reverend Collins' the day before.

Carla excitedly asked, "Well, did you call him?"

Lisa was in a daze over the recent announcements made by the White House.. She could not believe that on the first day of her new life these dramatic changes were occurring. She thought to herself, *Is this a sign? Is the world ending? Am I saved enough?*

Carla snapped her fingers in Lisa's face and asked, "Are you there, hello?"

Lisa answered, "I'm sorry. I just can't stop thinking about these announcements. What in the world is going on? This is supposed to be a good day for me."

Carla asked again, "So, did you talk to the Reverend?"
Lisa answered, "Yes and I gave my life to Jesus! I have been…born…again!"

Carla grabbed her and they both jumped up and down while shouting, "Hallelujah! Praise the Lord."

Then Carla said, "Praise the Lord, I am so happy for you girl. You have…"

One of their co-workers interrupted them and said, "Hey,

the UN is making another announcement. I have it up on my computer. You guys can come check it out."

Carla signed, "What now?"

They both started to walk over to the co-workers cubical when the co-worker said, "Uhh, not you Lisa. I'd just rather not take that chance. You know what I mean?"

Carla sternly said, "I can't believe you!"

She turned to Lisa and said, "Come on girl, we can watch it on my computer."

Lisa was down because people still judged her on her past. They were still afraid to be near her because of her affliction.

***

Johnny and Katrina were still in bed when the news reporter said the secretary general was about to make an announcement.

Johnny turned toward the television and said, "Another one? What is going on today?"
Katrina asked while hitting him on the arm, "Why did you stop? Come on, finish the job man."

Johnny replied, "Wait girl, this looks important."

35

Katrina got up and stormed off toward the kitchen, seemingly unconcerned with the world events.

***

After Calvin left Vanessa's house she got dressed and went to work. She arrived at her cube and overheard Lisa and Carla shouting.

Vanessa didn't like either of them. When she learned of Lisa's past she laughed at her. When Carla called Vanessa out on her Christianity, Vanessa threatened to beat her down. Vanessa's best friend Linda joined her at her cube.

Linda said smoothly, "Hey girl, did you have a morning snack?" Vanessa replied boastfully, "Yeah girl, you know I did.. Hubby left for work at three and my man came in at six, literally!"

Linda responded, "You're living dangerous. What if hubby came back and caught you?"

Vanessa answered, "Shoot girl, all his dirt? He's got no ground to stand on. I know he's sleeping with that hussy Katrina from church. Girl, she ain't nothin' but a tramp.. How many men have tapped that and dissed her?"

Linda answered, "Too many to count, girl!"

They both stopped and listened as Lisa and Carla celebrated.

36

Vanessa said with a sneaky voice, "Listen to them, I know she don't think she's saved. God gave her butt HIV because she's a demon. She won't see no part of my Heaven."

Linda replied, "I heard that, the ho'!. Ain't that much saving in the world!"

Vanessa responded laughing, "She might as well keep partying because she's gonna bust Hell wide open!"

Linda replied, "Amen sister! I don't want her up there with me!"

Carlos was in the cube next to Vanessa. He said, "Hey, are you guys going downstairs to hear the secretary general?"

Linda asked, "The who?"

Vanessa answered, "The head of the UN girl? I can't believe this, another announcement? Just give me the highlights. I got work to do." Linda joined in and said, "I'm gonna check it out. See ya girl." Vanessa replied, "Yeah, see ya, when I see ya!"

***

After hearing the news that the prices were frozen, transportation was being stopped, and martial law was imposed, Roger decided to stay at home and see what else would happen. They had just returned from the grocery store when Roger turned on the television.

The news reporter was speaking, "We have just received word that the secretary general will be delivering a special announcement to the world in a few minutes."

Roger shouted to Samantha, "Hey Sam, the secretary general is getting ready to make an announcement to the world."

Samantha shouted back, "What about?"

Roger answered, "I don't know, but he's gonna speak and

President Murphy will follow him."

Samantha responded, "Wow, it must be big."

She walked into the living room where Roger was sitting. Roger was intently watching television.

She asked, "What have I missed?"

Roger answered, "Nothing, he hasn't come to the podium yet. They're just speculating."

***

Brittney and Mia arrived at the Living Word Ministries

where her stepfather, Reverend Collins was the leader.

Brittney greeted some members who were standing at the door, "Hey, what's up y'all?"

One young man responded, "What's up B? You heard all the news this morning?"

Brittney answered, "Yeah, it's getting weird.. This is my roommate, Mia."

They all nodded or acknowledged Mia.

Brittney heard Kelvin whisper to his friend Jay, "She's tight."

Jay replied, "Yea."

Brittney laughed them off and asked, "Is my stepfather inside?"

Jay answered, "Yea, he's in there. Check you later B."
Brittney responded, "Alright."

They both walked in the church and Brittney saw Reverend Collins, gathered together with some members of the church. They were watching the news. Brittney's mom walked in the room just as Brittney came in.

"Hey baby," she said.

"Hi mom," Brittney responded.

Martha asked, "Are you okay? I thought you had class this morning?"

Brittney answered, "I'm okay and I didn't go to class after hearing all these announcements. I'm a little scared."

Martha replied, "We all are a little bit.. Who's this young lady?"

Brittney answered, "This is my new roommate, Mia Sanchez. Mia, this is my mom."

Mia said, "Hi, Ms. Collins."

Martha replied, "Hi, it's nice to finally meet you. Y'all come in here with the rest of us. There's another big announcement coming on the television. This one is coming from the secretary general."

Mia said, "Another one?"

They all walked over to the group, where Reverend Collins was standing, waiting for the next big announcement.

XXI

Bill had been at work all morning in his cubicle. He often kept to himself. His only visitor that morning had been Teddy. They talked about all the announcements that had occurred during the morning. Wendy and Teddy both came to Bill's cube this time.

Teddy asked, "Hey man you gonna check out the UN announcement."

Wendy interrupted, "Hey Bill."

Bill didn't even hear Teddy. As soon as Wendy spoke she had his undivided attention. He always admired her and wanted her. His Christianity was always challenged when she was near.

Bill responded, "Hey Wendy. How are you?"

Wendy responded, "I'm good."

Bill knew Wendy liked him but thought it best to hide the strong feelings he had for her. She was not a saved woman and that fact alone was enough for Bill not to date her. From time to time he did have to chastise himself for lusting for her. This was one of those times. When he looked up at Wendy he saw she had on a white low cut blouse and a blue skirt that ended just pass the halfway mark of her waist and knee. He loved seeing her in

41

skirts.. He soon found himself lusting for her again. He chastised himself. *Go away demon!"*

Bill said, "I'm gonna watch it here at my cube, on the Internet."

Teddy asked, "Want some company?" Bill replied, "You guys can join me."

Wendy said, "Let me go get my snacks. I'll be right back."

She smoothly walked to the other side of the office building and out of the ear shot of Bill and Teddy.

Teddy said, "Man, I wish I was you. You could get that easy."

Bill replied, "I'd rather go to Heaven."

Teddy responded, "Well, nothing wrong with going to Heaven knowing you had a little piece of that meat. Yeah, boy!"

Bill replied unemotionally, "Not my style brother. You know that."

After a few minutes Wendy rejoined them.

She said, "Okay, I'm ready. I hope this isn't more bad news. I already had to cancel my trip to Cali."

Teddy responded, "Yea, I know, I wanted to go with you."

Wendy smiled sarcastically and said, "I don't think so and you know it."

Bill said, "All we can do is pray."

Wendy and Teddy both looked at each other. They snickered, trying to hide it from Bill. He knew they were laughing at him but he didn't care. He loved the Lord with all his might.. Nothing was going to change that. They knew Bill was a devout Christian. Neither of them challenged his comment.

Wendy said, "Say one for me too, sweetheart."

She sat down in a chair where she could see Bill's monitor. The chair was behind Bill and to his left. Bill turned to answer Wendy and nearly passed out. Her legs were crossed and she was smiling at him.. He thought she was the most beautiful woman in the world. He quickly got himself together and replied, "Umm, I always do Wendy." He quickly turned back around, hoping no one noticed his behavior. *Dang it!. She's too fine. Get back Satan, get back I said!"*

***

President Murphy was sitting in his conference room

waiting on the announcement by the Secretary General of the United Nations. He often found himself in deep thought about these last few days. Now he was set to talk to the American people. He had to explain to them why he felt withholding knowledge that the world was going to end was necessary. *Many Americans were going to be angry.* But it was necessary and he knew it.

Twenty-seven hours remained. Just over a day, before the Earth would be destroyed. He remembered how his own son questioned the need to hide this information from the people. Tommy was adamant about informing the American people. It turned out to be the last straw in the dissolution of their relationship. He decided to get down on his knees and pray one more time. He knew God and grew up as a Christian. Like many others he strayed away when he got older.

His political positions conflicted with his belief in God.. He regretted allowing that conflict to remove him from Christ. Now, looking back, he wished he had stayed in Christ. He was thankful that he had a chance to repent. *How arrogant of us to think we have all the answers and don't need God. Now we find ourselves in a situation where only He can save us.*

President Murphy was surprised as several others in the room joined him in prayer. They were all side by side on their knees praying for help. President Murphy wondered if this was the first time such a sight was witnessed in the White House.

44

***

Alexander Engel, the Secretary General of the United Nations walked to the podium. All eyes in the room and around the world were focused directly on him. The announcement was also being streamed live on the Internet. He knew everyone in the world was watching and waiting to hear what he was going to say.

He was a tall, stout man. He had been in international politics for 20 years. He was also a Christian man and served as a minister at his church. It was hard for him to believe that the world was going to end this way. The Bible didn't say the world would end this way but his faith was strong and he feared not.

He prayed quietly to himself, *Father, help us in our time of need. We know we have strayed and not done right as a people. I come to you as one voice in the wind, help us Father.*

He raised his eyes slowly to meet the camera and started, "This is the toughest statement I have ever had to make in my life. I know that the world is listening.. You want to know what is happening to us. So many countries have announced that they are broke."

"Many people are asking, 'How could that be? How could so many of the world's leading countries now be broke?' Many of you are frustrated over the lack of transportation, the blockades of your cities, and the

45

military infiltrating your neighborhoods."

"You want answers. You want to know why this is happening. You want to know how this happened. It all started approximately one year ago when the world's most powerful leaders were briefed by a group of internationally renowned scientists."

These world renowned scientists informed us that an asteroid was headed our way. They also informed us that with the worlds combined resources, they were confident the asteroid could be destroyed or diverted."

"As the asteroid got closer and attempts to destroy or divert it were tried and failed, it became obvious that the scientist could not devise a way to destroy the asteroid. The drain of paying for these attempts caused the countries of the G8 to now face poverty."

"But I must stress, they are not to blame. No one could have anticipated the problem. As the asteroid got closer it became clear that the core of the asteroid was made up of a material that is not on our periodic table. This material could not be destroyed by any of our weapons."

"Yesterday the most powerful missile ever created by man was launched at the asteroid. It would be the last effort we could make to stop this asteroid. I am sorry to announce that this attempt--also-- failed."

"At 6:00 pm, Eastern Standard Time tomorrow, slightly

under 27 hours from now, the asteroid will strike Earth. All life, as we know it, will end. Let me make it clear. All life will end and no one will survive. There is no place on Earth to hide. If you have a God that you believe in, now is the time to pray to Him. I pray to Jesus for all of us."

XX

President Murphy stood emotionless at the podium. He stared out at the crowd of reporters, listening to them as they were launching a barrage of questions at him, and snapping shots of him over and over. He called up the strength from deep within him to start his farewell address.

No President before him had to deliver such a speech. He thought about the many presidents that simply left office after their term. But not him; he would be delivering his speech to a world that would not exist in just over a day.

He raised his hands in a motion to quiet the room and began, "Minutes ago, we learned the final piece of the story. We learned that about a year ago, the leaders of Earth discovered we were at the threshold of Armageddon."

"These reporters, they want answers. You may want answers. But, in the grand scheme of things, is any answer going to help?. Is any answer going to save us? Is it going to help knowing how we got to this point? Is it going to help explaining why you were not told until the 27th hour? Is it going to do you any good to know the country went broke trying to destroy an asteroid that eventually we learned could not be destroyed? No, my friends, it will not help you at all. What do I recommend?"

48

He paused to take a deep breath. "I recommend you go to your families and love ones. Spend these final hours together. If you have issues against another, settle it now for truly the day after tomorrow is not given to us. Our time is truly short."

"Let us not carry any ill will with us into the next life. If you pray, then let us pray together. Let us remember our laws. Let us not steal from one another. Let us not fight one another. Let us not murder each other.. Let us truly come together as brothers and sisters in these last hours."

"Our law enforcement and military personnel are on the job in these final hours to keep us safe. Let us not need them. Let us see that we, in our final hours, know how to be civilized."
"For today, we all know the day and the hour of our demise. Let us end this world with love in our hearts for all mankind, regardless of race, color, creed or national origin."

President Murphy looked down and with a sad voice said, "I will take three questions."

President Murphy looked back up as the reporters were raising their hands in an attempt to be first to ask a question. President Murphy said, "Al from WNN."

Al asked, "Sir, do we know where exactly the asteroid will strike?"

49

President Murphy answered, "It will strike the Western part of the United States. From what I understand, the impact will be so great that nothing anywhere will survive the after effects. You see, the impact of this asteroid is estimated to be the equivalent of a 1 million megaton bomb. Nothing on Earth will survive this devastation."

President Murphy continued, "Sarah from KWBC."

Sarah asked, "Sir, will the travel restrictions be lifted?" President Murphy answered, "No, I'm afraid they will not be lifted. The world leaders and I feel it will be best to restrict all movements at this time. I am staying here myself."

President Murphy said, "One last question." "How about Connie, from WUNC?"

Connie asked, "Sir, what will happen to the many prisoners we have incarcerated?"

President Murphy answered, "The nonviolent criminals will be processed for release. As for the others, they will remain imprisoned." "We cannot allow violent criminals to be released and loose on our streets. Controlling the movements of the people and keeping our streets safe is a tough enough job for our law enforcement officials in this time. Releasing a multitude of violent prisoners into the streets will only add to the problem. If family members want to visit them then we will relax visitation rules to see them but we will not release them."

As he was closing, his wife and small children came and stood next to him. He put his arm around his wife and smiled.

President Murphy concluded, "Now, please go and spend time with your family and friends. Now is not the time to be sitting around asking questions and debating issues. Now is the time to be with family and loved ones. Thank you and God bless you all."

***

Reverend Collins stood stunned at the news that the world was going to end in just over a day. He looked out across the room at his members and they appeared to be just as stunned and bewildered as he was. He glanced at the stepdaughter he'd raised from the age of six.

She was hugging her mom crying and asking, "Momma what is this? Could it be true?"

He walked over to his wife as she was saying, "Baby, momma don't even know."

Mia was standing with them and said, "My family is in Miami. I won't even see them again."

Reverend Collins consoled her, "You're a part of our family now."

He turned to the others standing with him and said,

"We're going to gather the membership and meet in the sanctuary at six. I want y'all to help with the calling."

***

Bill sat at his cube with Teddy and Wendy. He was deeply perplexed by the final announcement. He couldn't look at his two friends sitting with him because he felt like a fool. *Have I been a complete idiot? I need some answers.. I've been following the ways of the Lord all my life and now this is what I get? I'm an idiot, a complete idiot! Revelations is specific on how the world is to end and it says nothing about an asteroid!*

Wendy broke the ice, "I don't know about you guys but I'm gettin' out of here." She turned and emphasized, "Right, now!"

Teddy jumped up and said, "Can I go with you?"

Wendy frowned and sternly answered, "Not even with the world ending, buddy!"

Bill intently watched her body sway as she walked off toward her cube. His desires for her were growing with each step she took. He didn't even try and fight it off this time. Bill felt a release from what he considered bondage. His thoughts began to focus on worldly desires. He never allowed himself these thoughts before but now he didn't care. The ringing phone startled him for a second.

He answered, "This is Bill. Can I help you?"

A voice on the other end answered, "Hi, I'm from the Living Word Ministries. Reverend Collins is having a meeting at six this evening. Will you be able to attend?"

Bill replied, "Yeah, I'll be there. I got some questions."

The voice said, "Great. Thank you and have a blessed day."

Bill said to himself, *Yeah right!*

He hung up the phone, and looked up, as Teddy was making his way to him.

Bill said in a monotone voice, "Man, something ain't right."

Teddy asked, "Man, that Wendy is fine!" Then he looked at Bill and said, "Dude, what are you talking about?"

Bill answered, "I've spent all my life following the word of God and now I find out it isn't true."

Teddy responded, "What? Why are you saying that? I mean with the world ending, you're getting ready to go to Heaven. If anyone should go, it should be you. I thought you would be happy."

Bill answered, "Don't you see? The world is not supposed to end this way. Where's the rapture? If the world was going to end tomorrow then the rapture should have occurred seven years ago. The world doesn't end until seven years following the rapture. If we all die tomorrow no one is in Heaven but God and I bet He's laughing at us right now. I've been a complete fool, an idiot, one big fool!"

Teddy took a step back. Teddy's physical reaction made Bill realize how powerful his words were. He didn't think he would ever say anything remotely like that.

Teddy said, "Whoa, hold up brother. Aren't you jumping the gun a bit? I mean, don't give up now. Don't get me wrong I would love to party with you on the last day. Just think of all the tail we could chase. But, man, I'm concerned about 'cha."

Bill stood up and resoundingly bellowed, "I'm going to see what Reverend Collins has to say at six, then I'm going out and chase some tail with you, bro--tha! You down?"

Teddy happily responded, "Yeah man, I'm down.. What about Wendy? Are you gonna hit that? I shoooo wish I was you boy!"

Bill answered, "I've been holding back from saying this a long time, oh yes, I'm gonna hit it hard!"

***

Vanessa remembered her friend Linda was downstairs watching the announcement on the department's television screens. *Where's my girl, it's been a minute?* The phone rang. Her caller ID said it was from the lobby. She picked up and answered, "This is Vanessa."

Linda's voice was excited, "Girl, you're not gonna to believe this! The world is ending tomorrow at six!"

Vanessa was shocked, "Stop playin'."

Linda replied, "I'm not joking. Look on the Internet.. That's what the announcement was about. There's an asteroid headed for us and it will hit us tomorrow at six. You better go find Calvin and get that last bit of play time in! I'm dumping my husband and going out to find me someone else. Girl, this is going to be exciting!"

Vanessa said sadly, "Yeah, I gotta go." She quickly hung up the phone. Vanessa sat at her cube and verified what Linda said on the Internet. She couldn't believe the news. The world was going to end in just over a day. She thought about all the sin she had committed. She thought about her escapades with Calvin and two others before him. Her marriage was a sham and she had so much hate in her heart. She thought she had plenty of time to repent but now she found out that isn't true.

She started to cry. Vanessa was saddened by all the pain she caused herself and others. She felt she had to do something about it. Heaven was out of the question for

her, but she still felt she had to make amends. She was still crying when Carla and Lisa came back to Lisa's cube. Vanessa jumped up and quickly walked over to Lisa's cube.. Carla jumped back as if she thought Vanessa was going to start something.
Carla put both hands up and said, "Look V, we don't want any trouble."

Vanessa smiled and looked at Carla. She still had tears etched on her face. She calmly said, "I'm not here to cause any trouble, Carla."

Vanessa took a deep breath, then she continued, "Lisa, Carla, I know I haven't been right with both of you. For that I'm truly sorry. I can only beg your forgiveness and I understand if you don't give it. I just have to clear my heart of the wrongdoings I have done."

Carla and Lisa looked at each other. They were bewildered. Carla replied, "It's cool V. Jesus forgives us so we can forgive each other."

Lisa added, "Yeah, I'm new to this, but I forgive you too.. If I forgive my parents, then it's really easy to forgive you."

Vanessa still sensed some tension in the air so she explained herself, "You see, I think deep inside I'm probably jealous of you both."

Carla inquisitively asked, "Jealous?"

Vanessa continued, "Yeah, I think you're both closer to Jesus then I'll ever be. I messed my whole life up, and now I'm never going to see Heaven."

Carla put her arm around Vanessa. Vanessa felt more at ease that Carla was showing her some love.

Carla said, "That's not true. You have started to repent already and none of us, including me, are perfect. God has a special place in Heaven for those of us who recognize their wrongs and ask for forgiveness. You're gonna be right there with us girl."

A voice shouted from behind, "What are you doing?"

Vanessa jumped. She turned and saw Linda standing there, angry.

Vanessa tried to calm her down, "I'm asking for forgiveness, and so should you."
Linda shouted, "You're out of your freakin' mind. I will never ask them for anything!"
Linda put her hands on her hips and leaned her head to one side,"What? You think you can be saved now? Not with a million years of cleaning, girl! Remember, I know all your dirt!"

Vanessa replied softly and in an apologetic tone, "If I go to Hell then I deserve it, but I'm not going without making amends first."

Linda snorted, "Ump!"

Carla said softly, "God forgive her."

XIX

Katrina ran back to the bedroom when Johnny shouted the news to her. They both couldn't believe it. Katrina fell in Johnny's arms as she always did and started to cry.

Katrina asked, "So baby, what are we gonna do?"
Johnny looked at her and said, "We'll going to enjoy these last hours together."

Katrina asked, "What about the ball and chain?"

Johnny angrily replied, "What about her! She doesn't mean anything to me!"

Katrina apologetically responded, "I'm sorry baby." He didn't reply. She continued, "This is so sad. Now I will never get the chance to have a baby. I wanted to raise a cute little girl. I would have dressed her up in cute little outfits and we could have gone shopping together. We would probably look like twins."

She felt Johnny trying to comfort her. He squeezed her tightly and kissed her on the forehead. She hated it when he kissed her there; it made her feel like a child. She only tolerated it because she knew that was his way of showing affection.

Johnny softly said in her ear, "I'm sorry you'll never have that chance. But for the next day, we'll have so much fun making one. Check it out; I don't have to wear any protection!"

Katrina smoothly pulled Johnny down on the bed and affectionately said, "Come on baby, make me pregnant."

***

Vanessa went back to her cube and called Calvin at work. Despite knowing this was the right thing for her to do, making this call was still going to be hard. She knew Calvin would be mad.

She whispered, *I gotta do what I gotta do!*

She took a deep breath. Then she started to dial the number. As it started to ring she uttered under her breath, *here goes.*

Calvin answered the phone, "Intensity, Calvin, how may I help you?"

Vanessa said, "Calvin, this is V, have you heard the news?"

Calvin answered, "Yeah baby. I'm on my way home. Meet me there in an hour."

Vanessa replied, "No. I can't meet you." There was silence on the phone.

After a moment Calvin asked, "Where do you want to

meet?"

Vanessa could tell from his response that he didn't understand or he didn't want to understand.

She answered, "Calvin, I can't meet you anywhere. I'm going to spend the next day getting it right. There was a time in my life when I was right with God. I wasn't perfect, but I was right. In as much as it seems impossible, I'm going to try and recapture that time."

"I have to stop sinning, which means I have to stop seeing you. I'm going to try and convince my husband to join me. If he does, I will be happy, but if he doesn't, then I will have to do it myself. But no matter what, I can't see you anymore."

Calvin shouted into the phone, "V, you can't do this me!"

Vanessa moved the phone away from her ear.

He continued shouting, "With one day left in this world you think you can clean up ten years of mess? You have lost what little sense you had! Why are you trying to do this anyway? There's no God for you to please. Can't you see that?"

Vanessa tried to stay calm. She gathered herself together. She replied, "The God I know, have known, and will always know is there. He was always there.. It was me who wouldn't listen. I'm sorry I upset you, but I have to do this for me and my soul." All Vanessa heard was the sound of a phone going dead in her ear.

***

After Calvin slammed the phone down, he realized everyone in the area was looking at him. He shouted, "What y'all looking at!"

His supervisor walked over to him with his hands raise in front of him in a calming motion. He asked, "Where are you going? We have sales to make."

Calvin looked him up and down and smartly replied, "Sales? You stupid! The world is ending tomorrow. I'm outta here. Oh and by the way, you're a punk, and I never could stand you!"

Several other employees at Calvin's job started to get up and leave. As Calvin looked back, he laughed at the puzzled look on the supervisor's face. He turned and looked at his boss one more time, and said, "Punk!"

***

Vanessa left her job in search of Johnny. She had to try and make it right with him. She knew the project was a joke and that he was really with Katrina. She remembered how they fell in love with each other when they were in high school. They got married at a young age, but after ten years of happy marriage, Johnny met a woman named Sarah. This relationship destroyed their marriage.

Instead of divorce, Vanessa decided to get back at Johnny by having an affair of her own. Her friends wore her down by constantly encouraging her to have an affair behind Johnny's back. Now she wished she had not listened to them. The years of posing as a happily married couple in the church, while continuing to have extramarital affairs was hurting her deeply in the last hours.

She never forgave Johnny for that first affair. Now she had to forgive him, but was it too late? She knew the feeling was mutual but she had to try and reconcile their marriage.

Vanessa arrived at Katrina's house. She sat in her car for a couple of minutes and thought about her approach to this situation. She knew Katrina called herself in love, with Johnny.

Katrina often called herself in love but Vanessa knew the men were only with Katrina because she was easy. One of Vanessa's co- workers commented on how easy Katrina was, and how sick of her clinginess he was. Eventually he dumped her because she was so clingy.

Vanessa also knew Johnny was only with Katrina out of spite for her. She never forgot how angry Johnny was he found out that his childhood sweetheart was having an affair on him. He lost his mind. He threw furniture, dishes, anything he could get his hands on that day he

63

threw it. Vanessa laughed at his anger.

She often shouted at him, *That's what you get for cheating on me!* She remembered Johnny saying that he couldn't imagine her with another man and the pain it caused him. She couldn't make him see she would never have been with another man, if he hadn't first been with another woman.

She finally got up the courage to get out of the car and head toward the door. As she was walking she noticed Johnny's BMW in the parking lot. *He's not even trying to hide it!* Vanessa got to the door. She stood there for a minute, making sure this was what she wanted to do. She rang the doorbell. No one answered. She knew they were there and she was prepared to stand there all day if she had too. She continued ringing the doorbell.

Finally Katrina flung the door open and shouted angrily, "Why are you ringing my doorbell like that! Get off my freakin' property or get ready for a beat down!"

Vanessa surprised herself at her calmness. She replied, "I'm not here to fight you. I'm here to talk with my husband. Can you get him for me please? I'll wait right here."

Vanessa smiled while Katrina looked stunned. Katrina tried to reply.

She stumbled over her words,

"He's…not…uh…well…I…he's not here. What makes you think he's here?"

Vanessa answered, "Honey, I'm not as stupid as he has told you. I know there was no project. Plus, I can see his car right there.. For Heaven's sake, he didn't even try to hide it. I'm not here for trouble, and I have no issue with you. I just want to talk to my husband."

Katrina stopped fidgeting and said meekly, "Wait here."

Vanessa replied with a smile, "Thank you."

Katrina tried to slam the door closed but it didn't work. The door was open just enough for Vanessa to hear them talking.

Katrina said sternly, "You need to talk to her."

Johnny replied angrily, "I don't want to talk to her. Get rid of her!"

Katrina harshly responded, "No, she's crazy and she won't leave until you talk to her." She sternly added, "So go, talk to her!"

Johnny huffed as angrily flung the cracked door open and shouted, "What do you want?"

Vanessa looked at him, purposely blinked her eyes, and calmly said, "I want my husband back." She took a deep breath. "We have one day left…"

Johnny cut her off, "Not on your life! Get real V. I don't want you back. I don't care if the world is ending today, tomorrow or next week. I…don't…want…you!"

Vanessa continued, "Johnny, God is coming back tomorrow. Don't you see it?"

Johnny sternly shouted, "God? There is no God, stupid!"

Vanessa dropped her head in disbelief. She knew things weren't right between them, but Johnny was a minister. She thought he would never turn on God. She surmised he was totally engulfed in sin. Vanessa lifted her head back up.

She looked Johnny in the eye and said, "Johnny, let's go talk to Reverend Collins and make this right while we still have time."

Johnny sternly said, "You should have thought about that before you jumped in another man's bed. Go to Reverend Collins with that punk. I can't even stand to look at you…whore."

Vanessa continued, "Johnny let's renew our vows today." Johnny turned and vociferated, "Stupid. You're so stupid. I would never marry you again!"

Vanessa replied while still being calm, "We have to at

least repent for our sins."

Johnny was shaking his head and said, "Repent? Get out of here V. Go repent for yourself. I'm spending my last day with the best thing that has ever happened to me...Katrina!"

Vanessa responded, "Johnny, Reverend Collins is meeting with everyone at six this evening. Can we please go? He can shed some light on this for us." She was starting to cry as she was speaking.

Johnny sternly replied, "You think crying is going to help? I'm not spending my last night in church listening to a bunch of garbage." He laughingly added, "You go, and send me a text!" Katrina joined him at the door smiling.

She said, "I heard everything you said babe." She smiled at him and continued, "With the world ending, I can openly and publicly show love for my man.. He doesn't have to pretend to be a minister for some religion that's not real. Hell, he only did it for the money and the notoriety anyway! I'm excited even if it is for only one day."

She turned to Vanessa and sternly said, "So, get off my porch and go find your own
man. I got mine."

They bellowed out a laugh that could be heard up and down the block. They both walked back in the house and slammed the door behind them. Vanessa stood there and cried some more.

***

Roger and Samantha's marital problems seemed so irrelevant now. Roger sat there and thought about his life. He wasn't right over the last few months, but that was irrelevant now. He was on the right path now, and he was determined to make sure his family right in these last hours.

He remembered how he met Samantha through a mutual friend. Roger was in the military then, but from the first moment he saw Samantha, he knew he was in love. They dated for just over a year before they were married. Once Roger got out of the military, the two of them moved back to Rogers's hometown where they have lived since.

After five years of marriage, Roger ran into a woman he knew in high school. In high school Roger had a crush on her, but she didn't even notice him. After a few months of reminiscing, they ended up sleeping together. One day Roger was coming out of her apartment, and ran into Samantha's best friend Daisy.

Daisy lived next door to the woman Roger was sleeping with. She saw Roger coming out of the apartment, and right away she knew what was going on.. Roger was supposed to be at work. He had told Samantha that he couldn't go with her to look for a new car because he had to work that day.

Roger knew Daisy would tell Samantha what she saw. He hated himself for what he had done. He knew in his heart that it was wrong, and he never should have allowed it to happen. He promised himself and God that it would never happen again.

Samantha was so upset with Roger, she left with the kids. After several months, she returned home. They'd been attempting to patch things up since. Roger admired his wife because she was a strong Christian woman. She often told Roger it was a struggle for her not to divorce him.

Roger hated that she asked several her friends for their opinions. He knew that most of them advised her to leave him. Ironically, it was Daisy who advised Samantha to give God a chance to work on Roger. He was happy that she decided to listen to Daisy and trust God.

Samantha told Roger she would come back if they went through counseling with Reverend Collins. Roger was more than happy to do it to save his marriage. Samantha was folding clothes when Roger walked in. He looked at her with eyes full of love.

He said, "Honey, I think we should go to Reverend Collins' church and see what they're doing."

Samantha turned and smiled, "I was thinking the same thing."

***

Bill and Teddy were on their way to the Living Word
Ministries to hear what Reverend Collins had to say. Bill
was unusually quiet. He saw Teddy looking at him from
the corner of his eye. He figured Teddy was wondering
what to say.

Teddy finally said emphatically, "Boy, I'm glad you gonna
be partying with me! I mean, this is what I dreamed of;
you and me, partying all night. Yeah!"

Bill said shortly, "I'm looking forward to this man."

Teddy said, "I hope church don't last long. I want to be
in a club tonight."

Bill didn't answer. He was deep in thought about his life.
He felt he'd wasted so much time being a good Christian.
He thought about his days as a youth. His parents were
devout
Christians, and raised him to love and honor Jesus. Bill
accepted his call to Christ at six years old.. Many believed
he was too young.

Bill kept busy in the church. He sang in the choir,
ushered, and recently he decided to become a minister.
Most of all, Bill was still a virgin. He was often teased by
his non-Christian friends. He was admired by his
Christian friends. It didn't matter to him either way

70

because he was following God. That was the only important thing to him.

Now with the impending destruction of Earth, he was questioning everything he had grown to believe. He looked at his friend, Teddy, and admitted to himself that he admired Teddy's lifestyle more than his own. The only time he was this perplexed about his beliefs was after his parents died in a plane crash.

It was two years ago when he got the news. It deeply hurt him. Reverend Collins' was right there for him through the entire ordeal. That was the first time Bill had met the reverend's stepdaughter, Brittney. He liked her, but she was a senior high school at the time. He thought about Brittney. She would be in college now. Maybe his last day could be spent with her instead of Wendy.

Teddy broke the silence again, "Man, let's blow off this church thing and head to the club!"

Bill said, "No brother. I have to do this church thing. I have to see what the Rev is talking about. I owe him that much."

Teddy sarcastically said, "Owe him? Dude, you don't owe him nothin'."

Bill replied, "Yeah I do. He was there for me when my parents died."

Teddy said, "Oh, sorry."

71

Bill took a deep breath and continued, "I just don't know anymore. I did everything according to His word and it's all been a lie."

Teddy replied, "Yeah, I could have told you that year's ago."

Bill answered, "Sure but now I have absolute proof right before me. Who wouldn't see the truth now?"

Teddy said, "Yeah man, it's all bogus."

Bill answered, "I just think about all the lessons I was taught. I
was taught that the horn would sound in a twinkling of an eye and Jesus would come back like a thief in the night. All the believers would be called up and the world would go on for seven years. What a joke!"

Teddy replied, "Yeah I heard that crap too, comparing Jesus to a thief in the night? What up wit that?"

Bill smiled.

Teddy asked, "What you smiling about?"

Bill said, "Man, there's this babe at church named Brittney. She's soooo fine!. Wait till you see her. I know she'll be there because she's the Rev's daughter."

Teddy asked, "Is she finer than Wendy?"

Bill laughed and answered, "Yeah boyeeee!"

Teddy said, "Dang, I can't wait to see her! Finer than Wendy, dang, that's fine there boy!"

Bill said, "I'm gonna hear what Reverend Collins has to say, then I'm gonna see if I can hook up with Brittney.. If not then I'm gonna track down Wendy and see what I can get. As you like to say, 'yeah boy!'"

Teddy responded, "Sounds like a plan, brother!" Bill said, "Yeah brother"

***

Lisa arrived back home where she planned on waiting until the meeting at church. She was sitting on the living room floor of her apartment. She started crying while raising her hands up to Heaven.

Lisa shouted with enthusiasm, "Thank you Lord for forgiving me of all my sin in time to be saved. I know there are many on radio and TV saying, even laughing at Christians.. They're saying your word is a joke. I don't believe it Father. I believe in your promises. I don't know how and that's not for me to know. My job is to keep my faith and I'm not going to fail. I love you Lord."

As she finished there was a knock at the door. She went

to the door and peeped out the hole. She was shocked to see her mother there. They had fallen out a few years before and had not exchanged words since.

Lisa opened the door and asked with some apprehension, "Mom?"

Lisa's mom was Andrea Cook. Andrea responded, "Hi baby. I missed you. Can I come in?"

Lisa stepped to the side and let her mother in the apartment. She closed the door softly, stood there frozen for a second, and then turned toward her mother.

Lisa quietly said, "You're here because of the announcements, right? I mean, it's been three years."

Andrea answered, "Yes, but that doesn't mean I didn't think about coming a thousand times. I hate that I put you through so much turmoil in your life. I just want to try and make amends before it's over. I'm sorry about your HIV. It's all my fault."

Lisa replied, "No mom, it's my fault. You're not to blame." Andrea replied, "Yes I am. I steered you down that road, the road that led to your contracting that awful disease. I could, and should have been a better mom."

Lisa responded, "Mom, the Lord will care for me. I don't blame anyone."

Andrea shouted, "The Lord? Have you been watching TV? There is no God. It's all one big joke."
Lisa calmly replied, "Mom, I don't care what anyone says. My God is real and His word is no joke. My faith will not waiver for any reason."

Andrea walked toward the TV and said, "You need to watch that Bishop Carroll. He's coming on in a few minutes and he'll tell you the truth."

Lisa replied, "I don't need him or anyone else to tell me the truth. I already know the truth. Jesus is real."

She proudly shouted, "I should be dead already, but here I stand. Hallelujah!"

Andrea stubbornly said, "You're being a fool!"

Lisa responded, "No, I was a fool but now I'm saved. If you don't like my faith then you can leave. No one is going to put a wedge between me and Heaven."

Andrea looked down. When she looked back up, she said, "Okay baby, I'm sorry for questioning your beliefs. Can I make it up to you? How can I make any of this up to you?"

Lisa replied, "You can come to church with me and listen to Reverend Collins. He's a good man. He's a devoted man of God."

Andrea responded, "Okay, I'll do it for my little girl."

Lisa asked, "Where's dad?"

Andrea answered, "I don't know. I saw him about six months ago in a bar. He's still a jerk."

Lisa replied, "Mom, stop, how can I find him?"

Andrea answered, "I don't know baby."

***

Bishop Milton Carroll was getting ready to speak on national television. He was known as the most popular minster of the gospel in the world. Everyone knew and respected him. Presidents and kings had been known to seek his advice on matters of the cloth.

Bishop Carroll was born in a small town where he went to church seemingly every night. His father was a bricklayer by day and a deacon by night. His mother did everything in the church. She cooked, cleaned, sung, and ushered.

Bishop Carroll studied the Bible every day. By age 16 he was teaching Sunday school lessons at his parent's church. He answered his call to the ministry at age 18 and gave his first sermon at age 19.

While in college Bishop Carroll formed a gospel service at his school. When he was ready to graduate he had a flock of over a thousand people coming to his service. Everyone praised his style. He was charismatic, charming, hard when necessary, flamboyant, intelligent, and well-studied.

After getting his master's degree in theology, Bishop Carroll joined the AME church and rose to Bishop. He then separated from the AME church and started his own ministry known as the Divine Word Ministries. Bishop Carroll has over 4,000 churches in his ministry representing over 2 million members. Bishop Carroll is personified as a true man of God, untouched by sin.

He was sitting in his private office with his personal assistant, Clint Sessions. Clint had been with the Bishop for over seven years. He handled all of the Bishop's public and private matters.

Bishop Carroll asked Clint, "What do you think will be the response to my speech?"
Clint answered, "I think people have already agreed with you. I think you'll be fine."

Bishop Carroll said, "I don't want the public to become outraged at me but this is the word they need to hear."

Clint responded, "I don't think anyone will become outraged at you.. You're well respected and many will thank you for your word."

Bishop Carroll replied, "Thanks, Clint. You know my

reputation means everything to me. I just don't know what I would do without you. Come over and have a seat. You've been standing and working hard all day."

Clint responded, "Thanks, Bishop."

***

Roger and Samantha were at home getting ready to go to the Living Word Ministries when the Gospel Today show came on. The host of the show was a gospel personality named Mattie Jones.

She had several gold records to her credit and was well respected in the music business. She also was an Evangelist and a part of Bishop Carroll's Divine Word Ministries. Her show had been rated the number one gospel show for three years running. She had won several talk show host awards.

Evangelist Jones began her show by saying, "Today we all have heard the devastating news of our impending doom. I will be with you throughout the next day with different reports as we get close to the impact. My brothers and sisters do not lose hope in these last hours. As second Chronicles 15:7 says 'But as for you, be strong and do not give up, for your work will be rewarded.'"

"I, for one, believe that we will be saved by the grace and mercy of Jesus Christ, my Lord and Savior. This may not look like its lining up with scripture, but I trust God and

78

his word does not lie!"

"Okay, they're telling me we're ready to go to my pastor, Bishop Milton Carroll. You know you have to stop me, 'cause I'll preach all night, if you let me! Let's watch live as Bishop Carroll gives us what I know will be some uplifting and encouraging news from God.. Ladies and gentlemen, here's my pastor, Bishop Milton Carroll at the Divine Word Ministries."

Roger looked at his lovely wife. He took her hand and gave her a hug. *How could I have cheated on such a beautiful flower?* He hated himself every day for that few minutes of pleasure. He was thankful that his wife was giving him a second chance but he knew deep inside she still hurt from it.

***

Samantha smiled back at Roger. She was glad that despite it all, she was still with her husband. The Bible told her she could divorce him for his infidelity, but she decided to forgive him as God would. They had been through a lot, but she was foolish enough to go against the world and trust God.

She thought about all the people she knew who had chosen differently. One was her neighbor, Vanessa, who she knew was an usher at the Living Word Ministries. Vanessa told her that she was cheating on her husband. She didn't want the lifestyle that Vanessa was leading.

79

She thought that it would be better to trust that God would make it better for her and her family.

***

Bishop Carroll approached the podium to a loud and vigorous applause from the people in the Revelation room of his church. Bishop Carroll's church building was so large that this particular room could hold over 500 people. For a moment he paused as he looked out to the crowd of select members and reporters who greeted him.

He sat his papers on the podium, looked down, and stepped back for a moment, taking it all in. Then he stepped back up to the podium. He was gathering himself to deliver the biggest speech of his storied career. He lived for these moments. He loved the limelight. He smiled after seeing the camera was fixated on him. He knew that millions of people were watching him.

Bishop Carroll was a large man. He stood over six feet seven inches tall and weighed over 250 pounds. His mere presence intimidated most people with whom he came into contact. His voice was powerful and masterful.

Bishop Carroll slowly brought his eyes up to meet the crowd and began to speak, "Today…today we meet in this room because its name is significant. This room is called 'Revelation' and it's here that our eyes must open so we can see. The information provided to the multitude today concerning this Heavenly body called

Earth has us running to and fro looking for answers. Why is this…? Why is that…? Is Christianity a lie? Is there, a God and if so, has He forsaken us?"

A voice shouted, "Preach, brother preach!" Another shouted, "Tell us the truth Bishop! Tell us!" Others were clapping as the Bishop appeared to be revving up. He motioned to them to calm down so he could continue.

He paused for a second and continued, "These are some of the questions being asked, by Christians and non-Christians alike. We are all faced with something that doesn't seem to line up with scripture. We're looking at each other, perplexed, confused, astonished, astounded, if you may!"

"Awwww, are you listening to me! We're looking at each other and saying 'Something ain't right here!' I went to my office and I studied. I prayed. I called on the name…of the Lord. Then I prayed a little more. After spending some time doing that I felt it was time to come out here and tell you what I found."

Bishop Carroll felt everyone was on the edge of their seats waiting for his next words. These were the moments he lived for, and he cherished them. He looked out over the room and saw anticipation in the eyes of the people in the room. He believed the people worshiped him. They placed him on a pedestal, and he loved it.

In the beginning, he tried to correct them. He was not a

god, and he didn't want to be treated that way. As time went on he began to like it. Then he began to love it. The admiration consumed him. He felt he deserved it. He looked into the television camera, forcing a look on his face that he hoped would ease their pain.

He was used to giving the people something to keep them encouraged. This time wouldn't be different. In these last hours he was ready to give the world something they needed to hear. He knew they admired him and respected him as a true man of God. He knew his words would carry the necessary weight to lead millions in what he believed was the right direction.

Bishop Carroll continued, "After careful study and deep analytical thought I have concluded that there is only one possible conclusion to be derived from the information we have received today, the events of the past year, and the word of God."

A voice from the front rowed shouted, "Come on wit it Bishop!" Bishop Carroll again stepped back and adjusted his belt. He placed his hand on his chin and walked back to the podium. He looked over at Clint, and then he looked at his wife, Jessica. He wondered how his words would affect her. He had not discussed his speech with her, but he believed that she would follow him, no matter what.

He thought about his marriage of 25 years and how she always stood with him no matter what she truly believed.

Bishop Carroll placed each hand on the opposite edges of the podium. He then took a deep breath and said, "My fellow human beings, my brothers, my sisters in Christ, we have been deceived." He felt the air seemingly leave the room. The looks on the faces of the people in the room were clear. They couldn't believe what they'd just heard.

Bishop Carroll stood there nodding his head in the affirmative. He sealed the deal that he also believed Christianity was a hoax.

A loud voice broke the silence, "Liar!" It was followed by another, "You're the deceiver!" A third voice yelled, "I'm wit you Bishop!" Another voice shouted, "Bishop, how could you?"

Photo flashes were being taken all over as the Bishop attempted to restore order in the room. Bishop Carroll held the Bible up in the air.

Bishop Carroll continued, "This book, this book in which we have lived our lives, is nothing more than a fairy tale for children."

He tried to finish, but he was being booed by many of the believers in the audience. Others were yelling in support of his decision. The room seemed to be divided on the issue and no one was paying any attention to the Bishop. Yelling between people in the audience was evident.

83

One person was shouting, "I told you!. Yeah Bishop, you're right. I've been telling these idiots that for years!"

Another shouted, "Bishop, noooo! We'll pray for you, brother!" It got to the point where he could not continue and his security team had to usher him out of the room.

***

Jessica stood there stunned at her husband's comments. She had no idea that he was going to denounce Christianity as a fairy tale for children. Her thoughts were interrupted by her personal assistant grabbing her by the arm.

She shouted at Jessica, "Ma'am, we need to get you out of here."

Jessica responded, "Why? I don't support those comments." Jessica's assistant continued to push her along.
S
he said, "Ma'am, they don't know that. Let's get out of here."

She led Jessica out of the room and to safety. Jessica wanted to talk to her husband and ask him what in the world made him take that stance. She had never questioned his opinions before, but this one had to be questioned.

Back in the studio, Evangelist Jones was shocked. She didn't know what to say or do. When the TV cut back to her, she sternly ordered them to cut to a commercial.

Her producer, Zack Carter, came running up to her, "Evangelist we have the rest of the Bishop's speech. We want you to read it on air."

Evangelist Jones responded, "I would die before I read that garbage. Find someone else."

***

Evangelist Jones walked off, and Zack turned to Tess Minter, a young up-and-coming journalist, who relished the opportunity to get on the air. She stood behind Zack, excitedly waiting to be asked.

Zack started to ask, "Tess can..."

Tess excitedly answered, "Yes, I'll do it!"

The crew rushed to get Tess ready for her appearance. She couldn't wait to get on the air has the main host. This was her big break. She didn't care that the world was ending; she just wanted to get on the air.

Zack counted down to the live cut in, "And, 5...4...3...2...1..." Tess began, "Hi, this is Tess Minter

85

live from the Gospel Today studios. We have received the rest of the speech that was to be given by Bishop Carroll. I will read it to you."

'You have a revelation of your own, and that is all life will end in just under
25 hours.. You now have the opportunity to do that which you wanted to do in your
heart, but were afraid, because it didn't line up with the fairy tales of the Bible.
I am sorry for leading you all astray over the years. I will lead you astray no more. For the last 25 years, I have never done anything that would even remotely amount to sin. What a fool I have been. But for the next 25 hours, I will be a fool no more. Neither should you. I
love you all.. Go out and do as you may.. Enjoy your final hours, but be safe, and do no harm to your fellow human beings.'

Tess continued, "That's the remaining portion of the speech that Bishop Carroll was to give today before the Christians became unruly and belligerent preventing him from..."

***

Evangelist Jones was standing to the side listening and holding her peace. With every word, she was growing more upset. Her God was being crucified by one of his servants. His word was being trashed right in front of her, and she wasn't going to take it much longer. When Tess started attacking the Christians, Evangelist Jones

86

couldn't take it anymore. She boiled over.
Evangelist Jones interrupted, "Hold it a minute, sister girl.. How dare you attack Christians like that? Everyone was shocked and upset, but don't you try and put it all on Christians."

Evangelist Jones sternly said, "Move, Miss Thing, and let grown folk talk here."
She started with emphasis, "My brothers and sisters, First John four and one tells us 'Dear Friends, do not believe every spirit, but test the spirits to see whether they are from God, because many false prophets have gone out into the world.'"

"My friends, we all love the Bishop but clearly he has lost his way. We must pray for him and others like him. He used this medium to sway the minds of millions of believers. I beseech each of you who still believe to encourage your brother and sister to stick it out."

"God will never leave us nor will He forsake us. I will believe that to my grave and beyond! If I'm wrong then let me be wrong but ohhhhhh…if I'm right, ohhhhh if I'm right!"

"We will be rejoicing in the house of the Lord forrr…ever! Let's
keep the faith and pray for our fallen. As a reminder, we will be staying on the air all the way to the end so keep your TV tuned in to us as we keep reporting on the Gospel of Jesus Christ."

The camera went away from Evangelist Jones. She stepped off the set and Tess was standing there in tears.

She tried to say something to Evangelist Jones, "Ma'am, I'm…"

Evangelist Jones interrupted, "Look, we don't take sides on this show. That's something you need learn."

Evangelist Jones walked away, headed to her dressing room. She had to pray over the recent events. The world was ending, and her bishop just trashed her God to millions. There was nothing else to do except pray.

**

Roger and Samantha looked at each other. Roger decided to speak first, "I don't care what he says. I'm with Evangelist Jones. There is a God and his name is Jehovah. My faith isn't wrong."

Samantha stood up and said, "I'm glad to hear you say that because he isn't going to lead me anywhere. I'm with you. Let's go hear what Reverend Collins has to say. If he agrees with the Bishop, then we'll be on our own."

Roger responded, "Amen sister." They kissed, and Roger was happier than the day he got married. He knew now that God had delivered his marriage, and no one could make him mess it up again.

XVIII

Bill and Teddy arrived at the Living Word after the Bishop's speech. They listened to the speech on the radio, and now Bill was even more revved up to walk away from Christianity. They were getting out of the car as they were talking.

Bill's voice gradually got louder as he said, "Man, I'm done with this mess."

He pointed at the building and shouted, "I shouldn't even go in there".

Teddy responded, "Naw, bro, let's hear what the old dude has to say. We got 15 minutes; why don't you give Wendy a call. If you're so sure, you might as well get her primed and ready. I know I would!"

"Bill asked, "What's her number?"

Teddy answered, "555-8619, good luck."

Bill pulled out his cell phone and dialed Wendy's number. He was nervous. He had never called a woman to ask her out before. While he was dialing he asked Teddy, "How'd you get her number?"

Teddy smiled and said, "I got my ways. Playas don't tell

89

their game."

Bill recognized Wendy voice. He always thought she had a pretty. He thought, *Man, her voice is soooo sexy!*

She answered the phone, "Hello."

Bill responded nervously, "Hi Wendy. This is Bill."

Wendy said, "Well, this is a shock. You've never called me." It was true he liked her, but he never expected to get with her because of the difference in their beliefs.

Bill replied, "Yeah I know. But things have changed, I have changed. I'm a different man now. I'm a man that can call you and ask you out."

Wendy responded with shock evident in her voice, "Now I'm stunned twice over. Sure, but with this being the last night and all, me and my girls are going out. I kinda thought you would be in church until the end."

Bill replied, "Like the Bishop said, I had a revelation! I agree with him and the time for deceit is over. I've been lied too all my life and I'm not about to spend one more minute believing in it."

Wendy replied, "Wow, this is truly unexpected. I never thought I would hear this from you. I even admired you for always standing firm in your beliefs. Dang, you're even a virgin."

Bill responded with a growing confidence, "Don't remind me. Look baby, the only thing that got in the way of me and you was my beliefs. I'm not chained to those anymore. There's nothing to stop us now."

Wendy asked, "Well, if you're interested in me, then you need to know that I'm not a freak like your friend Teddy tells everyone. If you want to be down with me in the last hours, then you're gonna have to prove it buddy. I'm not down with you getting yourself off with me. I'm not that kinda girl."

Bill replied, "I don't think like Teddy. I'm not looking to do the whole town in one night.. I just want to be with you. Are you down?" Wendy answered, "Yeah, I'm down. Do you know where the Peachtree is?

Bill replied, "Yeah, I know of it. Who doesn't?" He really didn't know but he didn't want to her to know that.

Wendy responded, "Yeah I know. Meet me there at eight."

Bill replied, "I wanted us to be alone."

Wendy explained, "We will be later. I just need to hang out with my girls for a minute. Then we can go to my place. It's close to the club."

Bill responded, "Bet, I'll see you at eight, baby."

Wendy replied, "Okay, bye."

Bill said, "Bye." Then he turned to Teddy and smiled. Teddy was standing a few feet away.

After Bill hung up the phone Teddy stepped to him and slapped five with him and asked, "So what's the deal my brother?"

Bill answered, "You know she wants me. I'm meeting her at eight. Some place called the Peachtree. You know it?

Teddy answered, "Know it! Man, that's my main joint!"

Bill replied, "I never heard of it." Teddy snickered and kicked his leg up. He said, "I heard you tell her you did." Bill was smiling now as well.

He answered, "Yeah, you know how it is. I couldn't let her think I was a nerd or something. We need to be there at eight. Let's turn this church out; then get ready for the Peacetree and my girl!"

Teddy responded, "You got it, brother."

As they started walking in the church they were met by Roger and Samantha.
Roger asked Bill, "So what's your take on this man?"

Bill answered, "Man, Bishop hit the nail on the head. I'm just here to give Rev a chance. I owe him that much. After that I'm out. I already got me a date lined up for the evening."

Roger said, "No man, Bishop got it wrong, brother."

Bill turned and said, "Let me see, he's got two million members under him. How many you got? 'Nuff said." Bill turned back around and began to walk in the church.

Roger said, "Bill, man wait…"

Teddy pushed his way between Bill and Roger. He made a gesture with his hands which suggested that Roger move away from Bill. Bill smiled. He was glad to see Teddy had his back. They had been friends for so long, but they never really hung out. Bill had his faith. Teddy chased women and drank all night. Their personalities were like oil and water, but Bill enjoyed hanging out with Teddy when they were doing things that didn't cause him to test his faith. Now, he didn't need to worry about that. They were on the same page, and Bill loved it.

Teddy said laughingly, "Back off, my brother. He doesn't want to hear it, and frankly, neither do I."

Samantha said, "Come on Roger."

Teddy said, "Whoa, now I can see myself chatting with you, Sweetheart."

Samantha grabbed Roger and said, "No Honey, don't even entertain him. Let's go get a seat."

Bill watched as Roger and Teddy eyed each other up and down.

Teddy said, "What up? Let's do it brother. Yeah, better step off. Punk."

Samantha looked at Bill as he was laughing over the exchange. Bill cringed at the look in her eyes. For a minute he felt bad. He turned and saw a familiar face. It was Brittney, and he knew she'd watched the exchange. Bill immediately felt engulfed by lust. He had hoped that he could go out with Brittney after Wendy. Brittney stepped in front of Bill and stared him in his eyes.

She said disappointingly, "Why? Why have you changed? You were stronger than anyone here."

Bill started to reply, "Because…"
Teddy slid between them. He placed his hand on Bill's chest and slightly pushed him back. He interrupted with excitement, "Whoa, what do we have here my brother?"

Bill answered sternly, "This is Brittney. I told you about her."

Teddy smoothly said, "Well you left out a few details, like 36-24-36."

Teddy glanced lustily at Brittney, "Hey baby how about us hooking up?"

Brittney looked at Teddy with disgust. Bill saw the look on her face. She then looked at Bill and he saw the look change to disappointment.

Brittney said to Bill, "To think, I wanted to go out with you." Bill replied, "It's not too late baby."
She turned and said, "Not with your new beliefs."

She walked away. Again Bill felt like he was making a mistake. He started to reconsider what he was doing.

Teddy interrupted his thoughts, "Come on man, Wendy is much better than her. Can I have your seconds?"

He started laughing as Bill starred at him.

Teddy continued, "You know I'm just kidding man."

Bill finally said, "Come on, let's go in this sanctuary and tell this man off a time or two."

Teddy replied, "Yo, I'm game!"

***

Vanessa was sitting in her car at the Living Word Ministries. She knew she had to confess her sins and make things right. She witnessed the exchange between Bill, Roger and another man she didn't recognize. Tempers were high even at church.

After a few more minutes she prayed and asked God for strength. She got ready to get out the car, when her favorite gospel song, "Jesus is my Rock", by Evangelist Jones came on the radio. She smiled and knew then that she was already saved, and nothing would stop that. She had the confidence she needed. Jesus was with her, and she would not be confessing alone.

***

The Living Word Praise and Worship Team was leading the congregation in songs. Most of the members were standing on their feet, clapping and praising the Lord. Bill looked around the sanctuary, and for the first time in his life, hated being there.
That feeling that he was making a mistake was starting to return. He tried his best to suppress it. *I can't wait to get out of this disgusting place. Look at them! They think they know everything. They don't know Jack. All of them are so phony. Look at 'em, jumping up and down like there's a God! Fools, there's no God!*

Bill sat down near the front of the church with Teddy at his side. He knew his face said what he was thinking, but he didn't care at all. He wasn't trying to hide it any longer. He looked at Teddy, who was yawning noticeably, and making loud noises.

96

Reverend Collins walked in and silenced the Praise and Worship Team. He stood poised at the podium. Bill started fidgeting in his seat.

Reverend Collins began, "Saints of God, you have received a lot of information on this day, most of it bad. But I'm here to tell you not to fear, for the Lord has not forsaken us. Contrary to popular belief, God is still alive and He is still God."

Bill couldn't take any longer and he stood up and shouted, "Bull…"

Reverend Collins removed his glasses. He started to step down from the small stage.
He said, "Bill…"

Bill cut him off, "No Rev, I heard this crap for too long! I'm not listening any longer. Bishop Carroll got it right. We have been deceived! If any of you want to sit here and believe the crap that's coming out of this man's mouth, well, you're a fool!"

Reverend Collins stopped in his tracks. Bill was startled for a moment as Teddy rose his foot in the air, stomping it to the ground, laughing hysterically. Bill chuckled. He knew Teddy was getting more and more excited as Bill turned on his God.

Bill heard another voice from the back of the sanctuary

shout, "Tell him, brother! Let's bolt from this joint!"

Everyone turned around. Bill saw Johnny walking in the sanctuary with Katrina hanging on his arm.

Bill looked at Teddy and mumbled, "I knew it!"

Reverend Collins asked surprisingly, "Minister Johnny? What are you doing with Sister Katrina? Where's your wife?"

Johnny said, "I'm not a stupid minister anymore, and I'm not with that stupid woman anymore. I'm with Bishop Carroll and this woman here? She's the best thing that's ever happened to me. Now, I can tell the world who I truly love."

He reached over and kissed Katrina in the mouth. Bill could see the nervousness and excitement on Katrina's face. He admired both of them for telling the world the truth. It inspired him to continue on his path.

Teddy's laughter rose to a higher level. Bill was constantly giving high fives to Teddy and laughing loudly with him. He was starting to feel more comfortable in his new lifestyle. He looked over at Brittney and she got up and walked out the sanctuary. Bill pointed at her leaving, and gave another high five to Teddy. He acted happy, but deep in his heart, he was sad that Brittney hated him.

***

Vanessa walked in when Johnny was proclaiming his love for Katrina. It sickened her stomach, but she understood it. She was ashamed of what Johnny was saying, but she knew, in her heart, he didn't believe it.

She noticed her neighbors in the audience. She remembered when Samantha talked to her about her husband, and his adulterous relationship. She told Samantha to get back at him by finding someone to have a relationship with as well.

Samantha told her that she appreciated her advice, but she wasn't going that route. Later Vanessa found out that Samantha sought God and forgave her husband. Vanessa thought she was a fool at the time.

She made fun of her to Linda and their friends. Vanessa remembered the hours of time they spent laughing and making jokes at Samantha's expense. Now she admired Samantha.

Vanessa's face soured as Bill shouted at Reverend Collins, "I don't have time to sit around here. I got things to do and a beautiful woman, uh, I mean, women, to see!"

Teddy jumped up and said, "Finally! What he said!"

Johnny looked at the audience and said, "You're all fools if you stay here. I dare any of you to find in the Bible where it talks about destroying the world with an asteroid.

If you don't find it, you should join me, the Bishop, Bill and his good friend here. It's party time baby!"

Vanessa stood up and took a microphone. She couldn't stand it anymore. She had something to say, and she was going to say it.

She shouted with intensity, "Wait, don't anyone leave until I say something."

Johnny shouted loudly and sarcastically, "Oh Lord, here we go!"

Bill looked at Johnny and asked, "Man, can't you shut her up?" Katrina said half laughing, "No one can shut that mouth up!" Johnny replied laughing also, "Now you see why I left her butt!" Vanessa frowned at them.. She wasn't going to let them stop her from doing what she had to do.

She continued, "Ten years ago I found out my husband had an affair with another woman."
Johnny screamed, "Shut up woman! Stop telling my business!"

Katrina said, "Don't worry baby, she just hatin'."

Vanessa looked at them both and continued, "I vowed I would get him back by having an affair behind his back. From that point on my marriage has been a sham. We were lying to each other and the world. It became a daily game. We came to church each Sunday making everyone

100

believe that we were a happily married couple when the truth was we haven't even been together in ten years. I became an evil person. I treated others bad."

"When I saw someone moving closer to God I tried my best to
hinder their growth. I talked about them, I berated them, and I treated them like second class Christians."

"Today when the end of the world news came out, I decided that I needed to spend my last hours cleaning my act up. If I was to have any chance to get to Heaven, I needed to clean my heart."

Johnny yawned loudly. Bill looked at Johnny and said impatiently, "Come on man!"

Katrina said loudly, "Ha! That will never happen. V? In Heaven? That's a joke. If there is a Heaven she won't be there with us!"

Vanessa blocked their actions and comments out. She continued, "I went to several people who I know I offended. Lisa and Carla sitting over there are two prime examples. I apologized for what I did to them over the years. I especially needed to apologize to Lisa who is a new Christian. Again Lisa, I am truly sorry for what I did."

Lisa nodded her head in acknowledgment of her apology.

Vanessa smiled like she had a new friend and continued, "I went to my husband and tried to make amends to him. You can see how far I got with that. But now I come before God and all of you to ask for forgiveness. To anyone I have offended over the years I am sorry. To God, I am truly sorry. I know there is less than a day remaining but I ask God for His grace and mercy and I repent for all my sins."

Johnny laughed out loud and said, "How sickening. You're nothing but a fool. There is no God and if there was a God, He wouldn't forgive the likes of a whore like you."

Johnny turned to Katrina and said, "Let's go baby." Bill and Teddy said together, "Finally!"
They both broke laughing hysterically.

Reverend Collins said, "Wait, Johnny, Bill, let me talk to you both."

Bill replied, "Not on your life Rev. The time for talking is over. I'm going out to get me some, over and over, baby! Later!"

Johnny turned to the audience and said, "If you want to be a fool then stay, otherwise you should get out of here and have some fun!"

Reverend Collins held up his hands and said, "Wait, let me talk to you. Don't leave, we must have faith. Don't listen to them!'"

It was too late. Vanessa watched, and her heart grew sad at the sight of over 300 members filing out of the sanctuary. She thought that Bill, Johnny, and Bill's friend had lead most of them to follow them. The sanctuary was cleared in a matter of minutes. She looked around, and now there were only 15 members remaining.

XVII

Evangelist Jones was on the air when she solemnly said, "Today, we have been given a choice. We can side with God and trust that His word is not a lie or we can be subdued by the world and give in to its pleasures. This is the epitome of free will."

She began to get excited, "I don't know about anyone of you out there, but as for me, I'm on the Lord's side. I plan to be in this studio sacrificing my last hours with my family to ensure the Word of God goes out to all that want to hear it."

"I don't know whose out there listening, but I know someone needs to hear that they are not alone. There are other believers here." She became businesslike, "Okay, we have a phone line open and you can call in with whatever comments you desire to make. Call us at 1-800-BLESSED. That's 1-800-B,L,E,S,S,E,D. Call us, and let's talk about what's on your mind. We have a report from Ralph who is downtown. Ralph, what's going on in the streets?"

Ralph answered, "Evangelist Jones, it's crazy down here. People are running around without a care in the world. Businesses have been abandoned, and people are drinking and doing drugs openly and publicly." Ralph continued, "I have one man here. Sir? What's your name?"

The man answered, "Tim...at least I think its Tim."

Ralph asked, "Tim, where's your family? Why aren't you with them?"

Tim answered, "Man, liquor is everywhere...and free! I don't want to be co...cohe...awake when we die! I'm gonna be smashed...when that thing hits!"

Ralph continued, "There you have it Evangelist. Some people don't even want to be coherent, when the asteroid hits."

The camera cut back to Evangelist Jones. She was shaking her head in disbelief. *This world has lost its mind and people are truly showing what they believe. God have you forsaken us?*

She said, "Thank you Ralph for that report. We need to pray for that man and others like him."

Ralph said, "Evangelist, there isn't any praying going on down here. In fact, I think I'm going to join the festivities. Sorry, but being saved isn't working for me anymore."

Evangelist Jones's head dropped and she said, "Ralph, try and think about what you're doing?"
She could only see Ralph's back as he was running away. She saw the camera move around as if the cameraman

were doing something. He set up the camera and picked up the microphone.

He said to Evangelist Jones, "Ma'am, Ralph's been chomping at the bit to get out there all day. It was only a matter of time. I'll stay down here as long as you need me."

Evangelist Jones said, "Thanks Conrad. Come on back to the studio. I don't think those people want anything we have to offer." Conrad responded, "Yes ma'am."

Evangelist Jones sighed and said, "Well, we have another report from Mark here in the studio. Mark?"

The camera moved to Mark Sims, who Evangelist Jones knew as one of the show's best investigative journalist.

Mark began his report, "Evangelist, it's a sad day for Christians all over the world. It was estimated that there were approximately 2.1 billion Christians in the world prior to today. That number is reported to have significantly dropped."

"We had a pole on our website that asked Christians if they still believed and the results were astonishing. The early numbers show that only 2 percent of the Christians still believe! That's only 42 million out of 2.1 billion, and Evangelist, most of them are in the Middle East."

"The United States has experienced the greatest drop.

It's been estimated that the United States Christian population has dropped by over 93.7 percent. This is truly astounding! Back to you, Evangelist Jones."

The camera moved back to Evangelist Jones. She said, "That's sad, Mark, and most of the drop in believers probably occurred once Bishop Carroll denounced Christianity."

Mark replied, "That is true, Evangelist. We also asked if Bishop Carroll's denouncing Christianity had an impact on those who admitted no longer believing. Over 80 percent of the voters said 'yes'".

Evangelist Jones continued, "My grandmother once told me that most people will end up in Hell because of preachers. It looks like she was right. Twenty-three hours to go. We'll be right back."

XVI

The Living Word sanctuary was virtually empty. It once held over 200 souls who were looking for guidance and hope in the last hours. They were looking to hear an encouraging word from their leader, Reverend Collins. Instead they got encouragement from those who turned on their God. The encouragement caused them to turn on their God and go out and have fun. They lost their faith in God.

Now only 15 people remained in the church. Reverend Collins sat in disbelief at how some of his most prominent members turned against God. He could understand turning on him, but he couldn't understand them turning on God.

How could they turn on God? God, h*ow could these people turn on you? Lord, what would you have me do?* He turned and looked at the faces of the remaining people. All of them appeared scared, confused and without hope. Most were watching him, either overtly or covertly. He knew he had to say something to comfort them. But what could he say?

This was not a situation he was prepared for. In all his years of preaching, he surly never thought he would deliver a word that would have to comfort his people facing the end of the world. Inside, he felt something nudging him to tell the people God is here with them. He felt they had to know that God would not leave them nor would He forsake them.

He gathered himself together and said, "Where there are two or more believers, God is here too. My friends we are not alone. He is here with us. We will stay right here and continue our faith together, one family in the name of the Lord."

"We will keep each other strong until the end. If one of you starts to feel down the rest of us will pick you up. Together we will make it to the finish line! My faith tells me that God has something in store for his people, whether it appears to line up or not. I trust the Lord! Are you with me? Are you with God?"

Martha added, "Yes, Lord, 'cause I don't want nothing to do with that crazy world out there!"
Samantha said, "Amen sister."

Reverend Collins noticed Vanessa standing there sobbing. He went over to her, and put his arm around her. He said, "Sister we will pray for you. You are not in this alone." He motioned for his wife to come over to him.

When Martha got there he said to her, "Take Sister Vanessa to the back, and a couple of you pray for her, and with her." Martha replied, "Will do."

Martha looked at Vanessa and said, "Come on girl. We got you!" Roger said to Reverend Collins, "Reverend

Collins, I think we should tune in to the Gospel Today Show. Evangelist Jones is staying on the air until the end, and she is still a strong believer."

Reverend Collins said, "Yes, we can continue to get information on what's going on as well. Let's go to the cafeteria and turn the TV on there."

***

Bill and Teddy were laughing uproariously in the car as they left church. They were rejoicing over the carnage they left behind, and all the people that followed them out of the church. What Teddy didn't know was that Bill still had that awful feeling in his stomach.

He still wasn't totally happy with his deeds. Something was tugging at him, trying to make him see the error of his ways, but he was resisting. He knew was being convicted by the Holy Spirit, but he didn't want to hear it. *I'm doing the right thing here. There's no God so I might as well have all the fun I can until I die.*

The radio in the car blared out, "*Bishop Carroll has released the world from all of their inhabitations. I feel released and now I'm headed out to party. Join me, DJ Fever at the Peachtree. That's where it will all be happening tonight!*"

Bill reared back in his seat. *There you see. According to the Bishop, I'm a free man. He should know because he is a devout man of God. Reverend Collins couldn't hold the Bishop's Bible.*

He should be listening to the Bishop like the rest of us! There's nothing for me to feel convicted about.

Teddy shouted, "Yeah boy we're free! Telling that Pastor off was the best thing I've ever done. Yeeaaah!"

Bill laughed and joined in, "You were never bound brother, at least not like I was."

Teddy said, "You got that right."

Bill continued, "Did you see Brittney run out of the sanctuary?" He reared back holding his hand over his mouth and continued, "Man, she was pissed!"

Teddy said, "Man, you should have tapped that! She was soooo fine!"

Bill replied, "She's a goody two shoes."

Teddy responded, "Well, Wendy's no goody two shoes!" Teddy added with emphasis, "She's a freak…and I know it!

Bill slapped five with Teddy and said, "Yeah boy, I can't wait."

Teddy replied, "You're one lucky boy. I wanted that so bad I could taste it!"

Bill said, "Yeah, I can't wait until tonight. I have to be

honest with you; I did watch that fine body move around the office on the sly. Now I don't have to be sly anymore."

Teddy responded, "Man, you're human just like anyone else. No one would have said a thing if they saw you looking."

Bill said, "Well, I had an image to uphold." Teddy replied, "Yeah man." They both laughed.

Teddy continued, "I'm gonna turn the Peachtree out tonight! I know it's gonna be some honeys out there."

***

Wendy was sitting in her apartment watching the Gospel Today show. Two of her girlfriends, Barbara and Shan, were with her watching the show.

Barbara asked, "So why did that Bill guy all of sudden want to be with you?"

Wendy answered, "Said he's through with Christianity. I don't know. This guy was the epitome of Christianity."

Shan added, "He just wants to knock some boots before the end and he has his eye on you." She was moving her hips in a sexual manner and laughing as she was talking. "Girl, I wouldn't even waste my time. At least you know someone like Teddy only wants your body. This Bill guy is playing games. He wanted it all along. He's just using

112

the end of the world as an excuse. After he hits it, you won't see him again."

Wendy replied, "I know, but he won't get it until I'm sure it's me he wants, and not what Shan says. He's probably listening to that idiot Teddy. I know he told Bill I'm some kinda freak."

Shan shouted jokingly, "You are!" Shan and Barbara laughed.

Wendy said, "You must be talking about yourself."

Shan replied, "Hey, I know I'm a freak and I love it baby."

Barbara added, "Give me some cognac and I'll be a freak too!"

Barbara and Shan laughed again. Wendy turned and continued watching the show. She felt something within her changing. She didn't feel like going to Peachtree, but she had already promised her two best friends that she would go with them.

The Gospel Today show was making her feel something, and she wanted to stay there and watch the show.

Barbara said, "Hey Wendy, give it to him at 5:55. He should be finished by 6." Barbara and Shan continued to laugh. That was Wendy's cue to walk into the bedroom.

113

She sat on the bed. Her thoughts turned to her life, and how it was all going to end in less than a day. She reflected on her upbringing.

She was an only child raised by a single mother. Her mother took her to church every Sunday but she never joined. She never felt right about joining. She never felt that closeness with Jesus. She always knew about Christ, but she never got close to him.

Five years ago when Wendy was 18 she lost her mother. Graduating high school was supposed to be one of the highlights of her young life, but it turned out to be the worst day of her life.

After the graduation ceremony, everyone had gathered around outside the building. They were all happy and talking with family and friends. Wendy and her mom didn't have any other family, so they were just standing there talking to each other along with Wendy's best and only friend, Denise.

Denise didn't have any friends either. Her mother was an alcoholic, and didn't even come to the ceremony. Wendy was glad that her mother was there for Denise.

Greg was a highly touted running back at the high school and on his way to play major college football. Wendy had a crush on him, but didn't even know she was alive.

Greg was gathered with some of his friends in the parking

lot about 50 feet from Wendy. Wendy was gawking at him, when she saw some known gang members come over to Greg and his friends.

Wendy got worried. She could tell the gang members were saying something to the girls standing with the football players. The football players stepped in and forcibly backed the gang members down. The gang members went back to their vehicle. They were saying something to the players and pointing their fingers. She was happy they appeared to be leaving.

A few minutes later the gang members came back. When they got close enough, they opened fire on the crowd, trying to hit the football players and their friends.

The second the shots began, Wendy's mom grabbed her to shield her from the bullets. Wendy couldn't remember clearly; it happened so fast. Her mother sacrificed her life to save her only child. Wendy tensed, tears forming in her eyes, as she remembered the sound the bullets made as they cut into her mom, one by one.

As they both fell to the ground, Wendy could see the lights go out in her mother's eyes. In tears, Wendy looked for her best friend, who was frozen in place. She screamed for Denise to get down, to no avail.

It was too late. The bullets found Denise next. Wendy screamed as the bullets hit her best friend in the chest four quick times. Denise was dead before she hit the ground.

She remembered the sound Denise's body made when it hit the ground. That sound has continued to echo in her mind since that day. For years Wendy dreamed of that day.
Many nights she cried herself to sleep, thinking of her mom and

Denise. She cried on her bed one more time, as she remembered that on that day, everyone she loved died, along with 27 others in a blood bath. After that day, Wendy vowed to get her degree, and make her mother proud but she never visited the house of God, or sought His love again.

***

Bishop Carroll was flustered and restlessly pacing the floor of his private office. He heard Clint trying to calm him down, but his mind was on the reception he received when he delivered his message.

His image was everything to him. Hearing half the people in the audience shout their disappointment with him disturbed him to no end. He pounded his fist into his hand, angry with all of those who would insult him.

He desired to be loved by the multitude. Bishop Carroll could not get enough of the spotlight. The hatred and disappointment he heard and felt, angered him. He

116

slammed his huge fist on the table.

He shouted, "How dare they talk to me that way!"

Clint said, "Bishop, Bishop, calm down. You have to stop pacing the floor like that."
Bishop Carroll heard him but didn't immediately respond.

He pondered a little more than said, "Did you see how they acted. I couldn't even finish my speech!"

Clint replied, "They're animals. The true nature of a so called Christian is savagery! But Bishop, there were a lot of people in the audience who love you. Even on TV, they're showing love for you. Look, just look at Channel 2. The people love you."

Clint turned up the volume on the TV. Bishop Carroll heard people being interviewed on the street by news reporters. He listened as one news reporter asked a nearby woman, "How do you feel about the Bishop's comments?"

She excitedly answered, "Hey Pookie, Justine, momma! The Bishop is down and I agree with him all the way. If there was a God why would he destroy his own creation? I mean come on, let's be real!"

Bishop Carroll started to calm down. He then intently watched as another reporter asked a different person, "What's your take on the Bishop's comments?"

117

The man responded, "He said the Bible is a fairy tale right? Man, I've been saying that for years and no one listened to me! These so called Christians are fools…idiots…fools, I tell ya!"
"They talk about us for teaching our kids about Santa and they're the ones who turn out to be the fools. Ha! Now who's laughing? I'm with the Bishop."

Bishop Carroll motioned for Clint to turn down the volume. Clint said, "Bishop you're a hero to these people. You have freed them from their bondage. Only a few remaining fools are hanging on to their beliefs. Now, sit down in your big chair and take it easy for a while."

Bishop Carroll felt himself calming down. The news reports did make him feel better. *I guess I am a hero.* He sat down in the chair and tried to relax. He closed his eyes and started to reflect on the events of the day. A sensation of calm soothed across his body. Bam! The sudden slamming of the door to the office startled him. Angrily he stood up and shouted, "What the…"

In walked his wife, Jessica. She pushed her way into the office shouting and screaming at him. The Bishop's guards tried in vain to hold her back. She struggled mightily with them.

Bishop Carroll always admired her toughness. He then motioned for them to let her go.

Jessica shouted, "Are you stupid? Have you lost your ever loving mind? Why didn't you consult me before making such a drastic announcement?"

Bishop Carroll put his hands up in front of him in an attempt to calm her down. He answered her, "Just calm down a minute, Sweetie, and let me talk civilized to you. I know you're upset, but we can get pass this and move on."

Her stern look started to anger him. Jessica said through her teeth while patting her foot, "So talk." Her posture angered him even more.

How dare she talk though her teeth at me and pat her foot. I should throw
her out on her butt." Bishop Carroll motioned for her to sit and asked, "Would you
like a seat?"

Jessica didn't change her posture and said, "No, talk."

He was becoming incensed inside. Bishop Carroll harshly continued, "I told the world what it
needed to hear, the truth! The Bible is filled with fairy…"

Jessica shouted, "Don't you say it! Don't you blaspheme in front of me!" Bishop Carroll reluctantly moved from behind the desk and tried to hug her, but she pulled away from him.
Jessica said, "Don't touch me. I don't want anything to

119

do with you. You're a sinner and a fool."

That was it. That was the final thing he needed to hear. For several years he wanted out of his marriage. However, he didn't want his image tarnished. Now that the world was ending, he could leave this woman, and not think anything of it.

Bishop Carroll sternly said, "Fine. The world is ending tomorrow, so I don't need to put up with your evilness any longer. Get out of here."

Jessica replied, "My evilness? You…"

Bishop Carroll motioned to his men, "Get her out of here, you can continue to be a fool somewhere other than around me." He looked at his men again and shouted loudly, "Now get her out of here."

Jessica shouted at the men, "Let go of me. I know my way out. Good riddance!" She stormed out of the room and slammed the door behind her.

Bishop Carroll caught of glimpse of Clint chuckling quietly. He knew Clint was waiting for him to say something. Bishop Carroll finally said, "Sometimes she just gets on my last nerve!"

Clint said, "That was amusing. You know I can't stand her anyway. I had to tolerate her because she was your wife. Now I don't have to calm you down after

120

arguments with her anymore and you don't have to pretend to the world that you are a happy couple."

Bishop Carroll responded, "You're right, I'm free to do whatever I wish now."

Clint answered, "Yes sir, you are."

***

Roger was pouring some water for his young son when his wife, Samantha, walked up to him. He smiled at her while admiring how beautiful she was. He took every opportunity to admire what he almost lost. He thanked God for keeping his marriage together.

She said, "This is too much. I didn't imagine my day to be like this at all."

Roger replied as he was handing his son the water, "I know, me either."

Samantha asked, "We're all gonna spend the night here; can you go home, and get the kids some clothes to sleep in?"

He answered, "No problem."

She continued, "Oh yeah, and we need a change of clothes too. You can just grab my blue dress. You know the one I wear around the house a lot."

Roger pictured her walking around the house in that dress. She didn't know it but he loved that dress. He had to shake his head and gather himself to answer her.

Roger replied, "Sure. I'll be right back."

Samantha smiled and said seductively, "Oh, I'll need under clothes too."

Now he was really excited. He said, "Maybe you should come with me." She smiled and he smiled back at her. He liked flirting with his wife. As Roger walked away, he saw Lisa was coming out of the bathroom. He admired her for staying a believer. *Man, if anyone has a reason to go out into the world it's her.*

***

Samantha smiled at Lisa and Lisa smiled back at her. Samantha knew Lisa was HIV positive, but she was not afraid of her. She was proud that Lisa chose to give her life to God, and stick to it, despite the news that the world was ending.

Lisa asked her, "How long have you been coming here?"

Samantha replied, "Not long. My husband and I were having problems. A friend referred us to Reverend Collins. We liked it so much that we started attending the service. I know your situation. Are you doing okay?"

Lisa answered, "Yeah, not much can happen to me now. I mean, with the world ending in less than a day, and all."

Samantha said, "I admire you. You could easily be out partying the time away. No one would blame you. You are an inspiration to others, myself included."

Lisa smiled and replied, "Thanks. I'd rather be here with the Lord, than out there doing whatever. It was 'the whatever' part that got me positive. I guess the world doesn't care, since it's all going to be over with soon, but I'd rather have eternal life in Heaven."

Samantha responded, "Amen to that. I'm with you. There's no other place to be than with family and friends, praising the Lord to the end."

Samantha saw Vanessa and Carla coming toward them as they were talking. They appeared to be laughing as they approached.

Lisa said to them, "This is so odd; the two of you laughing and
talking together."

Carla responded, "You know, we actually like a lot of the same things. We just never knew it."
Vanessa added, "Yeah, imagine all the stuff we missed out on. We could have been shopping together…"

Carla interrupted, "…eating at the Colehouse…"

Vanessa sighed, "Oh, yes, my Lord! You like the Colehouse?"
Carla answered, "Yeah girl…"

As Carla was talking Samantha heard a loud noise from the front of the church. She thought it sounded like a door slamming. Then she heard shouting.

A voice shouted, "V! V, where are you? I know you're here, V!"

Samantha looked at Vanessa. Carla and Lisa were looking also.

Samantha knew trouble was brewing. She wished her husband was here.

***

Tommy stood outside of The Holy Place church. He really needed to see his dad now. The realization that the world was coming to an end hit him, and he wanted to make amends. He didn't want to talk on the phone with him; he wanted to see him in person.

Marcie came out of the church and asked Tommy, "Hey, are we still going to see dad in the morning?"

Tommy answered, "Yeah. I think we really need to see

him and bury the hatchet. What do you think?"

Marcie said, "I'm down. Service is getting ready to start, are you coming in?"

Tommy answered, "Yeah, in a minute."

Marcie replied, "K. See ya."

Tommy smiled. He loved his baby sister. He always protected her and she always admired him. He couldn't count the number of fights he had gotten into protecting his sister. Almost every man tried to hit on her, and some tried too hard. *Being a politician's child isn't easy.*

***

Vanessa recognized the voice that no one else did. She stood frozen in place as she saw Reverend Collins headed to the front to see what was going on. Fear for her safety, and everyone there, roared throughout her body.

She heard Reverend Collins ask, "Calvin, what are you doing? Why didn't you come to the meeting?

Vanessa realized that Carla had taken her arm and was tugging on her to go up front. The other ladies were already making their way to the front. When Vanessa got up front, she saw Reverend Collins standing between her and Calvin. For the first time he looked scary. His face was hard and displayed true anger. For the first

time, she saw what he truly was, and it scared her to
death.

When her eyes meet Calvin's he shouted, "I need to talk
to you, now!"

She saw him pointing his finger angrily at her and in a
downward motion.

Reverend Collins said, "Well come on into my office."

Calvin sharply replied, "Not you fool! V, come here. I
can't just let you go like its nothing. You're my woman!"

Vanessa was truly afraid for all their lives. Calvin was
angry. He towered over the much shorter Reverend
Collins. Calvin had a temper, and could get violent, but
this was the first time she witnessed it in action.

Vanessa's eyes met Samantha's, and the two locked for a
second. The look told Vanessa she was afraid. She knew
Samantha had two young kids at the church, and her
husband wasn't there. She had to say something to get rid
of Calvin before anyone got hurt. She looked at Calvin
and said in a meek voice, "Calvin, I told you on the
phone that we were through. I'm saved again and I can't
run around with you. Please respect that I am a saved,
married woman."

Calvin harshly responded, "I don't care about that crap.
Your husband doesn't even you. You're coming with me

and that's final!"

Reverend Collins stepped toward Calvin and chimed in, "Calvin let me..."

Vanessa jumped in shock and utter fear. She backed against a nearby wall, and held her hands over her mouth. In one quick motion, Calvin hit Reverend Collins with a punch to the chin. Vanessa was not really one for violence. She could talk a good game, but when it came to it, she really didn't have the stomach for it.

Reverend Collins fell to the ground. As he fell, everyone gasped, as his head hit the end of a table, and he appeared to be unconscious. Vanessa was scared that Reverend Collins might be severely injured. Martha and Brittney came running into the room and past Vanessa.

Brittney yelled, "Daddy! What have you done to my daddy?"

Calvin shouted, "He got in my way, and if you get in my way, I'll do the same to you!"

Martha began taking off her earrings and shoes. Martha said, in a serious, street like tone, "Oh no Lord, we gonna have to beat some Holy Ghost love into this man."

Vanessa couldn't move. She saw Samantha quickly reached past her kids to grab Martha. The other ladies grabbed her as well. Vanessa didn't want anything to

happen to Martha, especially
after seeing what happen to Reverend Collins.

Brittney shouted at her mom, "No momma, he's crazy!"

Martha said back, "No baby, he's just a punk."

Calvin yelled, "Come on old lady! I'll show you a punk,
and knock you out too!"

It was so much going on now that Vanessa didn't know
what emotion to feel. She knew she had to do something
to put a stop the insanity. She screamed so loudly,
everyone froze. Vanessa yelled, "Stop!"

They all stopped yelling, and posturing for a fight, to look
at Vanessa. Vanessa's back was against the wall and she
was noticeably scared. She continued, "Now…Sister
Martha I can't let you fight him. Look at him. He'll kill
you. You need to tend to your husband."

She turned to Calvin, as she was fixing her clothes on her
body. She continued, "Calvin, I'll come with you only if
you promise to leave them alone."

Calvin sternly said, "I got no beef with them. It's you I
want." Lisa spoke up, "V, no, don't go with this clown."

Carla added, "Yeah V, he can't take us all."

Calvin pointed his finger at Lisa and Carla. He said,

"Shut up, or I'm gonna put my foot up both your butts. Lisa, you're dead anyway. What does any of this matter to you? You're a dead whore walking. Now, come on V. I don't have any time for this mess."

Before Vanessa could take a step, she saw Roger walk in with a bag in his hands. Vanessa looked back at Samantha. Samantha and her kids ran out the door behind them. Vanessa assumed she was going to meet her husband through the sanctuary.

Roger walked in, and Vanessa looked at him, panic in her eyes. She saw Roger look down at Reverend Collins, then back at Calvin. Calvin turned around and looked at Roger. Samantha had made it to the other side.

Vanessa could see Samantha saying something to Roger, but she couldn't hear what they were saying. She assumed she was warning him about Calvin.

Calvin shouted, "Come on bro, what you got!"

Roger was equal in stature to Calvin. Secretly, Vanessa hoped Roger would stop Calvin from taking her away, but she didn't want to risk another person getting hurt. Vanessa began to move toward Calvin.

Roger shouted, "Wait V. You're not going with him."

Vanessa stopped and watched, as Roger and Calvin stared at one another. She didn't know what to feel. She didn't want to go with Calvin, but she didn't want Roger to get hurt. She silently prayed, *Father, help us. Please send your Angels down and protect this house from this evil man. Help us to show him the error of his ways Father. In your wonderful son, Jesus' name I pray. Amen.* Calvin postured toward Roger, as if he were expecting a fight.

Roger said, "Calvin, I don't want to fight you but I can't let you take anyone out of this church."

Calvin replied, "Come on dude, let's do this."

Vanessa still didn't want anyone else to get hurt. She said, "No Roger, I'll go if he promises not to hurt anyone else."

Roger responded, "No V, you're not going anywhere."

Calvin said, "Enough of this!" Vanessa shuttered as Calvin stepped toward Roger, and swung a hard over hand right at his face. Roger side-stepped the punch, counting with a jab to the jaw, and a quick blow to the stomach.

The women gasped as the fight began. The kids started crying. Vanessa was secretly happy to see Calvin stumble backwards. He grabbed the end of a table, flinging it between himself and Roger. Roger kicked the table out his way. Calvin lunged at Roger.

Samantha yelled, "Roger, look out!" It was too late.

Calvin hit him in the stomach with his shoulder, and tried to lift Roger in the air. Vanessa felt a twinge of fear course through her body, as Calvin got the advantage. Roger forced Calvin to the ground, and punched him in the side several times.

Vanessa felt some relief. Calvin struggled to his feet, and the two stood facing each other again. Calvin's back was to the ladies. Vanessa watched Samantha. She was behind her husband, holding on to her kids for dear life. The kids were crying for their daddy.

Calvin reached around his back. Vanessa was truly scared now as she saw him pull out a knife. She yelled, "He's got a knife!" One of the kids shouted, "Daddy!"

Calvin pointed the knife at Roger and said, "Now, I'm gonna cut you into little pieces. Then I'm gonna cut your wife and kids into little pieces. Then I'm gonna take my woman out of here!"

Vanessa felt someone rush past her, almost knocking her down. Before she could realize it, she heard a loud thump that filled the air. She happily watched Calvin fall to the ground; apparently unconscious.

The next thing Vanessa saw was Martha standing there, holding a two by four in her hands.
She said, while moving her head side to side, "I'm 'bout tired of him!"

Roger replied, "Thanks, First Lady. I thought I was done."

Martha responded, "I couldn't let that happen, brother. This idiot hurt my husband, and I can't stand by and let anyone else get hurt."

She turned to Vanessa and said, "Are you okay girl?"

Vanessa was crying as she said, "I'm so sorry!"

The women all gathered around Vanessa.

Carla said, "V, this isn't your fault. He's to blame."

Vanessa was without words. She was happy that Calvin had been subdued, but the fear of what he truly was still revolved within her. She finally said, "I can't believe I thought I loved him." She cried as she saw Samantha run to her husband. As they embraced, Vanessa silently prayed, and asked God to forgive her for all the trouble she had caused.

She continued to watch as Roger and Samantha kiss and hugged as if it were the last time they would ever be together. Samantha was crying, but it was tears of joy. Vanessa smiled as the kids hugged their father. It was a blessing to all of them...a family still together in this time.

Brittney was kneeling over her dad. She said, "We need to see about my Daddy."

Vanessa replied, "She's right, and we need to tie Calvin up somewhere. Do we have any rope?"

Martha responded, "We got some in the back closet. I'll get it."

Lisa said, "Can somebody bring me some ice? I think he's just unconscious."

Carla replied, "I'll get it."

Everyone was busy at the church. Vanessa went and sat down. She was still trying to calm herself down. She looked at everyone, trying hard not to discuss what just happen. She didn't want to talk about it either. She did know she was grateful Roger and Martha saved her from having to go with Calvin.

XV

Johnny and Katrina returned to her home. He was excited about the last day, and the events that were lining up. He decided to have sex with Katrina one more time before they hit the Peachtree.

He pulled her close to him, and whispered in her ear, "I love you baby. Come on down here with me."

She smiled, as he pulled her down to the bed. He knew it wouldn't be difficult. She always gave it to him whenever he asked. As ironic as it seemed, that's what he hated most about her. It wasn't a challenge when it came to Katrina. She was needed and clingy. But Johnny liked her performance in the bedroom, so he stayed with her.

Katrina shouted, "Whoa, my Lord, baby that was so good."

Johnny smiled and thought to himself. *Of course it was.*

He said to Katrina, "Nothing but the best for you, baby." He laughed to himself, and fell back on the bed to rest. He felt Katrina shaking him.

She asked, "Are you still taking me to the Peachtree?"

Johnny answered, "Yeah, baby. Wake me in about an hour."

Katrina sighed and replied, "Men!"

Johnny laid on the bed, thinking about Vanessa. He knew in the back of his mind, his discontent for her was his own fault. He wondered if hadn't cheated on her in the first place, would they have continued being a happily married couple?

He glanced over at Katrina's picture on the nightstand, wondering if he really loved her. He knew she was just something to toy around with, because he had grown to hate Vanessa so much.

He quickly rationalized that everything was Vanessa's fault. She didn't have to cheat on him, even if he cheated first. *If she was any kind of a woman, she wouldn't have slept with another man, regardless of what I did. After all I'm just a man and that's what we do. Why couldn't she have been like that Samantha babe? She didn't cheat on her man even when he cheated on her. A good Christian woman would have known better.*

Katrina interrupted his thoughts, "I thought you were sleeping? Are you thinking about V again?"

He knocked the pillow down that she threw at him. He snickered under his breath, as he heard her stomp angrily out of the room. Johnny knew wherever she went, she was probably crying again. He hated her weak and clingy nature. That was one thing he admired about his V.

135

She wasn't a weak woman, and didn't need to cling to him. He hated the fact that Katrina always accused him of thinking about Vanessa, even though it was true most of the time. In his mind, Johnny felt Katrina knew how he felt about Vanessa. She should just learn to deal with it.

Should I dump her and find me some new women at the Peachtree? Naw, she might come in handy, if I don't get anyone else tonight. It's nice to have an old standby to kick around. His last thoughts, as he fell asleep, were on all the female companionship he dreamed he would have to choose from at the Peachtree. He couldn't wait to get there.

***

Evangelist Jones said, "I hope you enjoyed those moving videos. We now have a special interview for you. We have Bishop Carroll's wife, Sister Jessica Carroll right here, live in the studio."

The camera zoomed out, and now viewers could see both Evangelist Jones and Jessica on the screen. Evangelist Jones was excited for the opportunity to interview her friend. They meet ten years ago, and immediately became friends.

Evangelist Jones excitedly began, "Sister Carroll, how are you today?"

Jessica answered, "Tired, frustrated, shocked, you name

136

it. My emotions have been on a rollercoaster all day. I just don't know how much more I can take!"

Evangelist Jones said, "Well, Sister, that's why we're here. To help you, and anyone else out there who wants help. We just have to keep each other prayed up!"

Jessica replied, "Amen to that!"

Evangelist Jones inquired, "Sister Carroll, I have to ask you, do you agree with your husband's assessment of Christianity? I mean, do you feel Christianity is a lie?"

Jessica sharply answered, "I certainly do not agree with that crap!"

She then straightened up and continued, "I don't know what my husband's problem is, but what he said earlier is totally off base. I will die a devout Christian woman and no one…no one, not even my husband, will change my mind."

Evangelist Jones happily replied, "Amen sister, we have to stand for ourselves in these last hours. No one can get us to Heaven but ourselves. Do you have any idea where he got this or when he started believing this mess? I mean, in all the years I have known him, I have never seen anything like this in him."

Jessica answered, "Evangelist, I have lived with that man for 25 years, and I have never seen him like this before. I have seen him help people. I have seen him go to bat for people who sometimes even I didn't think he should. I have seen him go toe to toe with believers of other faiths in support of Christianity."

"I don't know where this came from, and I apologize, on his behalf, for all the disruption, and all the lost souls his opinions have caused."

Evangelist Jones replied, "Sister, you have no reason to apologize. His deception is all on him."

Jessica added, "I know, but at the end of the day, I am still his wife, and we are still one in the eyes of God. This means I must help him when he's down, and take the blame for what he has done. I have to try and save those who he has deceived."

Evangelist Jones replied, "Now, there's a truly supportive wife. Too bad she's married to a man who has lost his way. Oops, did I say that out loud?"

They both laughed. Evangelist Jones continued, "Thank you, Sister Carroll, for coming out, and answering some questions for us. Wait, I understand we have a couple of callers on the line. Go ahead caller?"

A voice on the phone said, "Yes, my name is Thomas, and I would like to ask if this is true and the world is to end tomorrow, why do you still hang on to your faith?" Evangelist Jones asked, "Sir, who are you directing your question to?"

Thomas answered, "Oh, I'm sorry. I'm asking Sister Carroll."

Jessica responded, "It's just what you said, faith. You see, my brother, it may not appear to line up with the word to us, but you just have to have faith in all things seen and unseen."

Thomas said, "Thanks, Sister, I'm hanging in there. I don't like the other choices, so I will stay with God."

Evangelist Jones joined in, "Amen brother. Hang in there, we're praying for you." Evangelist Jones pumped her fist in the air with excitement. She lived to inspire others to praise the Lord. Her days as a youth were spent singing in the choir.

When she was 11, she started directing the youth choir. Everyone knew she would be an exceptional musician and singer.

She continued, "Another caller; what's your name and what do you want to talk about today?"
A female voice said, "My name is Susan and my question is for Evangelist Jones. Why did you kick that other girl off the air? I think her name was Tess something. All she started doing was telling the truth about how ignorant those Christians started acting towards the Bishop."

"Christians are so two faced. When someone supports you, you're all shouting. Let someone have a different opinion, and you put them down and kick them off the air. I can see why the Bishop said what he said."

As the caller was speaking, Evangelist Jones was trying to hold her tongue. She didn't like it when Christians were attacked, but she had to remain cool.

Evangelist Jones took a breath then seriously answered, "First honey, I moved Tess off the show, because her views are not in line with this station's views. Secondly, for you to say Christians were 'acting ignorant', is totally misleading to people. Everyone was shocked at the news, but they were not acting ignorant, nor were they disrespectful to the Bishop." "Finally, I think I can speak for all Christians when I say we don't judge anyone, or put anyone down, because they don't believe as we do. I don't know who you're hanging with, but true Christians don't behave that way. Thank you for calling, and we love you! God bless you."

Evangelist Jones stood up and smiled. Jessica joined her, as they both pumped their fists in the shouted praise to the Lord.

Evangelist Jones continued to smiled and clap her hands. She continued, "Remember, you can call in to us at 1-800-BLESSED with your questions, comments, or concerns. As you can see, we don't shy away from anyone."

Jessica said, "God bless you Evangelist. You handled that well."

Evangelist Jones replied, "Why, thank you, my sister."

They both hugged. Evangelist Jones said, "Look, thanks for spending time with us.
It was fun. What are you going to do now?"

Jessica answered, "I'm going home, where I hope my three kids are now. We will pray, and ask God to dwell in our home all night until the end. Hallelujah!"

Evangelist Jones responded, "Thanks, Sister Carroll, and be sure to keep it tuned to us."

Jessica replied, "I sure will. Thank you for letting me express my side of the story. Be blessed, my sister!"

Evangelist Jones responded, "God bless you too, my sister." The camera zoomed in on Evangelist Jones. She kicked her foot up and said, "Now we are at the 22 hour mark. We're going to play some videos for your enjoyment, and when we return, which will be in about 30 minutes, we will bring Tess Minter back on the air. This is just for the caller who thought we did Tess wrong. Stay tuned."

***

Bill and Teddy were in Teddy's apartment, getting ready to head down to the Peachtree. They were watching a newscast and getting excited. Bill watched the television, as Howard Clark, of WWXY Channel 2, stood just off the main street across from the Peachtree. Bill was getting excited.

The reporter began, "This is Howard Clark, reporting live from the Peachtree. The atmosphere down here is one of excitement and anticipation, as the biggest party in our history is about to begin."

Bill looked at Teddy. They both smiled. Bill walked around in a small circle, hitting his chest. He could feel the excitement growing with every strike.

Howard Clark continued, "I have Carlos Davis here with me. Mr. Davis is the manager of the famous Peachtree. Mr. Davis, tell us what's in store for this area tonight."

Carlos Davis answered, "We got everything you could imagine down here. We have agreements with every establishment within eight blocks of the Peachtree. Everything you can imagine is here, and everything is free. All of these hotels have agreed to allow Peachtree customers free access to their rooms. The restaurants are open for your enjoyment."

"We have food, beer, wine, alcohol, drugs, anything you want, we got it! Just come on down to the Peachtree and do whatever you want. The only rule we have is that you must act civilized."

"Any rowdy behavior, and the security guards will throw your butt out. You won't be allowed back in, what I'm calling, the Peachtree Zone."

Bill smiled, jumping up and down. He was truly excited.

Howard asked Carlos, "So, are you saying that if I want to smoke pot on the street, then I can?"

Carlos answered, "Yeah, go ahead, do what you like! The worlds about to end, so who's gonna arrest you? Try all the things you have thought about, but didn't because of your morality."

Howard replied, "My goodness, this is going to be outrageous. How long will this last?"

Carlos answered, "Until the asteroid hits my friend. This party doesn't stop until it's over dude."

Howard responded, "Thank you Mr. Davis. I'm sure these streets will continue to get packed with people as the night progresses. Ladies and gentlemen the Peachtree is the number one place to be, until the asteroid strikes. As you can see behind me, things are revving up already."

"I will be reporting from here all the way until the end. With a party like this going on, I don't plan on leaving at all. Now, let's take it back to our studios."

Teddy shouted, "Yeah boy, that Carlos dude is the man. I can't wait to get down there and have some fun!"

Bill said, "Yeah, me too, brother. I hope that freak is ready to give it up. I don't have all night to be messing around with her."

Teddy replied, "Man, just hit that, then come on back to the Peachtree. There's plenty more where that came from. I bet there are so many freaks already down there. Just imagine, I bet a bunch of them are gonna be trying drugs for the first time. Those are going to be the really easy ones."

Bill laughed and responded, "Yeah boy. I won't be a virgin anymore and… that's for sure!" Bill jumped up and gave Teddy a high five in the middle of the living room. Both of them had started drinking already. Bill knew Teddy loved his gin and juice. He would always tell Bill about his exploits after the weekend.

In the past, Bill secretly admired those stories. Now he was ready to create some of his own. He had never tried alcohol before, and was already feeling the effects of it. His head felt light. Suddenly, he realized he hadn't eaten anything all day. Bill took another drink. He couldn't help but frown, because it was so strong.

Bill said, "Whew, man that's strong. So what do I do if she doesn't want to do it?"

Teddy answered, "Man, here's what you do. You tell her that she's the sweetest thing in the world! You tell her that you don't want to be with anyone else. Make her believe that she's the only one you're thinking about."

Bill was taking it all in as Teddy was talking. He couldn't believe he could be even more excited than he already was. All he could picture in his mind was Wendy. He thought about her walking seductively through the office. Now, she was going to be all his.

Teddy continued, "But, now this is it. When she has that look in her eye, that look that says, she's about to give it up but has just a little bit of doubt, you say, 'Wendy, I love you.'"

Bill jumped up, his hands covering the big smile on his face. Teddy grabbed him by the shoulders and said with emphasis, "Man, it works every time. After that she'll throw it at you."

Bill said, "Wow, for real?"

Teddy replied emotionless, "Yeah man. You see, you say whatever you think they want to hear. Your goal is to get laid. After you succeed then you get up and come on back down to the Peachtree, my brother."

Bill asked, "What if she doesn't want to come back to the Peachtree?"

Teddy shook his head negatively and said, "You're not hearing me. After you get what you want, you don't care what she wants. Leave her butt there. You don't care."

Bill put one hand in his pocket, the other covering his mouth. He was shaking his head up and down and walking around the room. He replied, "Oh, I got you now. Yeah, that's how it's done. Man, you're a pro."

Teddy responded, "Yeah, sometimes I amaze myself."

***

Wendy, Barbara and Shan were finished getting dressed at Wendy's apartment. They were leaving to walk down the street to where the festivities were being held. Wendy was thinking about Bill, and his change of attitude.

She asked, "Why should I even bother with Bill tonight? I mean, it's clear he only wants one thing."

Barbara answered, "What man doesn't, tonight, or any other night?"

Shan added, "Shoot, even women want that tonight"

Barbara replied, "Amen to that. For once we can be as footloose and free as a man. We don't have to worry about kids, disease, relationships, nothing. All we have to worry about is getting laid."

146

Wendy sneered as Barbara and Shan laughed. Shan said, "I know I'm down. I want to try some crack, and see what the fuss is all about."

Barbara asked, "Are you serious? I want to be in control of
myself."

Shan answered sarcastically, "Yeah that cognac will keep you in control alright."

Barbara sternly said, "Whatever!"

Shan continued, "Yeah, my cousin tried crack. She said it was the best aphrodisiac."

Barbara asked, "How much crack did she do to believe that?"

Wendy couldn't take it anymore, as Barbara and Shan continued to trivialize the situation, laughing. She stopped paying attention to them. Wendy went over to the couch and sat down. She was deep in thought.

Shan said, "I don't care. It's the last night, and I'm gonna try me some."

Barbara replied, "Okay, I'll try a little bit with you. Wendy, how 'bout you?" Wendy didn't answer, or even look in their direction. Barbara snapped her fingers in

Wendy's face and said, "Wendy, are you there?"

Wendy answered, "What?"

Barbara replied, "Where are you? Earth to Wendy, can you join the conversation?"

Wendy watched, sneering as Barbara and Shan laughed at her expense. She asked, "What if they're right, and we're wrong?" Shan responded, "What are you talking about?"

Wendy continued, "The Christians, what if they're right?" Barbara replied, "You trippin'."

Shan added, "Yeah, you trippin' hard. Bishop Carroll already put that notion to bed girl. If he says that there is no God and the Bible is a fairy tale then who are you to argue? He knows what he's talking about. What you need is a drink, and some crack, baby!"

Barbara and Shan broke out in laughter. Wendy was disgusted as they slapped five with each other. She continued to sit there, looking at them, shaking her head. She wondered if she should even go to the Peachtree.

Wendy glanced at her Bible, which she kept on a table in the living room. She noticed that it was covered with dust, from never being opened. *Ironically, Bill would have been the perfect person to talk to right about now. Why did he have to change? Now, I don't know who to talk to about Christianity. God, send me someone…please.* She thought about grabbing

148

the Bible, and reading a few pages, but her thoughts were quickly interrupted.

Shan said, "Come on girl."

Barbara added, "Yeah, let's go, before it gets too crowded."

Shan whispered, "Yeah, and the crack is gone!" Barbara said, "You stupid."

Wendy left the Bible on the table without reading it. Her apartment was on the second floor. After she locked the door, she turned to go down the stairs, where her friends were waiting.
When she turned, she saw a lady at the top of the next set of stairs above her. She had never seen her in the building before. The lady just stood there, smiling at Wendy. Wendy pondered the odd, but comforting behavior of the woman.

Wendy said, "Hello." The woman simply nodded her head in acknowledgement, and smiled at Wendy. Wendy felt a soothing sensation move throughout her body. She didn't know what it was, but it felt good to her.
She felt safe, as if she were in her mother's arms again. After a minute, she brushed it off, and went downstairs, where her friends were waiting, impatiently. Wendy got outside, and she could hear the music coming from the Peachtree Zone.

Things were cranked up at the Peachtree Zone. The closer they got, the more revved up Barbara and Shan became. It was like they were transforming right in front of her.

Wendy started feeling something in her stomach. She wasn't excited at all. She knew her life was not intended to end at the Peachtree. The thought of all the sex, drugs, and alcohol turned her stomach. She planned to use Bill as an excuse to leave. She silently prayed that Bill would convert back to his Christian roots, and help her find her way to salvation.

***

The Heston Plaza Hotel was a five star hotel, where many visiting dignitaries stayed when in town. A large, black limo pulled in front of the Heston. This particular hotel was located just outside the Peachtree Zone.

The driver of the limo stepped out of the vehicle, quickly walking to the rear passenger side door to open it. Out stepped a small, slender built man, who was the assistant for the next man to step out of the vehicle.

This man was a masterful, full of confidence, power, and intelligence. He was tall and strong. His presence commanded respect from all who knew him. He looked around, taking note of his surroundings.

He looked at the driver, who was almost as tall as the

client. The client reached in his pocket for a tip for the driver. He was confident that his assistant had already put the tip there. It was important that he give the tip personally. He was that way. He pulled out a hundred dollar bill, handing it to the driver and waited for the driver's acknowledgement. The driver said, "Thank you, Bishop. Is there anything else I can do?"

Bishop Carroll saw the driver was looking in the direction of the Peachtree Zone while asking this question. Bishop Carroll took note of the driver's desires. He placed his large and powerful hand on the driver's shoulder.

Then he answered, "No, there's nothing else I require at this moment. Go on to the Zone, son. Tell the manager, Carlos, you work for me. You'll get the best treatment in the house."
The driver excitedly replied, "Thank you, sir!"

He ran off into the night air. After the driver departed, Howard Clark, from WWXY, Channel 2, approached Bishop Carroll.

Bishop Carroll saw Clint attempting to stop the reporter and his crew, but being the vain man he was, Bishop Carroll wanted them to come over.

Howard asked Bishop Carroll, "Sir, are you participating in the festivities in the Zone?"

Bishop Carroll responded, "No, I'm staying here in the

Heston." "I will not be taking part in the festivities in the Zone. I'll leave that to the younger generation."

Howard asked, "Sir, do you have any words for the people who are attending the festivities in the Zone?"

Bishop Carroll answered, "They should enjoy every minute of it. Morality is not an issue any longer. Thine eyes have been shown the light. The fairy tales rule us no more."

"You should partake of the fun yourself Howard." Howard replied, "Yes sir, I plan on it."

Bishop Carroll felt Clint step in between him and the cameras. He said, "Okay, that's enough." "The Bishop has had a long day. He needs to retire for the evening."

Howard concluded, "There you heard the encouragement from Bishop Carroll, himself. I think he's right, and we will partake of the festivities. We'll be back in 30 minutes."

Bishop Carroll and Clint walked in the hotel. Clint already had the key, so he led the Bishop to a side elevator, which led to his private penthouse suite. On the ride up, the two men were silent, until Clint asked, "Bishop, do you think Sister Carroll will cause any more trouble for us?"
Bishop Carroll responded, "She doesn't know anything.

152

So don't worry. Just enjoy the evening.

Clint replied, "Yes sir."

***

The Carroll residence was one of the most beautiful homes in the city. They lived in a gated community, but somehow people got through security, and were outside the Carroll home, shouting obscenities at Jessica for not supporting her husband. As she drove by them to her house she thought, "*Why are people wasting their last hours in front of my house shouting at me when they could be at home with their families.*"
She knew the Bishop had a following, and they would protect him and his name at all cost. She wondered if they knew the truth would they truly support him. When she got in the house, she saw her three children, her mom and her dad watching TV.

She said to no one in particular, "Can you believe these people have nothing else to do, but shout at me?"

Milton Jr was the oldest of the Carroll children. He was 27 years old, and a pastor over his own service. Jessica knew that he was having issues with his father's announcement. She planned to talk to him in hope of offering comfort.
Milton answered, "They've been there since dad made his statement. When they heard you on the Gospel Today show, they turned on you."

Jessica didn't respond. She stood at the window while everyone was watching television. Melody, Jessica's daughter and middle child, came into the room. She was 22 years old and had just graduated Summa Cum Laude. Jessica was so proud of her.

She had just been accepted into medical school when the announcement was made. Melody said to the room, "I am so ashamed of Daddy. Everything he taught us revolved around Christ, and now he denounces it to the world!"

She walked over to her mother and put her arm around her. Jessica was happy to be comforted by her daughter, smiling at her in acknowledgement of her daughter's concern.

"Momma, don't worry; let's just pray that daddy will come to his senses," said Melody.

Jessica was drying her tears. She looked her daughter in her eyes and said, "I hope so, baby."
"I still love him so much. Nothing could change that. I know we fight sometimes but I love that man."

Jessica's youngest son was named Samuel. Samuel was a sophomore in college and the most energetic of the Carroll children. He shouted, "I hate Dad!"

The shouting startled Jessica. She walked over to Samuel

and hugged him. She said, "Sam, don't say that. You don't mean it."

Samuel said, "Forget him, Mom. Let him burn in Hell."

Jessica replied, "Don't you ever say that again, you hear me?"

Samuel answered, "Yes ma'am."

Jessica continued, "Now listen, all of you. Your dad made an awful decision today." "We have to pray for him. Okay? "We can't just turn off the love we have had for him. No, we must pray that he sees the light. That's all we can do."

"Mom, Dad's on TV," said Milton Junior

The TV was showing Bishop Carroll's interview with Howard in front of the Heston. Jessica went and retrieved her purse. She said, "I'm going down there and talk to your dad. Maybe I can get him to come home."

I'm going too, Mom," replied Milton Junior.

Melody said, "Me, too."

Samuel added, "I'm going, too."

Jessica said, "Hold up; all of you can't go. Milton baby, you're the oldest, you and I will go. You two stay here with your grandparents."

They both said together, "Mom!"

Jessica sternly said, "You heard me."

Samuel replied first, "Okay. I'll stay."

Melody joined in, "Me, too."

XIV

A voice over the sound system blared out, "Ladiessssssss and gentlemen. I am DJ Fever and it's time to parrrrrrrrrrrrrtyyyy!" The crowd sent up a thunderous roar as the smoke rose up from behind the DJ stand.

Just after the smoke started, two young ladies, dancing in red, white and blue bikinis, rose up on separate platforms: one on each side of the DJ stand. As the platforms reached their intended height, two more ladies, dancing in pure white bikinis, were lowered down to a height approximately 3 feet above the DJ stand.

With each movement, the crowd was sent further into a frenzy. The music reached a fever pitch as DJ Fever shouted, "They call me Fever because I'm soooo…"

The crowd yelled, "Hooooooooot!"

DJ Fever continued, "Tonight everyone who is anyone is in the Zone. We got it all for you. We have the best music, the best liquor, the best weed, the best rock, pills, and most of all the best…laaaaaaaaaadiesssssss!"

The crowd yelled to the top of their lungs. DJ Fever was excited to be the man chosen to lead off the celebration. He looked out at his audience and thought, *There have to be over*

5,000 people parading through the streets."

Each inch of the eight block zone seemed to be covered with people.

He continued, "Fellas find ya self a lady, or two! Ya heard the Bishop, there's no more morality on the planet." "If you got morals then…"
The crowd yelled, "Go hommmmeeeeeeeeeeee!"

DJ Fever recommenced, "The world is ending tomorrow so there's no reason to hold back. Do anything ya like! Let's paaaarrrty!"

***

Wendy, Barbara, and Shan all arrived as DJ Fever was speaking. Barbara and Shan were into full party mode. They hit the first refreshment stand they came to, dancing as they went.
Wendy was dragging along behind them. She was reluctant to go with each step, but she promised her friends and Bill that she would come.

Barbara said, "I think I'll start with a wine cooler." "What about you guys?"

Shan answered first, "Yeah, pass me one. Peach preferably." "I want some of that MJ too."

Barbara asked, "Wendy?"

158

Wendy looked at her and sternly said, "No thanks."

Barbara sternly replied, "Look, you need to drop that 'tude' girl. Tonight is no night to be so Holier than Thou. Drink this cooler. It'll help loosen you up."

Wendy sharply answered, "I said no, didn't you hear me?"

Shan asked, "What's your problem?" "Didn't you hear DJ Fever? No morals tonight baby!"

Wendy replied, "I shouldn't be here. I'm leaving."

Both Barbara and Shan said in unison, "What?"

Wendy responded with an attitude, "You heard me, I'm leaving. Bye."

Barbara shouted as Wendy started to head back home, "What about Bill?"

Wendy turned and remembered that she told him to meet her at eight. She started walking back. She wanted to keep her promise.

Shan smirkingly said, "Knew that would get you back."

Wendy replied with even more attitude, "Only because I don't want to make it a practice to lie. I'm trying to live right in my last hours."

Barbara responded sharply, "Right? Want some of this weed?"

Wendy angrily said, "Why are you trying to get me to sin? Didn't you just hear me say I'm trying to live my last day right?"

Barbara was visibly upset. She replied, "Whatever! I'm trying to give it to you so you can loosen up. What difference does it make to live right now? You might as well get off that ship. All these years, I've seen you in full party mode, weekend after weekend. Now, you wanna be saved? Nothing can save your butt now."

Wendy shouted angrily, "What…ever!"

Shan jumped in with a calm voice, "Come on, guys. Stop fighting. Look, those guys are checking us out."

Barbara quickly turned her head and asked, "Where?"

Shan tried to hide her finger as she pointed in the direction she wanted them to look. She replied sneakily, "Over there."
Wendy looked in the direction Shan was pointing and saw three men heading toward them. She signed, not wanting to be bothered by these guys. She thought to herself, *"Dang, how did I get into this situation?" "I should have stayed home."*

The three men approached Wendy and her friends. One of them spoke, "Hi ladies. You guys are looking quite good tonight. My name is Jeff. These dudes are my friends, TJ and Jump."

Shan confusingly asked, "Jump? What kind of name is that?"

Jump smiled and answered, "It's my nickname." "I used to jump off anything I could climb. My dad started calling me Jump, and everyone else got in on it. It kinda stuck."

Shan responded, "Okay, whatever!" "I'm Shan, this is Barbara and Wendy. Don't mind Wendy too much; she trippin' tonight."

Wendy frowned at Shan. She said under her breath, "Whatever, 'ho."

Barbara covered her mouth with one hand and gasped.

Shan said to Wendy, "Come on girl, you know I'm just playin'."

Jeff asked Shan, "Wanna dance, baby?"

Shan gave him the up and down look over. Wendy dreaded this moment. She knew one of them would be asking her soon. Shan smiled and answered, "Yeah, let's do it. Have you ever tried crack?"

TJ looked Barbara up and down. Wendy cringed. She knew she would be next. She watched Jump out of the corner of her eye as he got ready to make his way to her.

Barbara asked TJ, "Are you gonna ask, or just window shop?"

Wendy looked around, hoping Bill would show up just in time to save her from being asked to dance. TJ happily answered Barbara, "I was checking out how lucky I am. Wanna dance, baby?

Barbara tried to be cool as she replied, "Come on, let's see what 'cha got."

Jump looked at Wendy. The moment she dreaded had quickly arrived. She thought he was smiling as if hoping he would be the luckiest of the three. She was trying hard to find a reason to turn him down. She didn't want to dance, and she didn't want to spend another minute in the Zone.

Wendy looked around again, but no Bill. Jump tried to be suave when he said, "I guess that leaves you and me, sweetheart."

Wendy replied while half looking at him, "I don't wanna dance. I'm waiting for someone."

Jump asked, "Its Wendy, right?"

Wendy answered, "Yeah."

Jump continued, "You are such a beautiful woman. You're tall, slender, and I can see that you have style and grace. You just have that certain something that your friends don't have."

He paused for a moment then continued, "Look I can see you have class. Anyone can see that. Your friends are not like you. I get it, you're waiting on someone, and a woman like you wouldn't just go off with someone else. But, all I'm asking is, while you're waiting, why, don't we dance."

Wendy thought, *"I guess there's no harm in it. Afterall, he is nice and polite."* I don't have anything to do until Bill shows up, so I guess I can dance a bit.' She said to Jump, "Okay…one dance." Jump smiled and it sent a curl up Wendy's back.

***

In the skies above the Earth, a dark cloud-like figure roamed too and fro. The figure was on its way to the new body its master allowed it to inhabit.

The figure happily reminisced over the last body it inhabited. That body was a 22 year old female. The figure remembered how the body became so consumed by the power the evil figure made it feel.

Shortly after the figure inhabited the body, the woman killed herself to rid herself of the demon. The demon remembered how he laughed at her when he removed himself her body while she was falling to her death.

She thought she was killing the demon by killing herself, but she realized that she was only killing herself. The demon would continue to live and inhabit others. The demon loved the horror that appeared on her face.

The last words she would hear were the demon telling her that she was on her way to Hell. That had been a year ago, and the demon longed for another body to inhabit. Its master had given him permission to inhabit the body of a young man that craved sex.

Now the demon hovered over the man's apartment building, waiting for its appointed time to inhabit the body. It was smiling, waiting intently. Now the time had arrived. He lowered himself down into the man's apartment building. Through the cement walls of the building he went, one by one, until he arrived in the bathroom of its next host.

The host could not see the demon with his natural eye. Slowly, he entered the body of the man. The deeper he entered, the more pain he caused the man. The pain was so tremendous, it caused him to fall to his knees and grab his face. The man tried to scream in agony, but nothing came out of his mouth. The demon laughed as he continued to inflict pain on his new host. By slowly entering the body it caused the host the most pain. He enjoyed inflicting pain because it allowed him to control his host. The demon had now taken over the man's body. Now the man's writhed in pain; his chest pulsing in pain, as if something was burning into it.

The demon was placing the mark of possession of the body. After a few moments, the man looked down to see a symbol now resided on his chest. Instead of being afraid, the man was excited. His body felt like never before. The difference excited him. What he had originally resisted, causing him great pain, he now coveted. He felt stronger than ever. He rolled his fingers over the symbol on his chest, pleased with it.

Now he was ready for the evening to begin. He thought he would get lucky with one, maybe two, women at most. Now, he had the power to conquer as many women as he wanted. He had renewed confidence in himself. His confidence was not his alone. He looked into the mirror. With confidence he boldly said, "I am Asmodeus, Demon of Lust!"

***

Reverend Collins was starting to wake up. His blurred vision slowly came into focus. He saw his stepdaughter and wife sitting on each side of him. He smiled at them, happy to see them. He slowly started to remember what happened to him. Groggy and grabbing his head he urgently said, "What happened?"

165

Martha placed her arm around him and angrily replied, "That jerk hit you."

Reverend Collins responded, "Where is he? Did he take Vanessa?"

Brittney said with fear evident in her voice, "No Daddy. Mr. Stevens fought him off, and Momma hit him over the head with a two by four."

He smiled at his wife. The one thing he truly loved about her was her aggressive nature. She wouldn't sit back and let things happen. She was aggressive and took action.

Martha confidently added, "Yeah, I did, and he's lucky that's all I did. The jerk! He's tied up in the sanctuary."

Reverend Collins said as he tried to get up, "Now Martha, be a good Christian. Let's keep him tied up for a while." Martha sternly responded, "Ump!"

***

Roger was standing near the front door area, when two men tried to gain access to the church. Roger and Martha decided to lock all the doors, in case someone else tried to attack them. Roger didn't recognize the men, but he saw a limo with two flags at the front of it.

He thought it was a presidential limo, but he couldn't

imagine why the president, or anyone else of high status, would come to the Living Word Ministries church.

Through the glass door, Roger asked the men, "Who are you,and what do you want?"

One of the men answered, "We're secret service, open the door, Sir."

They both showed their badges to Roger as Samantha walked in. She asked Roger, "What's going on Honey?"

Roger said, "They said they're Secret Service, and they have badges."

Samantha said, "Let them in."

Roger replied, "I don't know."

Samantha responded, "Come on, they even look like G-Men."

Roger told the men, "Step , and I'll unlock the door."

The men complied, and Roger unlocked and opened the door. The two men came in immediately. One said to the other, "Go that way, I'll start over here."

Roger shouted as he followed one of them, "What's going on?" "Talk to me?"

Samantha followed Roger. The second agent's voice came over the radio and said, "All clear."

The agent with Roger replied, "I got something over here." He then looked at Roger and asked, "What's going on here?" He was pointing at Calvin as he was tied up.

Roger answered, "He tried to kidnap a woman here, so we tied him up."

The agent then got on the radio and made a call. The other agent walked in the door.
Roger looked at the agent as he surveyed the situation without any emotion apparent on his stern face.

The first agent said into the radio, "Sir, we have a man tied up here. One of the people here said he tried to kidnap someone."

The voice responded, "Is he secure?

The agent said, "Yes, sir."

The voice replied, "We're entering the building."

Roger didn't know who was coming in, but he thought it must be someone big, for all this attention.

***

Jessica arrived at the hotel with her son, Milton Junior.

The Bishops bodyguards quickly met her with force. She shouted at them, "Let me go! Do you know who I am?" They didn't respond. Instead, one of them pulled out a radio to contact someone. Jessica assumed they were calling Clint or her husband. She couldn't stand Clint. She tried to be coordinal with him, but inside she could not stand him.

She knew in her spirit that he wasn't right, but she knew her husband liked him. Jessica heard Clint's voice come over the radio, acknowledging the call. He sounded as if he were sleep.

He said, "This is Clint."

The bodyguard told him, "We have detained Sister Carroll and Pastor Carroll, Jr. What should we do with them?"

He answered, "Get rid of them…by any means."

The bodyguard replied, "Yes, sir."

Jessica was shocked at what she heard. She shouted, "Clint, I won't let you…" The bodyguard shoved her away. The bodyguards were rough with Jessica and her son. One of the bodyguards punched her son in the face, knocking him down.

The lead bodyguard shouted, "Get out of here, or we'll see to it that you aren't around when the asteroid hits."

Milton Jr said, "Come on, Mom. It's obvious that Dad doesn't want to see us."

Jessica was disgusted, but she knew her son was right. She needed to leave because Clint was prepared to take any action to get rid of her. She had to go back to her family. She had to figure out what to do next.

***

Evangelist Jones was back on the air. She was praise dancing as the camera focused on her. She stopped, reared her head back and shouted, "Hallelujah!" Evangelist Jones put her arm around Tess. She said, "I have sitting next to me, Tess Minter, who earlier placed the blame for the disruption at Devine Word Ministries solely on Christians."

"I removed her from the air, because that view doesn't support this station, nor are they proper for a journalist. Journalist should remain as impartial as they can. Tess is here to speak on her own behalf because we had a caller who felt we were wrong to remove her as we did."

She looked over at Tess with an honest smile on her face. Tess looked at her, smiling as well.
Evangelist Jones continued, "Tess, what would you like to say?" She motioned for Tess to go ahead.

Tess smiled at Evangelist Jones, then back at the camera. She started, "Evangelist, in short, I was wrong. I got

170

caught up in the moment, and spewed out words that were inappropriate, and in conflict with this station's views."

"My words were also in total conflict with my views. I was, and I continue to be, a strong Christian. For all I said, I do apologize. To the caller, I thank you for feeling the need to come to my aid but it was me who was wrong. In the end, I'm big enough to admit when I made a mistake. The excitement of being on the air should never conflict with my Christianity."

Evangelist Jones asked, "Tess, I must ask you, if you are speaking of your own free will?"

Tess answered, "Yes. My words are mine, and mine alone. I am not being coerced by anyone."

Evangelist Jones replied, "Thank you, Tess." The two hugged each other, and then turned back to the camera. Evangelist Jones excitedly said, "We have a caller. Yes!" "I love it when people call in, can't you tell?"

The caller's voice was slurred. He said, "Hey Tess baby, come on down to the Peachtree. You look sooooo fine, baby! I got a room just for me and you!"

Evangelist said, "Wooo…" She looked at Tess, hoping her response would be a Christian one.

Tess replied calmly, "No thank you, sir." "I'll take my

171

chances with Jesus."

Evangelist Jones gave a 'thumbs up' sign to Tess.

She excitedly said, "Good answer girl! We need to start screening those calls a little better."

Tess responded to Evangelist Jones while nodding her head, "Amen."

Evangelist Jones smiled and said, "Let's take another call." "God, I pray this one is better."

The voice on the phone said, "Evangelist Jones, thank you for staying on the air all this time. You could easily have returned to your family, but your sacrifice has helped me a great deal. You see, I'm here all alone."

"Watching your show is the only thing that I have to keep me going. "I'm in a wheelchair and have to care for myself. My caregivers left me here alone. I just want to say thank you for staying on the air."

Evangelist Jones sadly replied, "Oh my Lord, we cannot have that!" She turned to someone off camera and ordered, "Someone get his name and number, so we can get some people over there immediately!"

She then turned back to the camera and starting talking to the caller, "Sir, we're going to get someone to you quicker than ASAP."

The voice on the phone happily replied, "Thank you so much, Evangelist!"

Evangelist Jones energetically replied, "Well that's why we're here…to help people like you with this struggle. I can't believe your caregivers just left you all alone. God bless you and remember He has not forgotten you!"

The voice responded, "Amen, sister, and again, thank you so much."

Evangelist Jones said, "We understand things down at the Peachtree are in high gear. Saints we need to be in high gear as well. We are getting reports that all kinds of sin is going on down there. We all need to be in prayer for those souls. If only one is saved, Hallelujah, we should thank God for that one!"

"I'm told that Mark has another report for us." "Take it away, Mark!"

Mark said, "Yes, Evangelist. We are receiving reports that they're giving away free beer, wine, all kinds of alcohol, drugs, and hotel rooms down at the Zone. All of these things are free. Evangelist, they're giving everyone all the room they need, to be as immoral as possible."

"Evangelist Jones said, "My God; people don't care anymore. The devil is reigning in the Zone. We'll be back."

***

Johnny was dressed and ready. He was in the foyer, sipping on some cognac, waiting for Katrina. He was excited about the Peachtree. He had heard all the reports coming from there, and couldn't wait to get there. He was trying to restrain himself from jumping up and down in excitement. He finally shouted, "Come on baby, let's go."

Katrina yelled back, "I'm coming." She raced down the stairs and embraced him. She said, "I'm sorry, but I wanted to look my best on your arm."

He said to himself, *"Whatever."*

Johnny replied, "Yeah, let's get out of here and get down to the Peachtree."

She frowned. He thought, *"Dang it! There she goes again!"* He told her, "Katrina baby, you know I love you." "You look sooooo good!" He wondered how he could contain himself.
The ability to lie like that was an acquired specialty of his. He was the master at it.
They walked out the door and to Johnny's car. Once they got inside, Katrina was smiling at him. He knew the 'I love you' lie had worked wonders again. He hoped she wasn't going to start getting all mushy with him.

He wanted some freedom to be with other women, but just in case the Peachtree was all hype, he had to ensure that she still loved him. She broke the air of silence and asked, "Johnny, do we really need to go down there? I mean, I'm all you need, right? Johnny said to himself, *"Dang it!"*

He looked at her carefully, thinking about what words to use. After all, he did like her, but at the same time he was thinking about all the other fine women that would be down there. But, on the other hand, he thought, *"What if the reports are over exaggerated? Then, I'll need someone to spend my time with, and it might as well be her."*

Johnny replied, "Come on baby, I just told you how I feel. You know I love you." He continued to secretly smile as he uttered those words. Truthfully, he never believed he loved her, but when he realized that all she needed to hear from him, he said it.

He thought, *"Man, how long can I continue to lie like this? I'm good…man, I'm good."* Johnny continued, "I don't want to be with anyone else but you. I'm going down there for the music, and to get my drink on." "We'll have fun, together. Now come on Baby, loosen up!"
He outwardly smiled, but inside, he was laughing as hard as he could.

He wanted to meet some new women in the Zone. He was tired of Katrina. If the world weren't ending, he would have found him a new squeeze anyway. He

glanced at her as she smiled. She believed him again. She always believed him. They started on their way.
The Peachtree was a few miles away, so it wouldn't take them long to get there.

He had to contain himself, so Katrina wouldn't realize just how excited he was.

***

Unsuccessful in her attempt to see her husband, Jessica decided to head back home.
She let her son drive because she was too upset. Jessica said, "I don't understand what is going on with him. Why won't he even see us? I can somewhat understand why he wouldn't want to see me, but why not you?"

Milton Junior answered, "I don't understand it either Mom." "Why would you want the world to end without seeing your wife and children?"

Jessica says to her son, "Milton, I'm so proud of you. You have grown up to be a great man of God. Tomorrow, when life ends on this planet, I know you will be in Heaven."

Milton Junior looked at his mom and replied, "So will you mom. You have stood behind this man, even though he's lost his mind. Your reward will be the same as mine."

Jessica responded, "Thank you, Milton Jr. We have to

keep the others prayed up."

Milton Junior replied, "We will."

***

The 15 remaining members of the Living Word Ministries church, along with Calvin, who was still tied up, waited at the entrance for the person in the limo. Reverend Collins stood in front of the group, wondering who would garner all this security and special treatment at this last hour. As he waited patiently, he looked over at Calvin.

He could not believe what he witnessed earlier. Reverend Collins felt blessed when he hired Calvin for his music department. He hoped that Calvin's baggage would be behind him. The police told Reverend Collins about Calvin's history.

Calvin came to the Living Word Ministries after being released from jail. He was charged with domestic battery after he severely beat his girlfriend for coming home late. She had to be hospitalized for a week, with bruises and contusions all over her body. He also broke two of her ribs in the process.

Calvin's former girlfriend was so scared of him, she wouldn't testify against him in court. The district attorney in the case had no choice but to release Calvin. Calvin then moved near the Living Word Ministries, and that's when Reverend Collins met him.

Reverend Collins brought him into the service in the hope that he had changed.
He had suspicions Calvin and Vanessa were having an affair. He kicked himself for not handling the situation. He hoped that it would just blow over. Now, he realized that he should have done something then. The door swung open, interrupting Reverend Collins' thoughts.

Another secret service agent stepped in, quickly followed by an elegant and graceful woman, dressed in a beautifully designed, sleek blue dress. Reverend Collins didn't know if the dress was expensive, or if the woman wearing it was that beautiful. She was carrying one child, while another was walking beside her.

Once they were in, a tall, slender man entered the building followed by yet another agent.
Reverend Collins recognized them. He smiled and said, "Mr. President, of all the places you could go, you decided to come here to be with us?"

President Murphy answered, "Yes, Wilson. I always told you I would visit. There's no better time than now."

Reverend Collins turned to everyone and said, "Everyone meet my cousin, President Stan Murphy, and his lovely wife, Elizabeth. Can someone take the little ones? They look so tired."

Samantha said, "I'll take them."

Mia said, "I'll help."

Brittney added, "Me, too."

President Murphy and Reverend Collins shook hands, and the President met everyone in the room. Reverend Collins said to President Murphy, "Can we get you, or your men anything?"

President Murphy replied, "No, I think we're fine."

Reverend Collins said, "Have you been keeping track with what's going on down in the 'Zone', as they call it?"

President Murphy answered, "It's a shame. I was hoping everyone would be with their families at this time."

Elizabeth interrupted, "You men talk, I'm going with the ladies."

President Murphy responded, "Okay." He kissed his wife, then turned to Reverend Collins and continued, "Bishop Carroll is the cause of all this. If he had stayed a believer, many of those lost souls wouldn't be down there right now."

Reverend Collins replied, "I don't know. A lot of them might not, but I think most of them were just looking for an outlet; something to take their mind off the end. He gave it to them in spades."

President Murphy responded, "You're probably right. I thought he was stronger than that."

Reverend Collins replied, "To be honest, so did I."

***

Katrina proudly walked by Johnny's side as they approached the Zone. As they got closer, she felt a twinge of fear. She looked at Johnny. He was acting like a kid going to his first state fair.
Her mind traveled to the day they first met.

She was sitting outside of the Living Word Ministries crying. Her boyfriend at the time had just left her for her sister. Katrina was devastated. She planned to go home that afternoon and commit suicide. Her plan was to drink a bottle of wine, and take a bottle of sleeping pills. She no longer wanted to live.

She recalled Johnny coming to the window of her car, pointing down. She didn't know what he was talking about so she rolled down her window.

He said to her, "Your skirt is hanging out of the car door."

She chuckled, while wiping her, tears away. He comforted her and they agreed to meet later that day. She thought he would be the one. She remembered how much she admired him when he was up in that pulpit. She thought Vanessa was a lucky woman to have Johnny. Even though he was married, she believed God sent him to take care of her, like her father did.

She always needed the comfort of a man. It started when she was a little girl. She was close to her father. She remembered all the good times she had with him. He used to take her to the movies, the park, and the fair. Everywhere he went, he took his little girl.

One day, when Katrina was 15 years old, she was at home with her mother. She went to answer the door, and two police officers were standing there. They told Katrina and her mother that her father had died in a car accident.

The news devastated Katrina. From that day, she always felt she needed to have a man in her life. She went from one bad relationship to another, searching for a replacement for her father. When she was 18, she started using sex as a tool to get a man. She believed that if she gave herself to a man, he would stay with her.

After a while, Katrina couldn't keep her hands off of Johnny. She believed that some people at church suspected they were sleeping together, but no one could ever prove it. Now as they approached the Zone, Katrina wondered if she was going to lose another man, just before the end of the world. Her heart began to hurt as she watched Johnny's get moreexcited with each step.

She saw him jumping up and down in anticipation.

He said, "I can't wait to get in there, come on, Katrina."

Katrina replied, "I'm coming, I'm coming." What she was really trying to do was stall him, in the hope that he wouldn't go in there. She wanted to go home and be with her man until the end. Once inside, Johnny went straight to a bar.

Katrina frowned as she heard him say, "Hey man, give me a double rum and coke." He turned to her and excitedly asked, "What you want baby?" Katrina softly said, "I'll have a glass of white wine."

Johnny angrily replied, "That's all?"

Katrina stomped her foot and replied with anger, "You know I'm not a drinker."

Johnny turned his back sarcastically said, "Whatever!"

He got the drinks, and gave Katrina hers. He said, "Here baby, let's go." They headed into the Zone. They were no more than 100 feet into the Zone, when Katrina saw Johnny being approached by a seductively dressed young woman. She couldn't have been more than 20 years old.

She had on a black dress that barely covered her behind. The dress was so tight; it showed every curve of her body. Her breasts were large for her sleek body, and most of them were exposed by the dress.

She walked up to Johnny, reached up, and put her arms around Johnny's neck. She said, "Hey baby, my name is Missy, what's yours?"

Katrina went ballistic. She angrily shouted, "None of your business! Get out of here!"
She tried to push Missy in the shoulder, but Missy stood her ground, and squeezed Johnny's neck harder. Johnny put his hand on Katrina's shoulder, stopping her from causing any more trouble.

Missy sternly replied, while looking Katrina up and down, "Stop tripping mom!"

Katrina yelled, "Mom? I'll show you."

Johnny angrily shouted at Katrina, "Hey, chill out, Sweetheart. We're all here to have some fun and party. Get loose." Katrina's mouth was wide open. She was appalled, as Johnny hugged Missy around her tiny waist. The two kissed on the lips. Johnny's hands roamed around Missy's body, and Missy was grinding on him. Katrina was outraged.

She grabbed the first man that walked by, and kissed him tightly in the lips. The man kissed her back. She was trying to make Johnny jealous.

Johnny happily said, "Now that's more like it baby."

Katrina was shocked at his response. They were there for only ten minutes before all the lies Johnny told came out. He had him a new woman, and he didn't want Katrina anymore. She was feeling sick to her stomach again. Another man had dumped her. In the back of her mind, she knew Johnny didn't want her, with all the loose women running around the Zone.

Now he had proven it. She looked at the man, kissed him, and sharply said, "Take me to a hotel."

The man replied, "Let's go baby."

***

"Well, we have reached the 21 hour mark, and most people appear to be having a great time down here in the Zone," said Howard Clark. He continued, "I have even shared in some of the festivities myself. For the first time in my life I tried some marijuana or 'MJ' as they call it. It's a feeling or sensation that I have never felt before. I can see why people become addicted."

"There seems to be some of everything going on here. People are meeting and filling up the hotel rooms. They're dancing in the streets, smoking pot, drinking, you name it, it's being done down here. I'm feeling really hungry so let's return to our studios while I get me some that fried chicken. Hey dude over here!"

***

DJ Fever shouted, "They call me Fever because I'm soooooooo...."

The crowd finished his statement, "Hoooooooot!"

DJ Fever announced, "Fellas, we have a contest for you. Ladies listen up because this has to do with you as well. Fellas we have a beautiful 22 year-old virgin right here. She has agreed to give herself to one man before the end of the world."

The men began shouting, making cat calls, and screaming out loud with excitement.

DJ Fever knew they all wanted to be the one. He continued, "Now fellas, all you have to do is become the man who sleeps with the most women by 8:00 am."

The men shouted again, and began jumping around in hysteria. DJ Fever smirked as he realized how easy it was to get people to lower their morals. He then quieted the crowd and continued, "Now fellas, each woman will have to verify that sex actually occurred." In order for it to count the woman will have to verify it. Now ladies, you ask, 'what's in it for you?'
The women screamed with anticipation.

He continued, "The lady with the most sexual partners

will be set up with a presidential suite at the fabulous Charlton Hotel. She will be treated like a queen for the rest of Earth's existence. That means anything and everything she wants...she gets!"

The ladies in the zone began to scream with excitement. DJ Fever finished up, "There you have it; the man with the most female sexual partners by 8 am will win this beautiful 22 year old virgin. The woman with the most sexual partners by 8 am will be crowned 'Queen of the Earth' for the remaining 10 hours."

DJ Fever pumped his hands toward the sky and yelled, "Go for it my people!" After he finished his announcement, he stood there for a few minutes enjoying the screams. He then walked behind the DJ curtain, listening to the crowd as they screamed and yelled more and more.

He pulled out his favorite pack of cigarettes, lighting one up. After taking a deep puff, he smiled. Sensing satisfaction from his master he said, "Did I serve you well Master?"

He turned and watched, as a dark figure emerged from the shadows and moved toward him. The figure smiled.

Satan said, "You will cause many to sin. You have done well, Seth. Your Master is pleased."
DJ Fever replied, "That is all I desire, Master."

***

Wendy was tired of dancing. She was sitting down at a table as Barbara and Shan continued to party.

She watched Shan as she quickly graduated to crack. Her stomach churned as Barbara gulped down another cognac straight up.

Jump came to Wendy's table, sitting down in front of her.

Wendy thought, *"Here we go again. Will this guy get the message or what? Dang."*

Jump smiled and pleasantly asked, "Do you want to go to some place quiet?"

Wendy politely answered, "No, I'm still waiting for someone." She added emphatically, "Remember?"

Jump replied as he took her hand, "Look, it's been an hour and old boy hasn't shown. He's probably gettin' busy somewhere."

He reached across the table, placing his face directly in front of hers. She cringed because he was mere centimeters from her face. She hoped and prayed he didn't try and kiss her.

Jump continued, "I have a room saved over at the Tradewinds. Let's go over there."

187

Wendy was shocked at the blatant attempt to seduce her. She quickly and sternly asked, "For what?"

Jump sternly replied, "What's up with you? Why'd you come here if you're not down?"

Wendy sternly responded, "I came here because I agreed to meet someone here. That's it. I'm not down for all this…this sin! She got up and turned her back to Jump. At the touch of a hand on her shoulder, she quickly shrugged it off. She turned and sternly began to shout, "Look…"

As she swung around, she realized it wasn't Jump's hand. It was Bill's. Wendy meekly replied, "I thought you were someone else."

Bill asked sarcastically, "Oh, so you were replacing me?"

Wendy softly responded, "No…"

Bill quickly interrupted, "I'm kidding. You know, it was hard tracking you down over these eight blocks."

Wendy smiled and said, "You didn't give up."

Bill proudly answered, "No baby, I didn't. I'll never give up on you."

He pulled her close to him, lightly kissing her on the lips.

Wendy was tingling inside. She hadn't felt like that in years. She really liked Bill, but she wasn't sure he really liked her.

From out of nowhere, a voice shouted, "Yeah baby, Bill's first kiss."

Wendy dropped her head. Wendy knew that voice, and she shuddered at the thought of him seeing her kiss Bill.

Teddy looked different to her but she didn't know what it was. He looked evil, like something had taken control of him. When he got near, she tingled, and a chill ran up her spine. For some reason, more than at any other time, she didn't want to be around Teddy.

She saw Teddy was walking with Shan. They were arm and arm. When they got close to Wendy, Shan said, "Bill, I'm glad you're here, because Wendy's been trippin'. She's been zero fun so far. Please loosen her butt up."

Teddy said, "Oh, he's gonna loosen more than that up alright." Shan and Teddy burst into laughter.

Wendy said with disgust, "Shut up Teddy. Is that all you think about?"

Teddy put his hands in his pocket, reared back and said, "Yeah, pretty much." Teddy and Shan continued to laugh. Wendy looked at him with disgust. She pulled Shan by the hand, so they could talk by themselves.

Wendy said, "Shan, what are you doing?"

Shan answered, "What are you talking about? Teddy's the man." Wendy replied, "Are you kidding? Look at him. He looks evil or something. Shan don't go anywhere with him."

Shan proudly said, "Girl, you're crazy! Teddy looks hot! I don't know why I didn't see it before. He's too fine and so handsome. Whoa, I can't wait to get him to the Tradewinds. See you girl." She ran back over to Teddy. Wendy walked back over to the group. As Teddy and Shan were leaving Shan shouted back at Wendy, "I'm going to the Tradewinds with Teddy. I'm gonna get me some!"

Wendy stood there shocked, that Shan would sleep with Teddy. She asked herself, *"Why couldn't she see how evil he looked?"* She couldn't understand why Shan was acting like she just didn't care.

Things were starting to get strange. Barbara was walking off in the distance with TJ. They were headed in the same direction as Teddy and Shan. Wendy called out to Barbara, but she only turned, waving at Wendy.

Wendy just stood there with Bill. She didn't know what to say, so she waited for Bill to say something. After a few awkward moments Bill said, "So, what do we do now?"

Wendy answered, "We need to talk."

Bill asked, "Talk?"

After a brief moment he continued, "I thought we were here for more than talk."

Wendy was sensing something different about Bill as well. She knew he had turned on his Christian beliefs, but it was more than that. This was not the man she had known for the past five years. This was not the man she liked and respected so much. Wendy quickly looked him in the eyes and said, "I don't know what your maniac friend told you, but I'm no hoochie. In fact, I didn't want to come, because of all the things happening here. I need to be in church. She emphasized, "You need to be in church!"

Bill stepped closer to Wendy. Wendy started to step back and away from him but she was frozen in place. He took her arms and said, "I'm sorry. I'm no Teddy; no one could be Teddy." He smiled at her and rubbed her back. "Let me just walk you home. We don't have to do anything you don't want to do." She laid her head on his chest and felt at ease. She wondered if she was making a mountain out of a molehill.

***

Inside, Bill was laughing uproariously at the lies he so

easily told Wendy. He learned well from Teddy, and he hoped it would have the same results Teddy seemed to always get. Bill was shocked at his behavior. He used to care about Wendy. When no one was looking, he would watch her sway as she walked.

He often wondered if they could have a life together. He thought of her as sexy and intelligent. He actually thought she could be his wife. Now, he only looked at her as the object of his desire.

He had changed and he knew it. He liked it. He had little regard for Wendy now. She was only a means to end his virginity. He asked himself, *"Is my feelings a product of Teddy's coaching or is this how I really feel? Naw, Teddy had nothing to do with it. Like Bishop Carroll said 'thine eyes are open'!* He dreamed about what he would do after he finished with Wendy.

As they walked, he gazed at some of the women in the Zone. Bill couldn't wait to get his hands on them after Wendy. He wanted to look closer at them, but he didn't want to let Wendy know he was looking.

As they started walking toward Wendy's apartment, Bill wanted to put her more at ease. He said, "Wendy, I have to tell you a story about me. I've told no one else this story, so I hope over the next 20 plus hours, you can keep it to yourself."

Wendy replied, "I will. I probably won't even be around

anyone else. I feel like being alone."

Bill asked, surprised, "Without me?"

Wendy laughed, "No, silly, just you and me to the end."

Bill proudly replied, "Now, that sounds like a plan." Bill watched Wendy as she looked up to the sky. He was calculating his next move.

She asked Bill, "I wonder which one it is."

Bill answered, "I don't know. I've tried not to think about it."

Wendy responded, "You know it makes you think about your life."

Bill smiled inside. This was the direction he wanted the conversation to go. Bill replied, "I know. That's why I want to tell you some things about me. I just want to let you know I'm sincere about this." He thought to himself, *"Here we go."*

Wendy said under her breath, "We'll see."

Bill began to ease into his lie, "When I was a boy I was always picked on by the other kids. Girls wouldn't even talk to me because I was just so shy." "I think that was the reason I turned to Christ. Christ made me feel like I belonged and that someone loved me. I don't think I really believed any of it. I felt like it was all I had. I really threw myself into religion because I had no friends. At church, the other kids wouldn't even have anything to do with me."

"I really don't know why but no one has ever paid me any attention. That is, no one until you. You see Wendy; deep inside I've always enjoyed the fact that you had feelings for me. I didn't know how to respond to them, because I never had anyone interested in me. I want this night to be so special." He stopped to test how it was going. He saw her smile at him. He wished he could read minds to know what she was thinking.

She said, "Bill, you're a great person. I don't know why no one would be your friend. I certainly don't know why no one would want to go out with you. What I don't understand is how and why you hooked up with Teddy? Of all the people in the world, why would you be friends with that idiot?"

Bill pondered. Should he take up for Teddy or should he side with Wendy? If he sided with Teddy, that might turn Wendy against him, but if he sided with Wendy, it could all be good. But then again, if he showed some loyalty to Teddy, she might respect him more. He stopped and looked at her.

Bill continued, "Because Teddy is the only person who wanted to be my friend. I know he has his ways but he's been there for me over the years. But this isn't about

194

Teddy, it's about me and you till the end of time."

"That's so sweet. I just hope it's true," replied Wendy.

***

Shan and Teddy were in the room, ripping the clothes off each other. Shan was so zoned out on crack; she hardly knew what was going on. At times, the room was spinning, but she loved the high crack had given her.

She had never in her life felt this way. She had no worries at all. Shan was all over Teddy. She rubbed her hands over his shoulders and chest. She felt a mark on Teddy's chest. She asked him, "What's this baby?"

Teddy proudly answered, "It's my rebirth mark."

Shan was puzzled. She said, "Wow, it feels like three sixes. Were you reborn as the devil? She laughed loudly, throwing her head back. When her head returned to where she could look Teddy in his eyes she saw him smiling sheepishly. She turned her head sideways 90 degrees trying to focus on Teddy.

Something was different. Something was wrong. His eyes were fire red. Shan swallowed hard. Fear consumed her. Shan wanted to get out of the room, but she couldn't move. She was frozen in place. She feared for her life. Teddy pushed her down on the bed. Her back and head hit the mattress so hard, she was dazed.

She didn't know what to do as he lay on top of her. She felt him caressing her face. He wanted her badly, and she didn't want to fight. She couldn't resist. For some reason, she still wanted him. She was so scared, she couldn't utter a sound, nor could she move a muscle.

Teddy softly answered her question in her ear, "Not the devil, but he's a close friend of mine." His laugh filled her ears with pain and curled her blood. He entered her, and she wanted to scream, but again she couldn't.

The feeling was better than anything she felt in the past but she was so scared that she couldn't enjoy it. Then slowly she felt the essence of her life leaving her body. She screamed. For a minute, she could see her body as Teddy was laying on it. All of the life in her body was gone. The essence of what she was now hovered over the room. She cried, realizing she was dead. Shan saw several dark, evil looking characters surrounding her. She didn't know what to do.
Before she could move, they grabbed her and began dragging her downward. She screamed and screamed to no avail.

The demonic looking creatures only laughed as they handed her over to a large crow like bird. His claws dug deeply into her essence. She screamed even louder. The bird dragged her downward. She realized that she was headed to Hell. Shan screamed, "Jesus, Jesus, forgive me! I wanna be saved, Jesus save me!"

***

When it was over, Shan's body was laying there with all the life drained out of it. Her eyes were wide open. It appeared she died of pure fright. Teddy stood up and moved his head around, cracking the bones in his neck. He was pleased with his work. Teddy could feel the demon's power coursing throughout his veins.

He loved it. He was a different person now and he loved the feeling. Teddy and Asmodeus were becoming one. He liked the power, the lust, and the incredible sensation during sex; he wouldn't turn it away for anything. What he fought originally, he now coveted.

Teddy shouted, "Master, another soul is yours!" Slowly and mysteriously he watched as a figure emerged from a dark corner of the room. This figure spoke calmly, "Teddy, Asmodeus, demon of lust and sex, you have done well my friend." "You are now one. Now make sure Bill and Wendy's souls are mine as well! They both laughed with a cold evil.

***

Bill and Wendy arrived at Wendy's apartment. They started walking up the steps. Bill saw a Jamaican man looking at him. The Jamaican kept saying, "He coming back mon, he coming back soon."

197

Bill asked him, "Who? Who's coming back?"

Wendy asked Bill, "What are you talking about?"

Bill replied, "I was talking to that Jamaican guy over…"
He pointed in the direction where he saw the Jamaican
standing, but he wasn't there anymore.

Wendy responded, "Are you feeling okay? I don't see a
Jamaican guy." Bill said, "He was right there."

Bill thought maybe he was just anxious. Just then, his cell
phone rang. Bill answered, "Hello." He thought the
voice was Teddy's, but it sounded different.

The voice said, "Don't forget what I told you to do,
brother."

Bill motioned for Wendy, who was waiting on the steps,
to go on in the building. When she was gone Bill said,
"Teddy? Your voice sounds different."

Teddy answered, "I must be coming down with
something."

Bill excitedly said, "Oh, I haven't forgotten. It's been
working already. I got her primed. Now, it's time to go
for broke."

Teddy said sharply, "You need to hit that, and come back
to the party. We got plenty of work to do; many more

ladies to get wit."

Bill responded, "Trust me; I've practically got her clothes off now. "She thinks I only want her and that I want to be with her until the end. What a joke! Did you see some of those ladies walking around the Zone? Oh, my God, they were fine!" Bill couldn't remain still. He was walking around, excited at the thought of what was to come.

Teddy replied, "Good, my brother, good. You are right where I'd like you to be. Who said sinning was a bad thing?" They both laughed.

***

After Teddy hung up the phone with Bill, he said, "Both of their souls will soon be yours, Master." He then looked to another dark corner of the room and said, "Take this body and bury it." Two shadowy figures emerged from the darkness and took Shan's body to bury it.

Once the body was gone, Satan said to Asmodeus, "Wendy is a soul that I must have. She is that once in a generation beauty. Do whatever you have to in order to see that she is mine." Asmodeus replied as he bowed down on one knee, "Yes, Master."

***

The camera focused directly on Evangelist Jones as she readied herself to speak. The producer started the countdown to the start of the live broadcast. The producer said, "5...4...3...2...and you're live."

Evangelist Jones said, "We have come to find out that the Zone has instituted a contest. I thought I had heard all of the lowest, most despicable and immoral things in my life until I heard about this contest. Saints of God, Saints of God! We have to turn up the prayer! We may not save them all but maybe we can save one or some of them."

"This contest involves tracking how many women each man sleeps with until eight in the morning. The male who wins will receive a 22 year old virgin who actually agreed to this contest."

"And the women...the woman who wins will be anointed 'Queen of the Earth' for 10 hours! I was disgusted when I heard it, I get even more disgusted saying it, and my disgust grows even more with each passing moment."

"Let's take a call from a good friend of mine, Reverend C. Wilson Collins of the Living Word Ministries. Rev, how are you, my friend?"

"I'm doing fine but I am concerned about the rest of the world," answered Reverend Collins.

Evangelist Jones replied, "I hear you, Rev. How many people are with you?"

Reverend Collins answered, "We now have 23 souls here with us including four children. We had a little skirmish earlier but it's been contained. We're praying every chance we get." Evangelist Jones replied, "Amen. I won't ask what the skirmish was about but I'm glad everyone is alright. Have you heard about this contest?"

Reverend Collins answered, "I just heard it when you mention it. That is truly disgusting. I just can't believe someone would even want to be the prize in such a despicable contest. I also can't believe the women would allow themselves to be used like that."

Evangelist Jones said, "You know, Rev, these women are so high on drugs and alcohol, they'll do anything right now. Every immoral thing people have held inside is coming out, and the Peachtree is giving them the tools to do it."

Reverend Collins responded, "You are so right, and Bishop Carroll didn't help at all. I still can't believe he denounced Christianity. So many souls were lost with that announcement."

Evangelist Jones replied, "I still can't understand it. I have known him for so long, and to hear him make such an announcement was like a dagger in my heart. Well Rev, we thank you for talking with us and we're glad to hear that there are some Christians yet hanging on out there."

Reverend Collins responded, "Thank you, Evangelist, for staying on the air. We appreciate it."

Evangelist Jones said, "That was Reverend C. Wilson Collins of the Living Word Ministries. He has 23 people with him so if you're out there, take heart that there are others who still believe. We'll be right back."

XIII

Bill came up to Wendy's door. He looked at himself, impressed. He reveled in all the lies he had been able to tell Wendy that night. Now he had to close the deal. He had to make her really believe that he was down to be with her until the end.

He took a couple of deep breaths. He looked over and saw the Jamaican man again. He was standing there, shaking his head, displeased. Bill said, "What?" He knocked on the door. Bill looked again, and the man was gone.

Wendy opened the door almost immediately, and asked, "Hey, who was on the phone?" She paused, then sarcastically answered her own question, "Teddy!"

Bill held it together, and answered, "Yeah, you know Teddy, he had to tell me about his exploits."

Wendy sharply replied, "Yeah, he's a jerk, and an idiot. He better had done Shan right."

Bill said defensively, "Come on, he's not that bad. Shan was out of her head with that crack in her system. I know they're having a good time."

Wendy answered, "Are you serious? While that may be

true, she still should be treated with respect. Teddy's nothing but a liar. He has forever lied on me. You want to know the truth?" Bill didn't know what to say. She continued without letting him say anything, "I have only been with one man in my life. One, but he makes it sound like I have screwed everybody!"

Bill responded surprisingly, "One? That's all?" Bill saw Wendy's face hardened. He knew he made a mistake.

She answered him sternly, "Yes, one; and it wasn't your friend, either. In fact, he never will be 'one'."

Bill walked over to Wendy and took her in his arms. He looked deeply in her eyes, his forehead touch hers. They smiled at each other. Wendy giggled. Bill had her where he wanted her.
He was getting so excited, he could hardly contain himself. He asked, "Now let's not talk about Teddy any longer. Let's talk about you and me, okay?"

Wendy softly answered, "Okay, I promise I won't bring his name up again."

Bill replied, "Good, now it's all about us." He began to let his hands go down her back until they reached her behind. She swatted them away and sharply said, "Stop."

Bill said, "Why? Let's just do this baby. Let's see how many times we can do it before the world ends."

Wendy responded, "I don't know for sure if you really want to be with me until the end. We have 20 hours remaining. That's more than enough time for you to become number two if you really want too."

Bill asked, "You don't believe me?"

Wendy was smiling.

She kissed him softly on the cheek as she answered, "I do but there's no need to rush, right?"

Bill replied, "I'm a virgin, there's plenty of reason to rush." Wendy laughed. Bill quickly snapped, "Oh, that's funny!"

Wendy recovered and said, "No, it's not funny. It is funny that you are ready to jump in the bed and get some."

Bill interrupted, "Yeah, you're right!"

Wendy replied, "But I'm not ready yet. I really don't know you. So let's take it a little bit at a time."

Bill tried to conceal his anger. His plan wasn't working. He thought he would have her by now. He thought to himself, *"Teddy would have her eating out of the palm of his hands by now. What's my problem?"* He couldn't contain it anymore and snapped, "You don't like me. You're just like the kids I grew up with. You're just leading me on.

You're leading me to believe that you wanted to be with me and only me!"

"Then, you'll get with your girls and laugh about it. I thought you were different. If you really wanted me, we would be in the bed by now!" He felt Wendy jerk away from him. He knew he made another mistake.

She had her hands up, waving them back and forth in a negative manner. She started saying, "No, this is not what I want, and I think…"

Bill interrupted, "I'm sorry Wendy. I, I just lost it for a minute."

Wendy responded, "Yeah you did, and now I know I don't want this right now. If you want me, you're going to have to show me something, and that's not going to happen in a few minutes."

Bill took a depth breath and said, "Okay, how long are we talking?"

Wendy let out a deep sigh and said, "I can't believe you."

Bill managed to keep his calm this time. He was ready to drop a major card on her, but he knew he had to do it smoothly. This was his ace, and he couldn't mess it up. Wendy was turning away from him, so now was as good a time as any to play the card. Bill said calmly, "Wendy, you don't understand." "I love you."

***

The station break was over and the camera's returned to Evangelist Jones, as she danced in the studio. She said, "I don't know 'bout y'all, but I'm getting my praise on right now! We don't have much time left to praise Him, so I'm getting it in."

"Alright, its midnight Eastern Standard Time and that means we now have 18 hours remaining until the asteroid strikes. We continue to receive reports from the Zone that things are continuing their ungodliness but we're just going to keep on praising the Lord. Tess has compiled a story for us. Take it away my sister!"

Tess began her report, "Good morning Evangelist Jones and everyone watching us. I have been working with an informant, who has told me about a major story breaking from the Bishop Carroll camp."

"We don't know all of the details as of yet, but from what I understand, it could be Earth shattering for the Bishop. It could also shed some much needed light on his earlier statements. Stay tune as we develop this story. That's all from here; now back to you, Evangelist."

"Excellent job, my dear," said Evangelist Jones.

Tess responded, "Thank you."

Evangelist Jones continued, "Well, that's all we have right now. Here are some more encouraging and uplifting videos from the Gospel Today Show."

***

Clint was in the hotel room, hysterical over the news of a breaking story concerning Bishop Carroll. He knew what that story would be, and he knew the Bishop would be devastated. He had to stop it. He had to track down the source of the story.

Clint called in the only bodyguard he trusted with his life. Aaron and Clint met in college, and instantly became good friends. They often double dated, and after college they kept in contact with each other.

When Clint got the position as assistant to Bishop Carroll, he ensured that Aaron was hired as a bodyguard on the Bishop's team. Clint asked Aaron, "Do you know the source of this leak?" Aaron answered, "I don't know, but I will do some research." Clint said, "We have to find out who it is, and we have to shut them up...permanently. You understand what I mean?"

Aaron replied, "I do and I'll take care of it."

Clint responded, "Good, and make sure it's far away from the Bishop. He can't be attached to it in any way."

Aaron replied, "You can count on me."

Clint said, "I know. Thanks, my friend." Aaron gave Clint that knowing smile as he left to find the leak. Clint was still nervous that a negative story would come out concerning the Bishop. It was his job to protect the Bishop from anything negative, even in these last hours.

Bishop Carroll walked into the room, interrupting Clint's thoughts. Bishop Carroll asked, "Clint, that was a good rest. Anything going on I need to know about?"

Clint turned suddenly. The Bishop scared him. Clint was shocked that he asked that question. He replied, "No, Bishop. Everything is under control."

Bishop Carroll replied, "Are you sure? You seem nervous about something."

Clint answered, "Yes sir, I'm sure. Everything is okay."

Bishop Carroll responded, "Good. I'm a bit hungry. Can you find me some fried shrimp, catfish, and okra?"

Clint asked, "But what about your cholesterol?" The Bishop held his hands up in a questioning manner. Clint realized that it was the end of the world, and that wasn't a concern. He answered his own question as he grabbed his jacket, "That was a dumb question, my apologies."

Clint smiled and continued, "I will be back in two hours, depending on the lines."

Bishop Carroll had a newspaper in his hand and his reading glasses on. He responded, "Thanks Clint, I love you."

Clint replied, "I love you too, Bishop."

***

Wendy's head snapped around quickly. Bill smiled inside. He had used his ace card, and now he was set to go in for the kill. She said, "Bill, you...you really feel that way?"

Bill looked in her eyes and said smoothly, "Yes baby, I really love you. I knew it from the minute I first saw you, but I couldn't express it. You see, I was bound by all that Bible stuff. Now I'm not tied to that crap anymore. Now I can tell you how I really feel."

Bill could see in her eyes that he had her. Her eyes were glazed over with excitement and appreciation that someone she admired, like Bill, loved her. He had her. Teddy was right, and now Bill was going to lose his virginity...to Wendy.

It was time to move in. He stepped closer to her, taking her into his arms again. Bill kissed Wendy on the lips, and she returned the kiss. They were deeply locked together. Bill slowly grinded on Wendy, and this time, she didn't stop him.

He put his hands on her backside again. She still didn't stop him. Bill sensed she was ready. Wendy stepped back from Bill, and said, "Let me go to the bathroom and get myself together. Then I'll be ready."

Bill couldn't suppress the smile. Bill replied, "Do that, baby. I'll be right here waiting for you." As soon as she was out of the room, Bill pulled out his cell and tried to dial Teddy's number. He was so excited to tell his friend the news, that he almost dropped the phone.

He was about to get laid for the first time in his life. He fumbled over the phone again. Once he finally got the number dialed, he waited with excitement for Teddy to answer. It seemed to take forever for the phone to ring, and for Teddy to answer.

Teddy picked up after the fourth ring and asked, "Is it over?" Bill looked at the phone again and asked himself, *"Is this Teddy?"* Bill said, "She's in the bathroom getting it ready for me. Man, I can't wait.

Teddy reaffirmed, "And you're going to hit it and come right back here, right? Leave her lying there in bed all alone, right?"

Bill answered, "You got it brother. She actually thinks I love her. Man, as soon as I hit this, I'm coming back to the Zone. Make sure you got something beautiful lined up for me."

Teddy responded, "I already do, my brother. You should see her; she's half Asian and half Black. Her skin is so soft it will make you scream! Yeah baby...she'sssss hot! I'm almost tempted to take her for myself."

Bill replied, "Oh yeah. Let me hit this, and I'll be right down there."

Teddy sternly said, "Bill, you might have to take it. Don't be afraid to use force. Sometimes women need help making up their minds. That's when we help them along. Afterwards they're happy you helped them out."

Bill responded, "What? I don't..."

Teddy interrupted, "Listen to me. Have I ever lied to you?" His voice sounded chilling.

Bill answered, "No, my brother, you haven't."

Teddy responded, "Then, do as I say, and you'll be a happy man. I promise."
"

Bill replied, "I will, my brother."

Teddy responded, "Good." "See you soon, brother." Bill hung up the phone. He had doubts that he could do that to anyone, even Wendy. He slowly turned around, and Wendy was standing right there. She was angry.

He didn't know how long she had been standing there. A chill ran up and down his spine. He was fearful she'd heard his conversation with Teddy.

Wendy broke the silence, "So you love me, huh?" "You're one big fat liar just like your friend, Teddy. I can't believe I almost fell for that BS."

Bill saw tears rolling down her face. She was visibly upset, and angry at Bill. She continued, "I can't believe I...get out, Bill. Get out of my apartment and my life!"

Bill said, "You don't mean that, let me just..."

She pushed him away, but Bill grabbed her arms tightly. Wendy yelled, "Let me go, you're hurting me!"

Bill said, "It's okay baby, you'll enjoy this. When it's over you'll thank me and we'll laugh about this." He threw Wendy down on the couch, ripping her blouse open in one move. He proceeded to rip her bra off, and looked excitedly at her breasts.

It was the first time he saw a woman's breasts. Wendy was trying to fight back, but he forced his way on top of her, and held her down with his body. He was shocked that he had no trouble enacting what Teddy wanted.

He was going to take it from Wendy, and he was going to make sure she enjoyed it. Wendy continued to fight back, and Bill slapped her across her face two quick times. He didn't understand how he'd gotten into this. It wasn't even hard for him to do this to Wendy.

She was dazed. After admiring her breasts again, he decided to force her pants off of her. A sudden, sharp pain traveled quickly through his head. It stopped him from removing her pants.
Now it was Bill's turn to be dazed.

He didn't realize that he had just been hit in the head with a vase. He staggered to the side, and Wendy pushed him off of her. She ran into the kitchen. He struggled to get his bearings. He got up to follow her into the kitchen.

When Bill got to the kitchen, he saw Wendy standing there, holding a large kitchen knife. Bill couldn't tell if it was his imagination or not but the knife appeared to be the biggest knife he'd ever seen.

He could taste the blood as it streamed down the side of his face and into his mouth. Wendy shouted at him, "Get out of here. I'm not afraid to use this knife."

Bill replied, "You're not worth it! There are too many fine women in the Zone for me to be messing with a slut like you!" Bill adjusted his clothes and left the apartment.

***

Wendy followed him to the door, the knife still in her hand. She made sure he left, and locked the door behind him. She went back to the couch, dropped the knife to the floor, and slumped down on the couch, in tears.

She slowly put her blouse back on, crying throughout. She couldn't believe what happened. She couldn't believe that the man she thought was the one for her, had just tried to rape her in her apartment.

She wondered if this was somehow her fault. She thought, *"Did I lead him on? Is this my fault? Am I to blame? Lord, why is this happening to me? Please Lord, help me? I can't do this by myself anymore?* She grew tired. She felt a great desire to sleep overwhelm her. The struggle against a man much stronger than her tired her out. After a few moments, her eyes closed and she fell asleep.

***

Johnny and Missy were in the Tradewinds Hotel. They got a room from a friend of Missy's. Johnny couldn't believe the fun he was having. He truly felt like he was living a dream. He had only been in the Zone for a few minutes when he latched on to Missy. Now Missy was calling a friend of hers over to the room.

Johnny's was having more fun with each passing minute. This was the life he only dreamed about. He had forgotten all about Katrina. Missy's friend, Loren came in the room. She looked younger than Missy. Johnny realized he had a strong attraction for younger women.

He suspected it was because it reminded him of a time when he was happy with Vanessa. The older they got, the more problems they had together. Missy and Loren were both young and they both reminded him of his young Vanessa. Johnny said, "Peel off those clothes baby, and come on over here. We're gonna have a great time together."

Missy said, "I'm going to get us some ice, so we can make some drinks. I got some rum and vodka just waiting."

Johnny replied, "We'll be right here sweetheart. His ministerial days were long forgotten. He turned to Loren and said, "Woooooooo baby, look at you!"

***

Missy left the room and went down the hall to where the ice machine was kept. She stopped at the machine and said, "His soul is all yours baby."

Satan stepped from the shadows and replied, "Good job my sweet. Keep him occupied until the end."

Missy responded, "I will. Then, I can be with you forever?"

Satan answered as he gently touched her chin, "Yes, my love. You will be right next to me, forever!"

***

Everyone was asleep at Living Word Ministries, except for two of the Secret Service agents, Reverend Collins, and President Murphy. Reverend Collins asked President Murphy, "You can't sleep either?"

President Murphy answered, "Kind of hard when your impending doom is coming."

Reverend Collins replied, "I know what you mean. Where are your older children?"

President Murphy answered, "I don't know. They both were angry because I didn't tell the world when we first found out about the asteroid. I was hoping they would show up here. I told my secretary to leak the information that I was coming here to them."

Reverend Collins said, "Are you sure she did it?"

President Murphy answered, "Yes. I did talk to Marcie briefly but I didn't get a chance to talk to Tommy. I felt that if I had told them directly that I was coming here they wouldn't have come. Tommy likes to be sneaky."

Reverend Collins replied, "There's still time. I'm praying they come."

***

Calvin was still fuming. His desire to get his woman was

217

deeply rooted inside of him. He wasn't going to stop until he had her back. His plan was to pretend to be sleep. Once he worked his hands free of the ropes, and one of the agents was near, he would strike. Calvin watched and noted where the agents kept their guns. When the right moment came, he planned to pounce on one of them, take their weapon, and get his woman.

His hands were now free, but he still had to wait until one of the agents came close enough to him to make his move.

***

Bill arrived back in the Zone. He looked around for Teddy. Initially, he couldn't find him. He did find a young lady he was interested in meeting. He walked over to her, talking to her to see if she was interested in hooking up. Bill said, "Hi, my name is Bill."

Tammi halfheartedly replied, "Tammi, with an 'i'. How'd you get that bump and scratch?"

Bill answered, "Well, some hoochie said she wanted to get down then she decided she didn't want to. She scratched my face up and hit me with a vase."

Tammi replied, "What was she doing in the Zone, if she wasn't down?"

Bill answered, "Don't ask me. I'm here with you." "Want

218

to hit the Tradewinds?"

Tammi responded, "Hmmm, how many notches do you have?

Bill replied, "None baby! I have never been with a woman in my life."

Tammi screamed, "What? You're lying."

Bill answered, "No I'm not. Now let's go get a room."

Tammi said, "Okay, I guess I can be your first. I hope you can handle it Sweetie."

Bill confidently responded, "Oh, I can handle it." The two of them left to go to the Tradewinds. Bill was excited. He was finally going to lose his virginity. It wasn't going to be with Wendy, but Tammi would do just fine. From out of nowhere, Bill heard a voice, "Bill!"

Bill turned around, and saw Teddy standing with two beautiful women. One of them he knew as Wendy's friend, Barbara. He didn't know the other one, but he suspected it was the woman Teddy referred to earlier. She looked mixed, and she was fine.

Bill said under his breath, "Oh my God!"

Tammi angrily asked, "What?"

Bill quickly said, "Huh, nothing Baby. It's just my friend, Teddy. Hold on a sec, I need to talk to him for a minute."

Tammi responded, "I won't wait long, there are a lot of opportunities out here."

Bill replied, "Just one sec, girl, hold on." Bill ran over to Teddy. Teddy was changing. He couldn't tell exactly what it was, but he looked and sounded different...

Teddy sternly asked, "Did you do it?"

Bill replied, "She fought, and chased me out of her apartment with a knife."

Teddy sternly shouted, "Did you do it?"

Bill yelled back, "No, I didn't!"

Teddy sighed, turning his back on Bill, visibly angry. Bill looked at Barbara and other woman; both shaking their heads showing their dissatisfaction of Bill. Teddy turned back around and got in Bill's face. Teddy had really changed now and Bill was getting scared of him.

He said, "I thought you had what it takes. You have failed me."

Bill sharply replied, "What? I 'failed you'? I didn't know I worked for you?"

Teddy looked down and paused for a moment, smiled, then said, "You're right my brother. I do apologize." He turned to Barbara, saying, "Barbara, why don't you go talk to Wendy? You might be able to talk some sense into your friend. In the meantime Bill, this is Aaliyah, and she desires you so much."

Bill replied, "Hey, my brother, I got a fine honey over there waiting for me." Bill pointed to Tammi.

Teddy replied, "She's not for you. Take Aaliyah. Trust me, you will enjoy it."

Bill said, "But..."

Tammi shouted, "I waited long enough, now I'm gone."

Bill replied, "Hey wait...dang it!"

Teddy grabbed his arm and said, "I told you...she's not for you. Let her go and take Aaliyah."

Bill said, "I'm beginning to think no one is for me my brother. First Wendy, now Tammi. This girl won't want me either." Aaliyah walked over gracefully, reached up, and put her arms
around Bill's neck. She kissed him in the mouth and wouldn't stop. Bill's tongue danced with hers and he forgot all about Wendy and Tammi.

He felt hypnotized by Aaliyah's kiss. She pressed her body tightly against his and Bill couldn't contain himself. His tongue and body felt like it was on fire with lust and anticipation. He couldn't break away...he had to have her. Bill said, "Let's go Aaliyah."

Aaliyah happily replied, "I thought you would never invite me."

Bill excitedly responded, "I can't wait." Bill saw Teddy smile as he walked off with Aaliyah. For a minute it curled his stomach then he turned his attention by to Aaliyah.

***

Wendy was still slumped on the floor asleep. She slowly began to wake up. When she opened her eyes she was shocked. Someone was standing over her, smiling. It was the same woman Wendy saw in the stairwell earlier that evening. Wendy thought, *"How did she get in my apartment?"* *"I know I locked the door after that maniac left."* She asked, "How did you get in here?"

The woman smiled and said, "You let me in."

Wendy replied, "I did, when?"

The woman replied, "Does that matter? How do you feel?" "Are you better?"

Wendy answered, "I am. I feel so comfortable now. I seem to feel that way every time I see you." She sat next to Wendy and put her arm around her. Wendy laid her head on her shoulder.

For the first time in a long while she felt safe and free from any harm. Once again, she drifted off to a nice, quiet, and comfortable sleep.

***

Katrina was lying naked across the bed. The man she invited to the Tradewinds to make Johnny jealous, had his way with her and left her lying there. She spent the last hour crying.
She deeply hated and pitied herself. She couldn't understand why no one wanted her.

She questioned why God didn't love her anymore. As she laid there, she heard the voices of people partying in the hallway. Everyone but her was having a good time. A drunken man fell inside her room. He got up and saw her lying on the bed. He walked over to the bed, and she watched him pull his pants down.

She said to herself, *"Go ahead, do what you want. Everyone else has had their way with me so why not you?"* When he started to have sex with her, she turned her head to the side, and slowly closed her eyes. She said softly, "Daddy…why did you leave me?" She cried and didn't move, while the man had his way.

223

Once he was finished, he got up and pulled his clothes up. He staggered back into the hallway. Katrina heard him shout, "Man, I just got me some!" She felt another tear move from her eyes, down her face until it dropped on the bed. More and more followed. She was disgusted with herself as the last of her respect slipped away into the night. She wanted it all to end.

As she lay there, she kept hearing a voice telling her to end it. The voice was soft at first but kept getting louder. It said, *"End it. End your miserable life. No one loves you and no one acts like they care. But you can get them all by back killing yourself. They will all suffer then."*

The voice kept getting stronger and stronger, until she decided to give in, and listen to it. She walked over to her purse and removed a small .22 caliber handgun that she kept for protection. The voice said, *"Yes...do it...do it now! Make them pay...make them all pay!"* She stood there, looking out the window. The voice egged her on some more.

It said, *"End it, God doesn't love you. No one loves you! He took your father! God took your father from you. Make Him pay! Pull the trigger and end it all forever!"* She stared at the ungodly behavior going on in the Zone. The tears were streaming down her completely naked body. She slowly raised the gun to her temple.

The voice shouted loudly and with eagerness, *"Pull it, pull the trigger now!"* She squeezed the trigger. As she fell to the floor, her body kicked violently. The last thing she heard was the voice saying, *"Now you're mine."* Her body slowly relaxed, and she was dead. Some of the people in the hallway ran in the room to see what happened.

***

After the gunshot, Johnny heard a woman scream, "She killed herself!" He ran out into the hallway. He pushed past a man saying, "Dang, I just had some of that! It was good. What a shame."

As he run into the room, he buckled his pants, sensing that he desperately needed to see what happened. For some reason, he felt he already knew, but he needed to see first hand.

When he got inside the room, he found out that he was right. Katrina was lying on the floor, naked and dead. Johnny tried to hide his tears. He slowly walked over to her body, grabbing a blanket on the way. He wanted to cover her body. He owed her that much.

He never thought she would do such a thing. He felt a hand caress him. He looked back and saw Missy. She had come up behind him. Missy said, "Wow baby, you must be real good for someone to kill themselves over you."

Johnny was disgusted at her comments. He stood up, pushed her away and walked off. He didn't love her, but he felt she didn't deserve to die like that. Tears were forming in his eyes, as he realized that it was his behavior that pushed her over the edge. He should have known she was capable, because he stopped her from killing herself the day they met.

He wondered why he didn't remember that earlier. Johnny grabbed a bottle of rum and headed downstairs to the street. He didn't know what he was going to do, but he wanted to be alone for a while.

***

After everyone left the room, Satan emerged from the shadows. He stood over Katrina's body and smiled. He took in a deep breath and said, "Hmmm, the smell of suicide is sweet!"

***

Barbara arrived at Wendy's apartment, beating loudly on the door. The loud noise startled Wendy and woke her up. When she was fully awake, she realized the woman was no longer there. Just as mysteriously as she arrived, she was gone. Wendy yelled through the door, "Who is it?"

Barbara yelled back, "It's me! Let me in."

Wendy recognized Barbara's voice. Wendy hollered back,

226

"Are you alone?"

Barbara yelled again, "Yeah girl, open the door!"

Wendy opened the door. Barbara was so intoxicated, that she had to use the wall to hold herself up. Wendy asked, "What have you been drinking?"

Barbara answered, "Girl, what haven't I had?" "I've been having a great time. You need to come on down. Oh and, why don't you give that man some?"

Wendy responded, "Bill is a jerk, and he tried to rape me."

Barbara said, "No he didn't girl. It's the end of the world, why you trippin'? Give the man some of that stuff!" She stopped and pointed at Wendy then continued, "You ain't got the Holy Grail down there, you know."

Wendy replied, "Look Barbara you're drunk, and I know you don't fully understand what's going on here, but he tried to rape me. I will never give him anything and you need to go sleep it off."

Barbara responded, "Sleep it off? I've been banging everybody. I'm having the time of my life! I'm going back to the Zone, drink some more, smoke some crack and hopefully I'll get laid again...and again. When this thing hits I don't want to feel anything. Come with me."

Wendy sternly said, "I'm not going there ever again. That place is wicked. Where's Shan?"

Barbara replied, "I don't know. Somewhere having a good time I guess! I haven't seen her since she went off with Teddy. Girl, Teddy is the bomb. I don't know what your problem was with him but he's got the juice!"

Wendy responded, "What?" "You need to find Shan."

Barbara stumbled to the couch, falling on it. She said, "Why? She's off having fun.
"Besides she might take away some of my men. I can't have that. "You should try having some fun too!" "You need it. We've been telling you to loosen up all night."

Wendy replied, "I'm not going back in that Zone." "There's so much sin going on down there that it stinks. Stay here with me. We can read and study the Bible together."

Barbara quickly responded, "Oh, that's my cue." "I'm outta here, you done gone to that Bible. What happened to you? You use to be a partier like me. Now you done gone off and got saved!" Barbara started making dancing moves as she was sitting down. She continued, "It's the end of the world girl, now is the time to parrrrrrrty!"

Barbara stumbled as she tried to get to her feet. Wendy tried to help her up. Barbara sternly said, "I can do it on my own. Thank you."

Wendy said, "Look Barbara, with you as my witness, I believe in Jesus Christ. I believe he died for my sins and I accept Him as my Lord and Savior. Join me Barbara; we still have time to be saved."

Barbara responded, "Saved? Didn't you hear Bishop Carroll? There is no God. He told us all to have fun and stop worrying about fairy tales."

Wendy grabbed Barbara by the arm and said, "He's wrong, girl! Come on, stay here with me and be saved."

Barbara jerked her hand away, moving toward the door. She said, "Leave me alone with that stuff. If you want to stay here like a fool then go ahead. I'm going back to the Zone baby." She stumbled again, putting her hand against the wall to prevent her from falling.

Wendy knew she was totally out of it. Barbara didn't know what she was doing or saying. Wendy replied, "I'll be praying for you."

Barbara responded, "Go head girl, it can't hurt. Bye!"
***
Barbara stumbled her way through the streets. She tried to clear her head of the alcohol and drugs, but she couldn't. They had a strong hold on her. She tried to focus on what Wendy was saying, but she couldn't. She thought, *"Maybe there's some truth to what my girl was saying."* Try as she might, all she could think about was more

229

alcohol, more drugs and more sex.

The demons ruled her body, and wouldn't let her think of nothing else. She believed she was in love with Teddy. She had to have him. She thought to herself, *"After I have one more drink and just a taste more of crack...man that Shan was right about crack. After that I'll get saved. Yeah that's the plan. Oh wait, after I get with Teddy, then I'll get saved."* *"Now, that's the plan!"*

***

One of the secret service agents was in the process of making his rounds. Calvin saw him heading in his direction. He pretended to be sleep. When the agent was close enough, Calvin sprung up, and in one motion, grabbed the agent's gun, pulled it from his holster, and shot him twice in the chest.

The other agent jumped up, but it was too late. Calvin got off two shots, one to the agents thigh, and the other to his chest.

President Murphy and Reverend Collins hid in the choir stand, but Calvin saw them. He shouted, "This agent is still alive but I will put more bullets in him if you don't come out."

Reverend Collins stood up with his hands raised. President Murphy did the same. President Murphy said, "Son, do you know who I am?"

Calvin yelled, "Nobody. The world's going to end in a few hours so who cares if you're the President or not." Then he shot the agent twice more without even looking. The agent was dead.

He moved over towards Reverend Collins and President Murphy. Reverend Collins shouted, "You said you wouldn't kill him!"

Calvin said as he was moving, "I never said that. I said I would put more bullets in him if you didn't come out." He said, laughing, "I never said what I would do after you came

***

The last two agents took up a position outside the sanctuary, discussing how to get Reverend Collins and President Murphy out. Agent Kevin Charles was a veteran of 20 years with the Secret Service. He had been assigned to the President's team for the last five years.

His partner was a rookie named Agent Walker Thomas. Agent Charles asked Agent Thomas, "You're the better shot, do you think you can hit him?"

Agent Thomas responded, "Not yet. He's too close to the President."

Agent Charles said, "Okay. Stay here. If you get a shot,

231

take it."

Vanessa came up behind them and said, "Let me go in there and talk to him."

Agent Charles replied, "I can't do that ma'am. You're what he wants. If he gets you, there's nothing to stop him from killing President Murphy and the Reverend."

Vanessa asked, "Then, what do we do?"

Agent Charles answered, "We wait him out."

They heard Calvin yell, "I know you're out there. Get Vanessa in here and give me the keys to my car. Once I get these things, we'll leave and no one else will get hurt. However, if I don't get these things in 15 minutes, one of these fine upstanding gentlemen will die. Then 15 minutes after that, if I still don't have what I want, the other one will die. Don't test me; you see I'm willing to kill."

Agent Charles whispered to Agent Thomas, "How's that shot looking?"

Agent Thomas answered, "Still a no go. We've got to get him away from the President and the Reverend."

***

Barbara stumbled in the room as Teddy finished having sex with another woman from the Zone. The woman's

232

body lay motionless on the bed. Her eyes were wide open and she appeared to be dead.

Barbara gasped and wanted to run out of the room, but she just stood there. She could see Teddy for what he had become. His chest showed the mark of the devil on it. Barbara was scared.

She saw Teddy transform into Asmodeus, a hideous creature. He was tall, with scars all over his body. A new one was burning into his body as he stood there screeching, a hideous sound of joy.

She saw his wings span out across the room. His teeth were rotten and stained yellow. His eyes were fire red. He turned to her and said in a cold cracking voice, "It's unfortunate that you see me in my true form. I was saving you for later."

Barbara could only whisper, "Teddy no…no…what are you?" She tried to scream, but nothing came out.

He roared, "My name is no longer Teddy! It is Asmodeus, Demon of Lust and Sex!" He commanded, "Grab her!" Two figures emerged from the shadows and grabbed Barbara. She still couldn't scream. They dragged her over to Asmodeus and with hand, he swiped the body off the bed and onto the floor.

The figures threw Barbara on the bed. She struggled to free herself as Asmodeus looked into her eyes. He appeared as Teddy again and started to cry. He said meekly voice, "Barbara, help me. I can't get this thing out of me. Please help me."

Barbara was still fighting, struggling and crying. She shouted hysterically, "Teddy, how? How can I help you?"

Asmodeus answered, "Just give in to him. After sex he is weak. I can take my body back at that point and rid myself of him. Please don't fight Barbara. I can save us both."

Barbara replied, "Okay Teddy. I'll do it for you." She stopped fighting and allowed Asmodeus to have sex with her.

As Asmodeus started, she realized that she had been tricked. She screamed as loud as she could, but nothing came out. Asmodeus let out a hideous laugh. He whispered to her, "Scream all you wish. You gave me permission, and now I will have my way with you!" He shouted, "No one can hear you."

Barbara started to struggle and shouted, "You tricked me!" Visions of her childhood raced across her mind. She remembered being dragged to church as a child. She remembered the stories of Jesus Christ. She remembered how happy she was when she gave her life to Him. She saw a hand being held out to her. In her struggles she heard a soft voice say, "Come back to me!"

She remembered her pastor telling her that all she had to do was repent her sins and her slate would be clean. Slowly Barbara began to feel her life leaving her. She found the strength to yell, "Jesus is my Lord! I repent all my sins!"

Asmodeus jumped from her, shouting, "Noooooooooo!" The last of her life eased out of her.
Her spirit rose hovering over her body. She could see Asmodeus fall to his knees. A beautiful light, like Barbara never saw before in her life, appeared before her. She slowly moved toward it.

Barbara saw two angels descend beside her, each taking an arm. They were smiling. She felt safe and comforted. Barbara said, "Wendy was right." Without their lips moving, the angles said, "Your confession saved you."

***

Asmodeus stood with his head down, displeased with his work. He ordered his henchmen, "Dispose of these bodies!" He then turned to another corner of the room and asked, "I will not fail you again Master!"

Satan emerged with a cold stare etched on his face, visibly angry. He said, "Not only have you allowed Barbara to be saved, but the one in which I covet the most has given her life to Christ as well! The only reason I don't snatch you down to Hell is Bill. He must make her sin or he will die a violent death. See to it…now!"

Asmodeus replied, "Yes Master. Satan disappeared in the shadows again. Asmodeus now looked like Teddy again. For the first time since the demon possessed his body he was scared.

***

Wendy stood in her living room looking down at the floor. When she raised her head, she saw the woman again. Wendy was startled and stepped back. She asked sternly, "Who are you?" The woman replied, "I am a friend." Wendy was confused.

Wendy said, "But I don't know you." The woman simply smiled at Wendy. As confused as Wendy was, she always felt comfortable when the woman was around. Wendy flopped on the couch.

She was deeply disappointed that she couldn't get through to Barbara. The woman asked, "What has you troubled, my dear."

Wendy answered, "I couldn't get through to my friend. Both of them are out there, somewhere, doing who knows what. I wanted them to be here with me, reading the Bible."

The woman said, "The Bible is a good book."

Wendy asked, "You know the Bible?"

The woman answered, "I know it well."

Wendy asked, "What must I do to be saved?"

The woman smiled and said, "Profess with your mouth that Jesus is your Lord and Savior. Believe in your heart that God raised him from the dead. That is all that is required."

Wendy responded, "I've done that."

The woman replied, "Then, you are saved."

Wendy asked surprisingly, "Are you sure?" "It's that simple?"

The woman smiled again. She said, "Yes, dear. God made it that simple. It's right there in the Bible, Romans 10:9"

Wendy was happy. She looked the woman in her eyes and asked, "How can I save my friends?"

The woman answered, "Each person must come to the Father on their own."

Wendy said, "Then, I must convince them all." The woman stood up.

She said, "I must go now."

Wendy didn't want her to leave. She said, "Why? Can you stay a little longer?"

The woman replied, "It is my time to leave. You are saved and you know God. Beware the tricks of the enemy."

Wendy asked, "What tricks?"

The woman just smiled and walked toward the door. She turned and said, "Trust nothing but your faith. The enemy is powerful and has many tricks but your faith can guide you in the right path."

She then, opened the door and walked out. Wendy ran to the door and opened it wide. The woman was gone. There was no trace of her. Wendy ran out into the street, but she didn't see the woman anywhere.

She ran back in and up the stairs, to see if she went to the floors above, but she didn't find her anywhere. She mumbled, *"Who are you?"*

***

Vanessa said to Agent Charles, "Look, you have to let me go in there. Maybe I could get him far enough away from them so you guys can shoot."

Agent Charles replied, "I guess we have no other option."

Calvin yelled, "Time's up, let me see…"

Vanessa shouted, "Wait, Calvin, here I am, and I have the keys. I won't go with you unless you let them go."

Calvin said, "Come on, Baby, do you think I'm that stupid? If I let them go, they will kill me."

Vanessa said, "No they won't, I'll be your hostage."

Calvin laughingly replied, "Sorry baby, as much as I love you, you ain't as important as the President."

Vanessa responded, "I am, Calvin. I'm a living, breathing human being. They value that. Maybe you don't but everyone else in here does." She noticed Calvin was giving it some thought. She decided to take advantage of the moment. She said, "Come on baby; let's get out of here while we can. To be honest, I have been missing you. It wasn't easy seeing you all tied up like that. Let them go so we can get out of here."

He said, "Okay. Toss me the keys, and the Rev can go. Then you walk to me, and the President can go. But, I'm staying between you and those…"

Vanessa jumped at a sound of the shot that came from behind her. After gathering herself, she realized one of the agents shot Calvin. The bullet hit him in the shoulder

and he dropped the gun. President Murphy and
Reverend Collins both ran out of the way. Calvin went
for the gun, but another shot landed right in front of him.
Vanessa didn't move. She just stood there scared to
death.

After a second, she thought it would be prudent to get to
the ground. She went down, covering her ears. She saw
Calvin spin around with one hand on the ground. He ran
toward the side of the sanctuary and jumped out of the
stained glass window behind the choir stand.

Vanessa shouted, "Don't let him get away!" Agents
Charles and Walker ran to the window. They both fired
shots out the window. She heard tires screeching. Agent
Charles turned to Vanessa and said, "I'm sorry."

Vanessa asked, "He got away?"

Agent Charles said, "He jumped in a car and drove off.
We wouldn't have got to him in time."

Vanessa replied, "He'll be back."

Agent Charles responded, "We'll be ready."

Martha and Brittney ran into the sanctuary. They both
hugged Reverend Collins. President Murphy's family ran
in next. Vanessa just stood there in tears. She saw Roger
and Samantha embracing each other, and their children.

She felt empty inside. She had no family to hug, and she feared for her life. Vanessa knew Calvin would be back. He wouldn't give up. She had to leave so everyone would be safe. As long as she stayed, Calvin would come back there for her, and she didn't want anyone else hurt or killed because of her.

She wished Johnny was with her. He would know what to do. Lisa and Carla came up to her, embracing her. They all cried together. Vanessa never imagined she would be standing in the middle of the sanctuary hugging Lisa and Carla.

***

Aaron spent the last two hours looking for the source of the reports that were beginning to surface concerning the bishop. He found out it was one of the bodyguards who sold information to the Gospel Today Show. The bodyguard was a Christian, and felt people needed to know the truth about Bishop Carroll. Aaron thought, *"It didn't hurt that he was profiting from the providing the information either."*

Aaron confronted the man behind the Heston hotel. He asked him, "Look man, somebody told the Gospel Today Show about the Bishop; Do you know who it was?"

The man answered, "Naw bro, what makes you think I know?"

241

Aaron said, "No reason, I just think it's about time someone spoke out."

The man replied, "Really?"

Aaron responded, "Yeah, he's got so much in his closet and he gets away with it. Why should he be allowed to get away with it and why should he even care at this point? He should let it out like everyone else."

The man boldly said, "You're right. That's why I did it. Man, I told them everything I knew. In fact, that Tess lady is on her way down here right now. Once I give her the final details they're going to air the story and I will make a cool ten grand. Then that dog will be exposed!"

Aaron's expression totally changed. He looked at the man coldly. He already had his hand in his pocket, so he slowly pulled out his gun, aiming it at the bodyguard. The bodyguard saw the gun and his face totally changed.

He realized his mistake. Aaron's subterfuge tricked the man into revealing himself. Aaron cherished the look of fear on his face. The bodyguard tried to run, but it was too late. Aaron shot the man in the back. He walked over to the body and stood over it.

He flipped the body over with his foot and pumped two more bullets in him for spite. Then, he spit on the corpse. He said softly, "No, my friend, you have been exposed. Now, burn in Hell, like the coward you are."

242

Aaron then moved the body to the side, and waited for Tess to show up. He had to prevent the story from being aired.

***

Clint finally returned to the hotel with the Bishop's food. It took him longer than expected, due to the long food lines. Like everything else, food was free. People were eating anything and everything they could. Clint thought, *"Gluttony is truly a sin being violated tonight. At least the Bishop will be happy I got his food for him."*

Clint got back to the room, balancing the food and drink while opening the room door. He almost dropped the food on the floor, but successfully got it all in the room. The Bishop wasn't in the living room when Clint walked in, so he set the food down on the table and cheerfully headed for the bedroom area.

He was pleased that he had accomplished his mission. He was excited to spend this last day with the Bishop. He pushed open the bedroom door. Shock enveloped his entire body. He saw the Bishop standing there with his pants down, having sex with the young male bodyguard he only knew as Frank.

Clint shouted, "How…how could you do this to me? You said I was your one and only! How could you?"

Bishop Carroll calmly answered, "Clint, now take it easy. It's the last day my friend. There's nothing to get all upset about."

Clint yelled, "I hate you. You're going to pay for this, I promise you."

Bishop Carroll responded, "Clint, it's the end of the world. What damage could you do? Now, let's sit down and talk about this like friends."

Clint ran out of the bedroom, swiping the bags of food from the table and onto the floor. He then ran out of the penthouse. He was upset, tears running down his face as he got to the elevator.

On several occasions, Bishop Carroll told Clint that he only loved him.

Visions of those times raced through Clint's mind. Now, Clint believed it was all a lie. He thought in these last hours, he and the Bishop would be together until the end. Now, he felt betrayed.

He would get even. He would air all of the Bishop's dirty laundry out. He thought out loud, *"I'll make him pay for this. I'll tell the world what he did and what he has been doing. I'll air all of his dirty laundry starting with Cecil Williams' death. Yeah, that's what I'll do. I'll tell the world that Cecil's death wasn't an accident like it was reported. I'll tell them the truth…Bishop Carroll murdered him!"*

244

***

Bishop Carroll was sitting on the side of the bed. He knew that Clint was upset with him, and he didn't want to harm Clint. He did care for him. In fact, he loved him. He only wanted to experience other people since it was the last day.

Bishop Carroll wanted Clint to do the same. He thought, *"I should have talked to him earlier. Maybe this all could have been avoided."* He hoped Clint would see the light. The sound of the phone ringing broke his silence. He stared at it for a moment, almost believing it was a dream. Bishop Carroll answered in a commanding voice, "Bishop Carroll."

The voice on the other end said, "Sir, this is Craig. I have something on the monitor that you should hear."

Bishop Carroll asked, "Tell me what it is."

Craig replied, "It's Clint in the elevator, saying that he's going to make you pay by telling the world you murdered Cecil."

Bishop Carroll's head dropped. This was not the news he wanted to hear. There was only one day until the end of the world, but he wanted everyone to believe he was a stand up righteous man even if he wasn't. Most of all, he didn't want to harm Clint, but now it was apparent that it

245

would be necessary.

Bishop Carroll said, "Craig, I need you to see to it that he doesn't do anything. Do you understand me?"

Craig answered, "Yes sir, I'll take care of it."

Bishop Carroll continued, "Craig, you have to take care of Aaron also. If Clint knows something, then you can bet that Aaron knows."

Craig answered, "I will handle both of them personally, sir."

Bishop Carroll replied, "Thank you, Craig." He hung up the phone and sat quietly on the bed.

He sent Frank away so he could be all alone in his penthouse suite. He wondered for a moment if all that he had done was wrong, and there truly was a God who was punishing him.

***

Wendy sat on her couch, wondering about the pleasant and comforting woman. She didn't understand who she was, but she knew the woman loved her deeply. She got up and went to her bedroom.

She wanted to change her clothes, and go look for Bill. She felt that she was responsible for him turning his back on God. Now that she was saved, she had to do what she could to save him. She also wanted to find her friends, Barbara and Shan. Wendy hated the thought of going back in the Zone, but she remembered the 23rd Psalms and starting reciting it out loud.

She thought, "*Yea, though I walk through the valley of the shadow of*
death, I will fear no evil; for Thou art with me; Thy rod and Thy
staff, they comfort
me..."

She prayed for the strength to find her friends. She just hoped that she would be able to talk some sense into them. She needed to look for Bill first. The last time she saw him, he was uncontrollable. He was nothing like the Bill she remembered from work. Wendy found a nice conservative outfit to put on. She wanted to make sure she was fully covered and not send the wrong message.

She didn't want anyone to assume she was there to sin. After she gathered her purse and keys, she went out on her journey to save her friends.

***

Johnny found himself a table where he could be alone. He had a bottle of rum with him. He didn't even want a chaser. He was drinking the rum straight out of the bottle. Johnny was reminiscing over his life. He thought about how great it was when he first met Vanessa. They had such a great time together. He remembered his first

247

affair. He got away with that one, and two more, before Vanessa caught him.

He didn't really like any of the women. He just wanted to have sex with them, and his boys encouraged him. He wondered why they didn't stop him from making the greatest mistake of his life.

He remembered the pain on Vanessa's face when she discovered Johnny's affair. She would have been more hurt if she knew it wasn't the first time he did it was with Linda, her best friend at work. He kept that fact to himself.

He knew he really hurt her, but he couldn't believe that she went out and had an affair behind his back. He just couldn't picture his V in the arms of any other man. He thought about how those acts of indiscretion cost him his wife, and now led to Katrina, an innocent woman, killing herself.

He asked himself, *"Was it all worth it man?"* He took a drink. *"Were all the sex, drugs, and alcohol really worth it?"* He took another drink. *Man, you really screwed up your life!"* He answered his own question, *"No, I should have been faithful. I should have stayed with my wife. I love you V!"* He sobbed profusely at the table. Then he passed out.

The thought of asking God for forgiveness never entered his
drunken mind.

***

Aaron watched as a light blue sedan approached the back of the hotel.

He was waiting for it to stop. He wondered if Tess was in the vehicle. He didn't know if Tess had met her informant before, but he was willing to take the chance she hadn't. As the vehicle got closer, he could see there was only one person in it.

He recognized Tess from the Gospel Today Show. Once the vehicle stopped, he came out and stood about ten feet away. Tess stepped out and looked at him. She said, "Are you Malcolm?"

Aaron realized his plan was going to work. She had never seen Malcolm before. He answered, "Yes."

She walked over with an object in her hands. Aaron believed it was a recorder. She held the recorder out and asked, "Are you ready?" Aaron nodded.

He looked to see if anyone was around. He asked, "Is there anyone else with you?"

She answered, "No, it's just like you asked…only you and me."

Aaron smiled as he she fell to her knees. Tess was

shocked. He walked up on her as she looked up at him. His faced held a slight grin of success. He pulled out his gun, and shot her twice in the stomach.

She asked, "Why?"

Aaron answered, "The Bishop's closet must remain closed. I killed Malcolm and now you. The closet is closed." Tess' eyes closed.

XII

Wendy looked at her watch. It read 4 am Eastern Standard time. She shuddered at the thought of the asteroid impacting Earth in 14 hours. All these people in the Zone, and none of them care about their actions. She thought, *"The wages of sin is death."* She saw the sun trying to overcome the night. Wendy was racing across the Zone, looking for any hint of where Bill might be hanging out.

She had been looking for nearly four hours, when finally she found someone that knew who he was, and where he was hanging out. She ran over to the Tradewinds hotel, room 206, to see if she could talk to him.

She hoped and prayed that he would at least listen to what she had to say. After Bill, she had to find Barbara and Shan. She prayed they weren't with Teddy. She shuddered at the thought of Teddy and her friends. She said under her breath, *"How could they?"*

She finally got to the room where Bill was located. When she first arrived, she didn't hear any noise coming from the room. The door was cracked. After a momentary pause, she decided to go ahead and walk in the room.

Once she was in the room, she saw Bill's back as he was kneeling on the bed, completely naked. One woman was draped over him, kissing him. She saw Wendy and she

251

flicked her tongue at Wendy seductively.

Wendy almost threw up. Another woman was lying in front of Bill naked, and with her legs wide open. Wendy could see Bill's face in the mirror in front of the bed. Her hand shot up to her mouth. She was in shock and gasped aloud. The noise startled Bill. He looked up, and saw Wendy in the mirror.

He pushed the woman away, and turned to Wendy, grabbing his pants in the process. He said, "Wendy! Wait just a…"

She cut him off, saying, "I'll be out here." She caught a glimpse of one of the women as she grabbed Bill trying to prevent him from leaving. The woman said, "Bill, no, you're mine! You invited me! Bill!"

Wendy was still in shock, as she stood in the hallway with her hand over her mouth. She could not believe this was the man she admired for so long. Everything he stood for had gone out of the window. She thought how ironic it was that all the things he stood for, she now believed.

Bill met Wendy in the hallway buttoning his shirt. Wendy was standing a few feet from the door, pacing. She still couldn't believe what she saw Bill doing. Never in million years, did she imagine him like that. She was asking herself, *'Was this worth it? He's too far out there to save.'*

Bill came up to her and said, "Wendy, I never expected to

see you here."

Wendy sharply replied sharply, "That…I can tell."

Bill asked, "Did you change your mind? I mean, I'm so sorry for how I acted earlier."

Wendy responded sternly, "Bill, I'm not here to have sex with you. In fact, I can't have sex until I'm married, and we both know that's not going to happen in the next 14 hours."

Bill abruptly asked, "Then, why you come looking for me?"

Wendy pointedly answered, "Because, I want to save you Bill."

Bill heatedly said, "Whatever! Save me? I don't want to be saved baby! You see me in there? I'm having the time of my life! I stopped to hear this crap!"

Wendy replied, "Bill, everything you stood for was right. Heaven is real. Jesus is real. You have sinned but you still have a chance to be saved. You can repent!" She grabbed his arm, trying to impress upon him that it wasn't too late. Wendy passionately continued, "Please, Bill, just come back to the apartment with me. We can pray together, and you can repent. Then both of us will be saved."

Bill sarcastically asked, "Then will you give it up?"

Wendy sighed and vigorously responded, "No, Bill. Then we will wait until the end comes but both of us will be saved."

One of the women stepped partially into the hallway. She appeared to be impatient. She intently said, "Bill, come on baby!"

Bill placed his hand on the wall, looking Wendy in her eyes. He said softly, "If there's no sex at the end of this road, then why travel it? You see Aaliyah over there?" Wendy looked in the direction Bill was pointing. She saw the naked woman halfway in the hallway. He continued softly, "She's exposed me to a world that I like baby. My body has never felt this good before. The touch of Aaliyah and her friend ump; I just can't describe how good it feels. I can't turn back now for some fairy tales."

"Yeah, didn't you hear the Bishop? All that crap is a joke? It's all lies, and fairy tales. You, baby, you fell for it. Sorry baby but I've got work to do with Aaliyah and her friend. I'll see you when I see you."

Wendy watched as Bill walked away, disappearing back into the room. She stood there for a few minutes, wondering if she should go back in there and try to talk to him some more. Then, she heard loud moans emanating from the room. A tall muscular woman walked out of the room Wendy was standing next to.

Wendy was a little frightened. The woman stopped, and looked Wendy up and down. Wendy felt something crawl up her spine. The woman asked, "Wanna hook up?" Wendy almost vomited again. She quietly said, "No thanks" and quickly got out of there.

***

Evangelist Jones was in her dressing room sleeping before she went back on the air. She couldn't believe she was going to be on for an entire day, but if one soul was saved she knew it would be worth it. A loud and sudden knock at the door woke her.

Evangelist Jones startlingly asked, "Who is it?"

The voice answered, "Its Dave."

She knew Dave was another producer on the Gospel Today Show. Evangelist Jones opened the door and asked, "Dave, when'd you get here?"

He answered with concern, "About an hour ago. Have you seen Tess?"

Evangelist Jones replied, "No, I haven't. Is she missing?"

Dave answered, "Her story is supposed to air in a few minutes, but no one has seen her since she left about four hours ago."

Evangelist Jones thought for a minute. She then said, "I

255

haven't seen her since she left. I just assumed she was putting together the final pieces." She walked out of her dressing room with Dave. When they got to the studio she asked, "Has anyone seen or heard from Tess since she left?

Dave answered, "No, no one has heard a peep out of her."

Evangelist Jones and Dave ran into Mark. Evangelist Jones asked Mark, "Do you have Tess' cell number?"

Mark answered, "No ma'am. I think Diana over there has it. They're good friends."

Evangelist Jones and Dave walked over to Diana, one of the sound personnel. Evangelist Jones saw the worried look on Diana's face. She asked Diana, "Do you have Tess' cell number?" Evangelist Jones waited while Diana gathered herself. She continued, "Take your time, Sweetie."

Diana got herself together and answered, "Yes, I've tried to call her, but she doesn't answer. It just goes to voice mail."

Evangelist Jones said, "Okay, enough of this I'll call my friend, Alan. He's a police officer. I know they aren't doing much now, but he can go by and check on Tess. Do we know where she went?"

Diana replied, "She was going to interview her informant. This was a major story to her; she wouldn't just disappear."

Evangelist Jones asked, "Do you know where she's meeting her informant?"

Diana answered, "The Heston, in the back."

Evangelist Jones said urgently, "I'll call Alan and have him take a look. Then we'll go from there. Does anyone know what the story was about?"

Dave answered, "No one has a clue. She kept a lid on it." Diana replied, "She didn't tell me, either. She said she didn't want to tell anyone until it broke. She wanted to have all the facts, because she felt bad about what happened earlier, when she said that about Christians. She wanted to be sure of everything this time."

Evangelist Jones said, "Okay, we're going to find her."

Diana nervously responded, "I hope so."

***

Clint was sitting in the hotel bar, drowning his sorrows with a gin and tonic.
He was so upset with Bishop Carroll that he didn't know what to do.

On one hand, he wanted to expose the Bishop for what

he was but on the other, he still felt a duty to protect him. The image of his lover betraying him would not stop playing out in his head. He made up his mind that he was going to make the Bishop pay. He saw Aaron walk through the door.

He motioned for him to come quickly.

Aaron said, as he got in range, "The job is done brother."

Clint looked at him and disappointedly said, "Too bad. I want the story to air now."

Clint nodded, taking in the look on his friend's face. Aaron responded, alarmed, "What?"

Clint seriously replied, "Yeah, I came back from getting the Bishop some food and found him with Frank."

Aaron questioned, "You mean...?"

Clint sternly answered, "Yeah, he betrayed me."

Aaron replied in surprise, "Wow, I guess he doesn't care anymore. Man, it's hard to believe the world is ending, and every bit of decency with it."

Clint sighed and said, "There are Christians that would say what we are isn't decent or moral."

Aaron sharply responded, "I know but they are fools.

Look who's turning out to be right. There's no rapture, no Heaven or Hell. We're all just going to die. At least we are who we are supposed to be, and didn't hide in a closet."

Clint said, "Yeah, but he's going to pay."

Aaron asked, "How?"

Clint answered, "I'm going on the Gospel Today show, and admit everything. I'm going to tell it all."

Aaron replied, "You can't be serious." Clint answered, "I am serious."

Clint emphasized, "In these last hours, he...will pay." He slammed his glass down to emphasize his point.

Clint continued, "It will be my last act. I will have my vengeance on my betrayer." Clint saw two men approaching out of the corner of his eye. He recognized the man in charge as Craig.

Craig said in a stern and commanding voice, "The Bishop wants both of you upstairs now."

Clint stood up and replied, "I don't care what he wants. I'm not going back to him, now or forever."

Aaron quickly responded, "Hold on Craig, just let me talk to my friend a minute."

Aaron turned to Clint and said, "Hey man, these dudes don't play. The best play here is to cooperate, and see what happens."

Clint looked at Aaron. He always trusted Aaron's judgment in these matters. For the first time Clint could see fear in his friend's eyes. The courage he had was gone. Now he feared for his own life. He turned to Craig and said, "Okay, but I'm not staying with that betrayer." They began walking towards the exit of the bar, Craig and the other man behind them. Clint hired Craig because he was a former Navy Seal. Now he regretted that decision and hoped his friend could take Craig in a fight.

Craig was cold-blooded and if instructed he wouldn't waste time killing them both if necessary. Suddenly he remembered how the Bishop told him to have Cecil come to his private vacation home in the mountains. He drove Cecil there personally. Before the meeting, he had Aaron set up surveillance in the house in case they needed evidence on Cecil.

When he and Cecil arrived the Bishop met them in the living room. Clint watched the Bishop and Cecil argue over the Bishop's secret lifestyle. Clint was angry with Cecil because Cecil was going to expose everyone in the Bishop's circle. Cecil was a minster under the Bishop and part of his inner circle. He had a congregation of over 25,000 members and was privy to the secret goings on of the ministry.

Clint knew Cecil was guilty of forging income tax returns and adultery. However, Cecil drew the line at the Bishop's homosexual behavior. Clint's job was to record the meeting with the Bishop, so he could have Cecil's admissions to his wrongdoings on video. The admissions Cecil would make on the DVD would cost him jail time and millions.

Even with the threat of the videotape, Cecil still threatened to expose the Bishop. When it seemed they were at an impasse, the Bishop motioned for Clint to take him back to the city. Clint turned his back to grab his gear.

The next thing he remembered was hearing a loud shot. He heard it today as clearly as he did when it happened. When Clint turned around, he saw the Bishop standing there holding a gun, smiling.

The Bishop had just murdered a man in cold blood and he ordered Clint to cover it up. Clint remembered fearing for his own life then. He created the cover story that Cecil died in an accident.

Now he wanted to expose the truth to the world. The Bishop was a homosexual, and a murderer. Now he didn't know if he will get the chance to see the Bishop exposed.

***

She was hurriedly trying to make her way out of the Zone. Wendy had forgotten that she wanted to search for Barbara and Shan. She hated the fact that the only way home was to travel through all the immorality taking place in the Zone. Her skin curled with each step. She was about a hundred feet from the edge of the Zone, when she heard, "Wendy!" She said under her breath, "*Dang! I almost made it!*"

She turned around and saw Jump running towards her. Not wanting to be rude, she decided to stop and wait for him. She figured that after she told him she was saved, he wouldn't want anything to do with her and leave. Out of breath, he asked, "Where are you headed?"

Wendy answered, "Back home."

Jump asked, "Want some company?"

Wendy smiled and said, "No, thank you."

She started walking again and he followed.

Jump replied, "Look, the end of the world is just about a half day away. You don't want to be alone, do you?"

Wendy stopped and responded, "Actually I do. You see I am a saved woman now and everywhere I look I see nothing but sin. I'd rather be alone in my apartment reading my Bible when the end comes."

Jump looked around for a second. Wendy was waiting for his response, but she really wanted to leave. She couldn't be rude. He asked, "How can I be saved?"

She was shocked that he asked about being saved. *Is he serious? How can I be sure?*

She hesitated before she started to speak, "Well, you must first accept Jesus Christ as your Lord and Savior, then..." She was puzzled as Jump backed up. Wendy thought he was excited.

He interrupted and asked, "Can you tell me about Him?"

Wendy was really shocked now. At the start of the evening, this man cared only about having sex with her, now he wants to be saved. She couldn't turn him away if this was what he really wanted. Wendy answered, "Yeah, we can talk about Jesus... She was more puzzled and confused as she watched him backed up again, as if he was staggering.

She carefully continued, "...on the way, but I can't let you into my apartment. I've already had one bad experience tonight."

Jump impatiently replied, "Wendy, I just want to learn, and be saved like you."

They started to walk away when they heard a voice behind

them, "Jump, wait up man." They turned around and saw TJ running behind them.

Jump said to Wendy, "Hold up a second. I need to let TJ know where I'm going."

Wendy replied, "Okay." She saw the two high five each other. *I hope he doesn't think he's getting laid. I'm not that type of girl.*

***

Jump was smiling broadly as he got to TJ. TJ asked, "Hey man, have you seen Jeff?"

Jump answered, "Not for a while. He went with some chick over to Carlton."

TJ asked, "Where you headed?"

Jump smiled more as he excitedly answered, "I'm still working on that babe over there." He used his head to point in the direction of Wendy as he continued, "Man, get this crap. Now she's talking about being saved and all. I'm pretending like I want that for myself."

TJ replied, "You sly dog."

Jump continued, "Yeah, if it works I'll be hitting that soon. I'm going to play the hurt brother who just got out of a bad relationship. I'm going to string her along with this, and in a couple hours or so, I should be hitting it!"

TJ laughed and said, "Yeah, my brother. Sounds like a plan. Good luck. I'm going over here and get my dance on a bit. Then I'm gonna see if I can find something new to hit. Later."

Jump happily responded, "Later!"

***

Wendy waited patiently. She saw Jump running back over to her. She made sure her face showed her impatience.

Jump said, "Sorry about that. He was looking for Jeff and wanted to know what I was getting into. I told him that I had enough of all this sin, and wanted to be saved. He laughed at me."

Wendy replied, "Everyone will laugh at you. You just have to be strong. That is, if you're really serious. I can tell you now, if you have an ulterior motive, then you might as well go off with your friend, because it's not going to happen."

Jump responded, "Wendy, come on; give a brother a break. You're beautiful and all, but I just want to learn to be saved."

Wendy looked at him. *I wonder.* Because of Bill, she had little trust in men. *What did he have to lose by lying? Nothing.*

She looked at her watch. Fourteen hours to the impact, and she was walking home with a stranger. He claimed he wanted to know about Jesus, but only time would tell.

***

Alan Harper was a 10-year, veteran of the Metropolitan Police Department. He knew the lay of the land better than most officers on the force. He arrived at the Heston around 5:30 am and looked around the back for any clues that might lead him to Tess' whereabouts.

About 30 meters down the street; he saw a vehicle matching the description of her vehicle. He approached it and saw no one inside. The door was unlocked so he opened the car and looked for clues.

Nothing was apparent, nothing appeared out of place. He checked the glove compartment and found the registration. The vehicle was registered to Tess L. Minter. *So where are you?*
He closed the car door and proceeded to the area directly behind the Heston Hotel. Once he arrived, he could smell a strong odor emanating from somewhere. The strength of the odor prevented him from getting a good sense of where it was coming from.

He saw a large trash bin near him and slowly made his way over to it. When he looked behind the bin he saw four bodies lying on the ground haphazardly thrown. One of the bodies belonged to Tess, one he recognized as

Bishop Carroll's personal assistant and the other two were not familiar to him.

They did have on jackets displaying the Bishop's logo. *What is going on here? Tess is dead and her body is found with three of Bishop Carroll's team. This looks like some sort of cover-up. But what is being covered up and does the Bishop have anything to do with it? If it wasn't the end of the world this would be a major investigation.*

He pulled out his cell phone and began to dial Evangelist Jones' number. He hated to tell his friend the bad news but he had no other choice. The phone rang twice before Evangelist Jones answered, "This is Evangelist Jones."

Alan responded, "Evangelist, Alan here."

Evangelist Jones replied, "Alan, good, did you find out anything?"

Alan answered, "Yes, but you're not going to like it." Evangelist Jones responded, "Go ahead and tell me."

Alan replied, "She's dead, Evangelist, along with three men. I recognize one of them as Bishop Carroll's personal assistant. I think his name is Clint."

Evangelist Jones said, "Oh my God!"

Alan continued, "I believe the other two worked for the Bishop as well. I think someone was cleaning up something here and whatever it was…" A female voice behind Alan sternly said, "Hang up the phone. Don't turn around; just hang up the phone now, or I'll shoot." Alan hung up the phone as he was told.

Before he hung up he could hear Evangelist Jones saying, "Alan, Alan…hello, are you there, Alan…?"

Alan said, "Are you going to kill me like you did these people?"

The voice calmly asked, "Who are you, and why are you back here?"

Alan tried to maintain his calm, but inside, he feared for his life. He smoothly answered, "I'm Alan Harper. I'm a sergeant with the Metropolitan Police Department."

The voice asked, "Where's your uniform and badge?"

Alan said, "My badge is in my inside left coat pocket. I'm not wearing my uniform because…frankly, it's the end of the world, and I'm here as a favor to a friend."

The voice said, "Use two fingers of your right hand to get your badge."

Alan did as he was told. The voice instructed, "Throw it toward my voice." Alan tossed the badge behind him and toward the voice. After a couple of minutes, the voice said, "Turn around slowly." Alan slowly turned around, as the voice asked him to do. When he could see her, he realized that it was Jessica Carroll.

He asked, "Sister Carroll? What are you doing back here? Did you kill these people?"

Sister Carroll said, "If you recognize me, then you know I'm not capable of that behavior. My husband is cleaning up."

Alan was puzzled, "Cleaning up?"

Sister Carroll continued, "Yes." She pulled out a case with a DVD in it and showed it to Alan. She continued, "He's cleaning up his mess. I approached one of my husband's bodyguards and asked him to contact Tess Minter with the story. He did and for that he died along with Tess. I regret that decision now. My husband had someone kill both the bodyguard and Tess before they could tell the truth about him."

"Then, out of the blue, Clint contacted me. He said he was going to tell the world about the Bishop. I was shocked, but I still ran down here to talk to him. I saw two of my husband's henchmen kill Clint and the Aaron."

"It was awful hearing Clint beg for his life. I didn't like the man, but he didn't deserve to die like that. They disposed of the bodies back here. After they left I came to see the bodies. I guess hoping they might still be alive or something. That's when I saw Tess' body and the

269

bodyguard I had spoken to earlier."

"In your hand is the DVD that exposes my husband's greatest secrets. He has and will kill to protect it."

Alan asked, "What do you want me to do with it?"

Jessica answered, "Get it to Evangelist Jones, and tell her to tell the world."

Alan asked, "Will you come on the air and authenticate the DVD?"

Jessica answered, "If you get it on the air, I will authenticate the disk, and I will tell what I know about these deaths." She looked at him with tears in her eyes. Then she said, "May God protect you."

Alan watched Jessica turn and hurry off. He continued to watch until she was out of sight. Alan looked down at the disk, wondering what was on it. He proceeded to get to his vehicle as fast as he could. Four people had already died because of what was on this disk. He wasn't going to give Bishop Carroll or his men a chance to make it five.

***

Jessica made it back to her car. She sat there for a minute, thinking about what she had done. She kept her husband's secret for the last three years and now she wanted badly to expose it. She suspected something was wrong long before the evidence arrived in the mail that day, but she never did anything about it. Now four people were dead because of it. She couldn't help but feel responsible.

In the midst of her thoughts, a loud thump hit her windshield, startling her. It was one of her husband's bodyguards. He said, "Ma'am you can't be here."

Jessica said through the window, "This is a public street. I can sit here if I want."

The bodyguard responded, "Ma'am please move the vehicle or we will have it moved."

She didn't want to cause any trouble. At this point, she knew it was more prudent to comply. Jessica sternly responded, "Fine." She started the car and drove off, headed back to her home. Once there, she would wait for a call from Evangelist Jones.

***

Alan hurried through the streets, trying to get to the Gospel Today Show's studios. It was across town, but thankfully there wasn't much traffic at this hour. Most people were either in the Zone, or with their families at this point.

He arrived at the studio 30 minutes later and got out of his car. The first shot caught him in the left shoulder and he fell to the ground. More shots rang out around him. He pulled out his gun and tried to returned fire.

***

Inside the studio Evangelist Jones had started her next segment, "Good morning everyone, I'm Evangelist Jones of the Gospel Today Show. It is with great and deep sadness that I must report that our sister in Christ, Tess L. Minter, has gone home to be with the Lord. We do not know all the circumstances at this time, but we are certain that she died somewhere near the Heston. We will..."

Someone shouted, "There's shooting outside!"

Evangelist Jones shouted, "What?"

Everyone ran to a window to see what was happening. Evangelist Jones yelled, "That's Alan!" One of the security guards ran out to help him. Alan had been shot, but he had his gun out, trying to return fire. A black sedan was about 10 meters away from Alan. The shots appeared to be coming from the sedan.

When the security guard came out shooting, the men from the sedan jumped back in their car and drove off. The guard went to Alan to see if he was okay. Evangelist Jones ran out to help. Alan was lying on the ground when Evangelist Jones said, "Alan, are you okay?"

Alan answered in pain, "I'm okay. I took one in my

shoulder."

Evangelist Jones turned and said, "Someone call a doctor." A voice replied, "I already called 9-1-1."

Alan said to Evangelist Jones, "You have got to get this on the air. It's what Tess died for. Sister Carroll said she would confirm everything if you get it on the air."

Evangelist Jones replied, "Oh my. Sister Carroll? Where did you see her?"

Alan replied, "She was at the Heston. She saw two men get murdered. Hurry, those guys won't stop until they get this DVD back."

Evangelist Jones pulled one of the crew over, "Stay with him until help comes." Evangelist Jones looked at the security guards and said, "I need one of you to stay with me, and the other to stay with Alan."

She didn't wait for a reply. She turned and started running back to the studio. Evangelist Jones couldn't wait to see what was so secret that her friend Bishop Carroll would kill to keep anyone from seeing it. Everything she thought she knew about the man was turning inside out. She couldn't believe how bad things were getting.

***

Jessica arrived home shortly after 6:00 am. Earth had only a half day remaining before the asteroid strike. She quietly said a prayer as she walked into the house. When she got in the house, she found everyone wide awake. They were sitting in the living room watching the Gospel Today Show.

Milton Junior shouted, "Mom, come here, quick."

Jessica sat her purse on a table and quickly ran into the living room, "What is it?"

Milton Junior answered, "There was gunfire down at the Gospel Today studios. We're waiting to see what happened."

Jessica sat down slowly beside her mother. She knew her mother could always sense when something was wrong with her baby girl. She remembered when she brought Bishop Carroll home for the first time.
Her mother told her she had a good Christian man. Over the years, Jessica could tell that her mother's opinion had changed, but she never mentioned it to Jessica.

For that, Jessica was glad. She didn't want to discuss it with her mother. Now Jessica knew the truth about her husband was going to be unveiled in front of the world. She had to be prepared to be strong for her family but she would be embarrassed for herself.

***

Bishop Carroll was in his penthouse suite when the phone rang. He answered, "Bishop, we didn't get the disc back." Without answering the Bishop slammed the phone on the hook. He was angry. The Bishop was a vain man. He cared greatly how people perceived him. He wanted them to admire him. He didn't want them to look at him with disdain. He had to get that DVD back.

He picked up the phone and called his old friend Pep Lewis, "Pep, how are you my friend?" Pep answered, "I'm doing good, for a man with a half day of life left."

Bishop Carroll laughed and asked, "Pep, I need the power shut off around the Gospel Today Studios. Can you do that for me?"

Pep answered, "Sure could. How long do you need it out?"

Bishop Carroll answered, "Until the asteroid strikes."

Pep replied, "I'm on my way down there now. It should be off at eight."

Bishop Carroll responded, "Thanks, old friend." Pep said, "Anything for you, Bishop."

***

Wendy and Jump made it back to Wendy's apartment

building. She told Jump everything she knew about Jesus Christ. She was surprised at how much she remembered from her Sunday school days. The rest, she believed God was giving her. She was also surprised by the fact that Jump didn't know anything at all about Jesus.

She wondered how someone could be in their 20's and not know about Jesus. Once outside her building Wendy stopped and sat on the stoop. Jump asked, "Can't we go inside?"

Wendy answered, "No. I feel better talking out here."

Jump replied, "Come on Wendy, haven't I proved myself to you? I just want to learn more."

Wendy said, "And I will tell you more, right out here. It's a nice morning, so we can sit here and take in some fresh air."

Jump responded, "You're impossible."

Wendy replied, "No, I'm not. I'm possible; it just takes a Christian man, following Christian ways to get me."

Jump asked, "You think all those rules in the Bible really apply? I mean, come on, what person can go without sex until they're married?"

Wendy answered, "Anyone can, if they put their mind to it. Why do you need sex? You should want a woman for her mind, heart, and personality; not what she can do in the bedroom."

Jump replied, "I wouldn't buy a car without test driving it, right?"

Wendy answered, "See that's your problem. You don't think of women as people. You only think of us as objects of your desire. What about our desires? If I want to go without sex until I'm married, and you truly love me, then you should wait."

Jump replied, "Love? Men don't fall in love until we're over 40.

Anything else is asking a lot of a man." He stepped close to her and tried to put his arms around her. Wendy took his arms in her hands, and quickly removed them. She said, "It's not going to happen. If you're looking for something to happen, you've come to the wrong place buddy."

Jump replied, "No baby, I didn't." He tried to press against her again and she pushed him away.

She said, "This is why I didn't invite you in my apartment. You guys are all the same. Did you think I would fall for you because you ask a few questions, and pretend you want to know about my Jesus? Think again, my friend."

Jump was looking down. Wendy was getting nervous.

277

She started to walk around him, trying to get to her apartment but he grabbed her arm.

Jump said coldly, "I have a gun on my waist. Now let's go inside your apartment. If you make a scene, you'll see Him first hand."

Wendy was truly frightened. *How did I manage to get into this situation again?* She quietly prayed for help.

***

Jessica received a phone call from Evangelist Jones. Evangelist Jones told her they were going on the air with Tess' story, and she desired Jessica to come down to the studio to authenticate it. Jessica agreed and tried to explain herself on the phone, but Evangelist Jones excused herself saying she had to get ready for the show.

Jessica hung up the phone, thinking about how she was going to tell her kids. She walked back into the living room where everyone was waiting patiently on the big story. Jessica said, "I have to go to the Gospel Today Studios."

Milton Junior asked, "Why, Mom? It's dangerous down there."

Jessica replied, "The story that's about to break concerning Milton is big. They want me to confirm that it's true. You're not going to like what they are going to say about your dad. I just want each of you to be strong, and please don't do anything crazy." She was crying through her words. She was scared one of them would be so angry that they might go confront their dad.

She looked at her mom and dad and said, "Mommy, Daddy, please don't let them leave after they hear the story. Please."

Her mother and father both nodded their heads. Milton Junior asked, "Why don't you just tell us?"

Mark added, "Yeah mom, why don't you tell us? We'd rather hear it from you anyway."

Jessica stood there, pondering the idea.

***

Bill was having a wild experience. He wondered how he allowed himself to miss out on so much pleasure in the past. He was outside smoking some marijuana, when he noticed two figures throwing a large item into a hole.

He was curious about what it was, so when the men walked away he went over to the hole. When he got to the hole he smelled a strong odor. *Whew! What the heck is that smell?* He looked down and saw bodies, numerous female bodies. He counted eight of them in all. He looked closer and could see two bodies he recognized.

Bill saw Barbara and Shan's dead bodies with their eyes still open. He felt a curl up his spine as it appeared they were pleading with him. He fell to his knees, throwing up what little food he had in him.

When he looked again, he saw Tammi's body. He got up and ran, stumbling back to the Tradewinds. Bill didn't know what to do. *The only person that could have killed them was Teddy. Oh my God, Teddy's a killer! But why?*

He got close to the Tradewinds and fell to his knees again. He thought about Wendy. He should have listened to her. He cried out her name, "Wendy! Wendy!" When he looked up Teddy was standing in front of him. Bill got up, and ran as fast as he could. He pushed several people away as he ran. He was terrified at the sight of Teddy.

He no longer saw the happy-go-lucky friend he came to admire. Now, what he saw scared him. Bill looked back as he ran down the streets of the Zone. After about a half mile, he stopped, thinking he had outrun Teddy. He wondered why no one else paying any attention to him. He turned, and Teddy was standing right in front of him again. He couldn't believe that Teddy had outrun him. He looked around him and everyone had an evil face. *Am I going crazy? Where have I gone? What evil place is this?*

Teddy asked, "Going somewhere, my brother?"

His voice was bone chilling and it scared Bill even more, "Get away from me! You killed them...you killed Shan,

Barbara, Tammi and those other girls."

Teddy replied, "Yes, I did, and you're going to help me convince Wendy to sin. My Master badly wants her soul. His voice rose as he shouted, "I'm tired of playing games with you." He grabbed Bill by the shoulders, pulling him to his feet and stared deeply into his eyes, "Help me or die!"

Bill responded, "It's real, all of it is real."

Teddy answered, "Yes, it's real; all of it. The best part is that your soul now belongs to my Master."

Bill replied, "No, I want to go to Heaven."

Teddy laughed loudly, but it seemed no one else in the Zone could hear it.

Then he said, "Are you serious, Heaven doesn't want you! You lost your chance when you gave your virginity to the beautiful Aaliyah." Teddy turned and pointed. "Remember the beautiful Aaliyah?"

Aaliyah walked around the corner, laughing hideously at Bill. She fell against the wall with her hands behind her back. She had an evil grin on her face. Bill took one look at her. He was appalled at what he saw. She was a wicked creature. Her face was wrinkled; her hair looked like tiny serpents. Her eyes were as yellow as the moon. Her skin was a lime green. When she laughed, it sent chills up and down Bill's back. He had never been so frightened in his life. *What have I done?*

Then he cried out, "Lord what have I done. Please, for…" Teddy didn't let him finish the sentence. He shouted, "Lord! He can't save you now. Your lord is Satan. My Master is now your Master. Help us get Wendy, and you won't burn in Hell when the asteroid strikes. It's a fair deal!"

Bill was scared, he didn't want to die. He cared about Wendy, but not enough to burn in Hell. Bill replied, "Okay, okay, I'll do it. I'll do it. But she won't have sex with me; I tried."
Teddy said, "Try harder! Beat her into submission, and then rape her. She will be so distraught, she will kill herself. Then, her soul will belong to my Master. Suicide is the best sin; there's no coming back from it."
Bill said through his tears, "I can't…I can't do that!"
He knocked Bill to the ground, "Then, you will die and burn in Hell!" Teddy raised his foot to stomp him.

Bill shouted in fear, "No, no…okay, I'll take the deal. I'll do it, I'll do it! I'll help you get Wendy's soul." Bill was feverishly sobbing and crying.

Teddy replied, "Let me be clear…" He leaned down, placing his face right in front of Bill's face. Bill could smell his breath on his face and he almost vomited. Teddy continued, "…do you freely give your soul to my Master, Satan, in return for life after the asteroid strikes?"

Sobbing and crying profusely, Bill answered, "Yeeeesss." Satan stepped from the shadows and said, "It is done." Bill fainted.

***

Evangelist Jones had just seen the DVD, and she was horrified at what she saw. She could not believe that, Bishop Carroll was a murderer and a homosexual. She thought maybe this happened in the last few hours, but the technicians confirmed that the DVD had been made three to five years prior.

She thought about the times Bishop Carroll spoke out against homosexual behavior. His sermons on Leviticus 18:22 often taught how the word of God unequivocally spoke against homosexual activity. Most of all, she could not believe that he not only ordered the death of several people, he actually killed a man in cold blood. She could not believe she followed this man, and worked under his covering for all these years.

She felt so betrayed and had to get herself together before going on the air; she didn't want the pain of her betrayal to come through. Instead, she wanted the Christians and those that turned from the word because of the Bishop see just who they were listening too.

As Evangelist Jones got ready for the story, Jessica Carroll came into the studio. Their eyes met for what seemed like an eternity. Jessica spoke first and said, "Now you know the whole story."

Evangelist Jones gathered herself together and asked, "How could you stay with him, knowing he was against our God all this time?"

Jessica answered, "I loved him."

Evangelist Jones responded, "But honey, he loved other men!" She then emphasized, "And, he's a killer."

Tears were streaming down Jessica's face. She was at a loss for words. Evangelist Jones couldn't forgive her right now. She could only think about the millions of Christians who could have been saved if he were exposed years ago. She was angry that Jessica had been so selfish.

Jessica squeezed out, "I...I'm sorry."

Evangelist Jones looked at her and started to walk away. She heard a voice within her remind her that if she judged she would be judged also. She suddenly stopped. For a moment she let the devil get the best of her. She slowly turned around and walked back to Jessica with her arms folded, pondering what she was going to say. She found herself standing right in front of Jessica. She unfolded her arms, and put them around Jessica. Jessica was crying freely.

Evangelist Jones said, "Honey, we're not here to judge.

Forgive me for almost doing just that. I'm here for you my friend."

Jessica didn't say anything. She tried to smile through her tears.

***

A black van pulled up near the Gospel Today studios. Inside were five men. Using binoculars, the leader noted that security had been stepped up around the studio. There were two metropolitan police officers in front of the building, and two in back.

He had been told earlier that there were two security guards on the premises. He figured they were inside. The leader of the group instructed the driver to drive around the corner. Once around the corner the van stopped, and the leader instructed one of the men to take up a position on top of a nearby building.

The leader didn't watch the man check his rifle and scope. He had complete confidence in the man. The leader of the group put him there because he knew he was capable of hitting a target over 400 yards away.

The van drove off and parked a half block from the studio. The leader instructed the driver to join him as they approached the back of the building. He instructed the other two men to go around front, and take up offensive positions.

285

He was positioning his men for an assault on the building. The leader pulled out his cell phone to make a call. The phone on the other end began to ring. The voice on the other end answered, "Bishop Carroll."

The leader asked, "Sir, can you confirm our objectives?"

Bishop Carroll answered, "Your first objective is to secure the DVD and any copies that were made. Second, check to see if any copies of the DVD were emailed. If so, find out who they were emailed to and write down that information. Third, destroy all computers in the building. Last and most importantly, there are to be no survivors. Understand?"

The leader replied, "Understood." They both hung up. The leader checked his watch for the time. He looked through his binoculars and ensured all of his men were in place. All he needed now was the power to be shut off.

XI

Jacob was a serious man. He worked hard to become the best mercenary in the world. He was an experienced leader of assault missions and called in only when the mission was serious. Jacob spent 20 years in the Army and his handpicked experts were all men capable of easily pulling off this assault. He was not about to let him down. He looked at his watch once more. It was almost eight in the morning.

Jacob crouched into position waiting for the power to go out. His team member and friend, JJ was waiting about 20 feet from him. He pulled out his binoculars and watched the building. He looked at his watch again. *Three more minutes.*

He looked over at JJ and held up three fingers. He nodded for him to get ready. Jacob's cell phone rang. It was a voice he didn't recognize. The voice said, "The power's out. It's a go."

Jacob hung up the phone without saying a word. He clicked his microphone on his ear and said, "It's a go. Tray, take your shot."

Tray was the sniper on top of the building. Immediately after giving the order, Jacob saw one of the Metropolitan police officers go down. He knew Tray had taken the shot. Jacob saw the other officer take cover.

He made his way over to him laying down fire on his way. He turned and motioned for JJ to follow him. Jacob fired at the officer as JJ made his way over. They encircled the officer, trying to take him out. Jacob could hear shots being fired on the other side of the building. His men were assaulting the front of the building as planned.

He tapped his microphone and barked instructions to JJ, "Draw his fire. When you do, I'll take him out." JJ responded, "Yes, sir."

He fired. The officer stood and tried to return fire. Jacob took aim and fired three quick shots into the officer's chest. He watched the officer slowly fall to the ground.

***

Tommy was driving to Marcie's house. It was the same route he had taken hundreds of times before, but today it seemed like the longest drive ever. His friend Jack wanted to go to the Living Word with them, so he was on the passenger side of the vehicle. Tommy knew the world was about to end later today, and in his mind he just couldn't rationalize it all.

He trusted and believed in God, but he couldn't see why the world was ending and it wasn't according to the Bible. He remembered what his sister told him about having faith in all things seen and unseen.

He thought this is the best situation to have that kind of faith. So he chose to have faith in the unseen. He pulled up in front of Marcie's apartment building and pulled out his cell. He hit speed dial number two, and her phone began to ring.

He said to Jack, "I bet she's not ready."

Jack replied, "You know how women are, anyway. But your sister is nice. I'll wait a hundred years for her!"

Tommy said, "Let it go man. She's not interested."

Jack replied, "I'm just waiting. One day, she'll see I'm the one for her."

Tommy half laughed and said, "Sure she will."

Marcie answered the phone, "Be down in a minute!"

Tommy replied, "Sure, more like half an hour."

She responded, "Whatever, Tommy. You're late anyway."

Tommy said, "Okay, okay, hurry up."

She replied, "Bye!"

Tommy responded, "Bye!"

For the last year she had been his only family. They had become closer than ever. He protected his baby sister, and she always had his back. Now in the end, he couldn't think of anyone else he'd rather be hanging out with, than his little sister. After a few minutes, she popped out of the building, ran over to Tommy's car and jumped in.

Marcie said, "See, I wasn't that long. Hi, Jack."

Tommy replied, "Surprisingly."

Jack answered, "Hi Marcie."

Marcie responded to Tommy, "Do you think they're still at the church?"

Tommy answered, "Yeah. Ms. D said they were going to stay there until the end."

Marcie said, "I can't believe he didn't try to call you."

Tommy replied, "He did, I just didn't answer. I need to see him face to face."

Marcie responded, "Well, I talked to him. I was getting ready to conference you in but as usual, he had to leave."

Tommy laughed and said, "That's good anyway. I need to see him face to face."

Marcie responded, "Okay, let's go."

***

Inside the studio, Evangelist Jones and the others were getting ready to go live with the story. Suddenly, the power went out throughout the building.

Mark shouted, "I'll go down and get the generator started!"

Evangelist Jones responded, "Okay! We're going to run this story no matter what!" She shouted, "Praise God and Hallelujah!"

Evangelist Jones heard shots being fired outside the studio. She looked at Jessica; both knew that they had to find a safe place.

Evangelist Jones shouted, "Mark, wait. Can we take a camera and laptop down to the generator room, and show the video there?"

Mark responded, "Yeah. Grab whatever we need and get down there."

Evangelist Jones looked at Sid and said, "What do you need us to do?"

Sid responded, "Each one of you grab a case. It's our emergency broadcast gear. Then go with Mark. I'll be

291

right behind you."

Evangelist Jones and Jessica each grabbed a case and ran after Mark. Evangelist Jones was praying they would be safe. She was running as fast as she could, when she heard a loud boom.

She stopped to see smoke rising from the front door. It appeared to have been blown open and shots were ringing out everywhere. She saw Sid go down. He was lying motionless on the floor. Jessica stopped with her. She grabbed Jessica by the arm and they both ran for the basement generator.

***

Bill woke up from his faint to see no one standing near him. He heard DJ Fever shouting in the background. He was revving up the crowd in his usual manner. Bill looked around for Teddy but didn't see him. He thought maybe it was all a dream, until he felt the burning sensation in his arm. The pain grew more and more excruciating by the second.

He fell on his side, trying somehow to stop the burning pain. Something felt as though it was ripping his arm apart. He rolled over and tried to grab his arm with his other hand, hoping that would stop the pain. As he screamed in agony, he could see three numbers burning in his arm.

It was three sixes. Bill recognized it as the sign of the devil and it was burned into his flesh. Nothing he experienced was a dream. He'd traded his soul to the devil. After the numbers burned into his flesh, he stood up and screamed out loud, but no one seemed to hear him.

He staggered a few feet and heard DJ Fever announce, "Ladies and gentlemen, the winner of our "Virginity and Queen" contest is Mr. Teddy Robinson and Ms. Aaliyah!" Bill couldn't believe his ears. They were awarding a virgin woman to Teddy. He thought he could save her from death, but deep inside, he knew he was a coward and only wanted to save himself.

He got up and began running toward Wendy's place. Teddy had charged him with helping to get Wendy's soul. If he did this, he would not die with everyone else. He had to make Wendy sin. He reasoned, if he did what Teddy said and raped Wendy, she would kill herself. Then he would live past the asteroid strike. He didn't understand how that could be, but he didn't care. All he cared about was living.

As he was running toward Wendy's place, he came to accept what he had to do. He was going to do it. He was going to force her to have sex with him. When he got to her stoop, he stopped for a second to catch his breath.

After a moment, he darted upstairs. He noticed the door was slightly opened. He eased it all the way open and went inside. Once inside, he heard shouting coming from the bedroom. He went down the hall and peeked into the room. Wendy was on the bed, and a dude he didn't recognize was standing over her.

He went in and shouted, "What's going on here?"

The dude turned around and said, "It's about time you got here. What took you so long?"

Bill was bewildered, "I don't know you!"

Jump said, "But I know you. I also know about the deal you made. Our Master has tasked us to do a job and unlike you I plan on doing it. I will not fail him."

Bill looked at Wendy. He could see that she was scared. Bill said, "Wendy, this will be easy for all of us if you just cooperate."

Wendy replied, "Bill, please don't do this to me. I was your friend."

Bill angrily replied, "You weren't my friend! You wouldn't even have sex with me. I told you I loved you and everything. It's your fault I'm in this mess. It's your fault you're in this mess."

Wendy said, "Bill, you can still be saved…" Suddenly Jump slapped her across her face and the force of the blow knocked her off the bed and onto the floor.

Bill shouted at Jump, "What are you doing?"

Jump said, "You're stalling! Do what you were sent here to do or I'll do it for you! Then, you'll die with everyone else!"

Bill said, "I'll do what I have to do in my time. Get out of here!"

Jump threw a quick punch to Bill's face, knocking him down. Bill suddenly felt energetic. He had to get Wendy to a safe place, even if it meant his own death. All of a sudden he found the courage to be a hero. Since he made the deal with the devil, he couldn't be saved. Now he had to save the only person he truly loved.

***

Calvin made it back to his place and was sitting in his living room, angry he didn't have his woman with him. He was going to get her back if it took the rest of the time he had. He searched through his desk drawer until he found his .9 mm handgun. He planned to go back there and get Vanessa. If necessary, he was going to kill everyone there to get her.

First, however, he had to get some alcohol in his system. Playing the 'saved' game kept him away from drinking for far too long. He thirsted for some whisky. He decided to head to the Zone for a drink, and then he would return to the Living Word Ministries to claim his woman.

***

The loud celebration in the Zone at the announcement of the winners of the contest woke Johnny from his drunken stupor. He carefully looked around and realized that he had passed out at some point during the night. He saw people running around the Zone celebrating the end of the world. *Fools, all of them are just…fools.*

He stood up; trying to figure out what direction his car was parked. He stumbled falling to his knees. Tears flowed from his eyes, racing down his face like a river. *V, I want you back V!* He felt a hand on his shoulder. He jumped up and said, "V…"

When he turned, he saw Missy standing there with a smile. She said, "No baby, but I know you'd rather have me than that trifling wench you're married to."

Johnny pushed her out of his way and said, "You don't know what you're talking about."

Missy followed behind him and said, "But, I do, baby. Come back to the room with me. I can make it all better. The world is ending in 10 hours, but I got another friend, and you will really like her!

Johnny stopped and turned to her. He slowly said, "Missy, I don't want to go back to the room with you or any of your friends. I shouldn't been with any of you; especially given you're only 18! God, what did I do?"

He paused for second and then continued, "I'm going to find my wife and patch things up with her. I've made a mess of things, but to God as my witness I can't leave this Earth without making it better."

Johnny started to walk away. Missy grabbed his arm and tried to pull him back. She screamed, "No, don't leave! No...he'll kill me!"

Johnny turned and said, "What are you talking about?"

Missy said, "I'll die if you leave."

Johnny replied, "I don't know what's wrong with you, but you won't die just because I'm leaving. We don't even know each other that well." Missy fell to her knees and started to cry. Johnny walked away and out of Missy's sight.

***

Missy stood eyes downcast. As she stood there, a figure formed behind her. She knew she had failed her master. She knew he would come for her. That cold chill running up and down her spine was familiar. He was there.

She heard his evil voice, "You have failed. Now it's time for you to come to Hell and serve your penitence!"

The force of being snatched downward was more painful than anything she had ever felt in her life. She screamed as loud as she could. She felt the claws of something clutched tightly to her. This birdlike creature was guiding her to her final destination. She could see her body as it lay on the ground, lifeless above her.

Down in Hell, her spirit immediately felt the burning wind roasting her. She had no body, in the sense of her understanding, but she could feel pain...immense pain. She screamed as the pain consumed her.

All around her was fire. It was like a lake with nothing but fire as far as she could see. Her pain was bad; she began to gnash her teeth together. She could see others around her screaming in agony, crying out for mercy, gnashing and gnawing sounds came from every direction. Some people she recognized, but they died years ago.

Satan appeared before her in his natural form. He looked nothing like he was portrayed on Earth. She continued to feel the immense pain; fear encompassed her body. Satan stood tall over her like a tall, bronze statue. His body was rippled with muscles, and his eyes glowed red, like the fires of Hell.
His hair was long, and sparkled like flames. She looked at his face; it was scarred with evil. When on Earth, she saw nothing but beauty when her master appeared before her. Now she could see the evil within him.

The first time she saw Satan was a year ago, when she was depressed because her boyfriend dumped her. He appeared and she fell in love with him. She was so engrossed in him; she would do anything for him. When he asked for her soul, in return for being with him forever, she didn't blink an eye.

Now she realized the truth, what she saw on Earth was just an illusion. Satan was a monster after her soul, and she let him have it for the illusion of love. He said to her, "For your failure, you will suffer in this pit forever! Unlike Jehovah I have no mercy for you."

She screamed, "No, please! Don't leave me here! You said you love me! Don't do this to me!"

Satan said softly, "Love? What do you know of it? I gave you what you wanted on Earth. Now, your soul is mine." Satan laughed loudly. She watched him look around at all the suffering souls, and laughing.

She shouted, "Please, I'll do anything!"

Satan said, "I have your soul. There is nothing you can do for me, except suffer!"

***

Johnny made it to his car. He grabbed the piece of paper off of his windshield and tossed it in the car, not bothering to read it. He got behind the wheel of the car and started the ignition. Once the car was started, he glanced down at the paper.

It read, *If we live, we are living for the LORD, and if we die, we are dying for the LORD, Romans 14:8*
Johnny said to himself, *That is so right.* He sped off down the street headed for the woman he truly loved. He didn't know what he was going to say to make it right. He had said so many hateful things, but now he realized that he was wrong. There was no one more important to him now than his wife. He had to make it right with Jesus as well.

***

Calvin's car raced to the Zone blasting loud music. He was listening to his favorite rap artist and getting primed for the mission at hand. He jumped out of the car, and went into the first bar he could find.

As he went to order his whiskey, he paid no attention to anyone around him. One lady came up to him and tried to put her arms around him, but he abruptly pushed her away. He half heard her voice behind him, "Jerk!"

He sat at the bar and ordered, "Whiskey, straight up." The bartender obliged and sat the drink in front of Calvin. Calvin sternly said, "Leave the bottle!"

The bartender again obliged, without saying a word. Calvin drank the whiskey; tuning out the voices and music

300

around him. He had one mission, and that was to get Vanessa back. Nothing was going to stop him.

It started getting colder. Calvin thought the temperature was dropping fast. He felt someone beside him. He didn't even look to see who it was...

He heard a man ask, "Looks like you're getting ready for something special my friend."

Calvin sneered and said angrily, "Mind your business, and I ain't your friend."

The voice said, "Oh, but you are my friend. You see, we got things in common. We both don't mind death."

Calvin looked straight at the man now. He was as cold as Calvin. For the first time in his life, Calvin saw evil in someone else's eyes. He couldn't figure this man out. Calvin looked the man straight in his eyes, but couldn't see anything.

Calvin asked, "Who are you?"

The man replied, "They call me Raven. Some people think I'm a demon. They think you're a demon too, friend." Calvin frowned not caring what anyone thought of him. The man continued, "You see these poor lost souls, I'm here for them. When they die, I will escort their souls to Hell. Funny, I just got back from Hell. I escorted a pretty little lady down there who failed her

301

mission. She was a fool, too. You see, she believed all the lies she was told. Funny how that always happens."

Calvin replied, "So you're here for me?"

Raven answered, "Here for you? Noooooo, my friend, not here, not right now. You see, where you're going, there's gonna be death. I like death, especially the death of the unsaved. So when you leave here I'm going with you. That's your intention isn't it, to create an atmosphere of death, right?"

Calvin responded, "You got that right. Anyone who gets in my way, I intend to kill. I'm going to get my woman back. So if you want to escort someone to Hell, come with me...friend."

Raven half smiled and replied, "I'm right with you, friend."

***

Evangelist Jones, Jessica and Mark made it to the basement. They went to the generator room and looked around. Mark asked, "Where's Sid?"

Evangelist Jones answered, "He's dead...I think, he wasn't moving."

Mark replied, the sadness evident on his face, "Okay." He paused for a moment taking in Sid's death, "We need

302

to get this stuff set up and barricade that door. Evangelist, do you know how to set this stuff up?"

Evangelist Jones answered, "A little."

Mark said, "Okay, you get started. I'll push this stuff over the door. Let's pray it holds them for a while."

Evangelist Jones replied, "You and me both." She looked at Jessica. Jessica was just standing there, frozen. She had to help Jessica get through this situation. She knew Jessica was blaming herself for all that was happening at the studio. Evangelist Jones said, "Jessica, give me a hand."

She didn't move. Evangelist Jones walked over to Jessica and took her by the arm. She said, "Come on girl. I need your help here. Stop blaming yourself for this mess."

Jessica looked at her and smiled. Evangelist Jones recognized that smile. She had seen it many times before. It was Jessica's way of saying 'you're joking, right?' Evangelist Jones said, "Jessica, you have to get it together. There are men with guns who are going to come through that door any minute, to try and kill us. We have to get this message out. That's the only chance we have to live. After that, you can feel sorry for yourself all you want."

Evangelist Jones winked at her, trying to lift her spirits. She then said with some force, "Now come on girl, help us!"

Jessica replied, "Okay, okay, what do I need to do?"

Evangelist Jones responded, "Okay, I need to connect these microphones to the soundboard using these cables. The connections are marked, so you shouldn't have any problems. I'll be setting up the computer and camera."

Both ladies rushed to get the system connected. Evangelist Jones glanced up to see what progress Mark was making in blocking the door. Mark came back over and said, "Okay, that should buy us some time. Hopefully they won't know where to look for us. How's it coming over here?"

Evangelist Jones answered, "We're almost there. The problem is, we don't have an internet connection down here."

She looked at Mark like it was hopeless to even try. Mark responded, "Okay, I can connect my tablet to the computer and we can burn a copy to it and send it." Evangelist Jones asked, "You have internet on your tablet?"

Mark answered, "Yeah, I just got this one. Its 4g and everything. Check it out..."

Evangelist Jones said, "Mark...?"

Mark replied, "Yeah, sorry, I guess that can wait. Let's

get going."

Evangelist Jones said, "I hope we have enough time."
Mark responded, "So do I. Let's get started."

***

Jacob and his men secured the Gospel Today studio,
"Search every inch of this place. Find anyone alive, and
bring them in here."

Jacob looked around. He turned to JJ and said, "Search
these computers and find out if any of them have a copy
of the disc. If you find one, destroy it. Find the email
server and check all of the accounts to see if anyone
emailed a copy of it. If they did, find out who received
the email. Write down any information on them, so we
can track them down."

JJ replied, "Yes sir."

Jacob then pulled out his cell phone and dialed a number.
The voice on the other end said, "Is it done?"

Jacob answered, "No sir. We are searching the premises
now. When I find them, I will report back to you."

The voice said, "No survivors, you got it?"

Jacob answered, "Yes sir." The line went dead and Jacob
hung up his phone. He surveyed

the room, deep in thought. Then it hit him. He turned to JJ and said rhetorically, "This is a studio, right?"

JJ sarcastically responded, "Uhh, yes sir."

Jacob continued ignoring JJ's response, "They must have a way to continue broadcasting, even if they lose all power." He snapped his fingers and turned toward JJ. He shouted, "I bet there's a generator somewhere in the building."

He clicked his radio and announced, "Find the generator room! They're likely hiding there." A voice responded over the radio, "Roger that."

X

Bill dove at Jump hitting, him in the stomach with his shoulder. The two of them went down as Wendy watched; surprised, happily surprised that Bill was coming to her aid. Jump and Bill each struggled to get the advantage. Jump fought his way to the top. He had Bill pinned on the floor with his hands around Bill's throat.

Wendy couldn't take it. She had to do something to help Bill. She grabbed a decorative walking stick from its stand and reared back as far as she could. She swung it at Jump's head and the impact caused the stick to break in half.

Jump fell to Bill's side. Bill pushed him completely off of him as he grasped for air. Wendy ran to Bill and grabbed him. She said, "Are you okay?"

Bill struggled to say, "I'm good. Are you okay?"

Wendy answered, "Yes, and thank you. You came to my aid."

Bill said, "It was the least I could do. I've been an idiot, Wendy."

Wendy replied, "It's okay."

Bill responded, "You're pretty good at knocking people over the head. We have to get out of here, now"

Wendy smiled then asked, "And go where?"

Bill said, "We can go to the Living Word. It's my church. At least, I hope it's still my church. If there's a place to go, it's there. The Rev will know what to do."

Wendy replied, "Okay, let's go." The two of them got up and headed out of the apartment. Wendy didn't know what to make of Bill now. Ever since the announcement all he wanted was to have sex with her. Now, he'd risked his life to save her. Now, he was taking her to his church with the hope that he could still be saved.

***

Tommy had to drive through a rough part of town in order to get to the Living Word Ministries. He never liked driving through this part of town at any time. Now, it was the end of the world, so he really hated it.

He couldn't imagine letting anything happen to his baby sister, and that's why he was glad his buddy, Jack was with him. Tommy admired Jack because he was a fighter. Jack didn't let anyone push him around.

At the same time, Jack stood up for his friends. He didn't let anyone push his friends around, either. They were getting closer to the warehouse district, and Tommy was looking around to ensure no one attacked them. Jack broke his silence. He shouted, "Watch out!"

Tommy swerved the car, but it hit the mechanism on the ground, and two of the tires burst. The car spun around in a half circle before it stopped. Before Tommy could come to understand what happened to his car, the door flung open and someone grabbed his arm. They dragged him out of the car pointing a gun at his head.

Tommy glanced over, and the same had happened to Jack and Marcie. They had been taken out of the car, and guns were now pointed at all of them. Tommy's nightmare became a reality.

***

It was 10:00 am, and Johnny sat outside the Living Word Ministries. He was getting ready to go inside and find his wife. He hoped that he could convince her to come back to him. Silently, he prayed for Jesus to be in the middle of this meeting.

After his prayer, he got out of the car and walked toward the church door. When he got there, he realized the doors were locked. He knocked on the door until someone came. He recognized the man from the previous day's meeting.

The man opened the door and said, "What do you want?"

Johnny paused for a second. He said, "I want to come home."

The man replied, "Come on in, my brother."

Johnny asked, "I remember you from yesterday. What's your name?"

He answered, "Roger. I'm glad you found the light, my brother."

Johnny replied, "So am I, but it was a high price to pay. Is my wife still here?"

Roger responded, "Yeah. Come this way." The two of them began to walk to the cafeteria, when they were met by Reverend Collins.

Reverend Collins said, "Minister Johnny, it's good to see you again."

Johnny replied, "Sir, I don't deserve to be called a minister, and I am truly sorry for my words and my actions."

Reverend Collins responded, "Nonsense. You are, and will always be, a minister. It's good to have you back on Jesus' side."

Johnny said, "Sir, I need to repent in front of everyone."

Reverend Collins replied, "You just did, my son. Matthew 18 and 20 says 'For where two or three come together in my name, there am I with them.' You have been cleansed by the blood of Jesus."

Johnny responded, "Sir, you don't understand. It's my fault she's dead."

Reverend Collins asked, "Who?"

Johnny sadly answered, "Katrina. She committed suicide last night."

Reverend Collins said, "There's nothing we can do for her now, but you are saved by the blood of Jesus. You have repented your sins."

Johnny replied, "Not completely. I need to see my wife."

Reverend Collins responded, "Come on. She's right this way." The three of them walked into the cafeteria where Johnny saw his wife, but her back was turned to him. She was at a table with three other ladies, and two young children.

Johnny also saw a man he recognized as the President. He thought that was a Presidential limo out front, but he couldn't believe the President was at his church. Johnny saw the ladies as they whispered something to Vanessa. Then Vanessa slowly turned around. Johnny saw the look of surprise on her face. He slowly walked over to her.

She was noticeably nervous as he approached.

Once he was close enough, he took her hands and got on one knee. He looked up at her with tears in his eyes. She started to cry also. He said, "Sweetheart, I know I haven't been right for years. This whole thing has been my fault. If I had never done you wrong, our marriage would have stayed on the right track. Can you please find it in your heart to forgive me?" Vanessa pulled him up and wrapped her arms around him. They both cried.

She said, "I forgive you, if you forgive me. I should have been like Samantha and trusted God to make everything right." They embraced like it was the first time. He had never been happier in his life. The woman he loved had just forgiven him for his mistakes. He excitedly asked, "Let's get married again to symbolize our fresh start?"

She answered with a smile on her face, "Are you proposing to me, Johnny?"

He asked again, "V, will you marry me?"

She smiled a smile that lit up the room and said, "Of course I will!" Everyone cheered. For the first time since the news of their impending destruction, there was reason for celebration. Carla stood up and announced, "What are we waiting here for, we have a wedding to put on!" Samantha joined her and said, "That's right; let's get this thing rolling."

Johnny held his wife in his arms, and nothing felt better to him than to be back with the one woman he truly loved. No one could ever replace that spot in his heart for her, and now they were back together. The world was going to end in less than eight hours, but he didn't care. He was with the one and only person that mattered to him, his wife. Nothing else mattered to him now.

***

Tommy, Jack, and Marcie were on their knees in the street. Tommy's car was disabled, with two flat tires. He focused on finding a way out of this mess. There were five men against them, and they were all armed. He didn't fear for himself, but he did fear for his sister.

The leader stepped up and said, "Well, it appears we have hit the jackpot." He turned and laughed with his gang members. He continued as he walked up to Tommy, and bent down inches from Tommy's face, "You...you are the President's son.

He looked over at Marcie. "And you are his daughter. I bet you thought I wouldn't recognize you. I bet you thought I was an old, uneducated thug. Wrong!"

Tommy said, "Just let us go, man. We've done nothing to you."

The leader said, "Can't do that."

He egotistically added, "Or better yet, I don't want to."

He held his hands as if to say 'why' and looked at his men. They all continued to laugh.

He continued, "You see, I think your sister here is soooo fine. I remembered seeing her on TV and thought 'if I had that...'" He caressed her chin while speaking then continued, "Now, I don't have to dream anymore. I'm about to have it!"

He began moving his hips in a circular motion. He continued, "Over and over again!" The men laughed even harder than before.

Jack shouted through his teeth, "Leave her alone!"

The leader struck him with the back of his hand. Jack's head turned quickly at the force of the blow, but he quickly turned back to the leader. Tommy admired him for not backing down.

One of the men tapped the leader on the shoulder. He whispered something to him and pointed down the street. Tommy looked. He saw a police vehicle headed toward them. *Good timing, this is our chance.*

The men tried to grab Marcie, but Jack sprung up and pushed them back. Tommy seized that moment to swing hard at the leader. He then grabbed Marcie, and ran across the street. At the same moment, he heard Jack say,

"Tommy, get Marcie out of here!"

Tommy heard the shots ring out behind him. He thought they would surely get hit by one of the bullets. They made it behind one of the vehicles and Tommy peeked out. The shooting was between the two police officers and the gang. Jack was fighting with the leader. Tommy grabbed Marcie, and they ran toward an abandon building. He had to get her to safety.

Once inside the building, he looked out again to see the shooting. One of the officers had gone down. The other one was still fighting, but Tommy saw a man coming up behind him. The man squeezed out two shots, and the officer appeared dead. Tommy then looked back at Jack. Two men were holding him and the leader was pounding him repeatedly, with furious blows to the face.

Blood was all over Jack's face, and the leader's knuckles were covered with it. Tommy didn't know what to do. He knew he couldn't take all those men, and he had to protect his sister. He turned to Marcie and said, "We have to get out of here."

Marcie responded, "But what about Jack?"

Tommy paused looking out at the street, "We can't help him. We have to get to a phone and call dad. He'll send help." They both ran as fast as they could to the other end of the building, and escaped out a back door. They hoped they had seen the last of the rape gang.

315

***

Jump woke up and realized that Bill and Wendy had left the apartment. He was angry that he failed his master. He had to find them and make it right. As he started to leave the apartment, Satan appeared before him. He fell to his knees.

Jump begged, "Master, please spare me. Spare my life, Oh Mighty One. I will make it right. I will find them."

Satan looked at him and said angrily, "I will grant you one more chance. If you fail me, I will snatch you down to Hell, like I did your sister Missy."

Satan smiled, "You will remain there forever! Is that clear?"

Jump answered solemnly, "Yes, Master."

After Satan disappeared, Jump cried for his sister, "Missy!"

***

Wendy was running as fast as she could, with Bill leading the way. She hoped Bill was not leading her to another trick. She believed in him because he risked his life to save her, but she was still scared.

She couldn't understand why everyone wanted her to sin. *Why am I so special? I'm just an average girl. There's nothing special about me.* Bill came to a stop and Wendy asked, "Why are we stopping?"

Bill answered, "I'm not in the best shape. Let's stop here for a minute."

Wendy said, "Okay, but only for a minute. I don't want that jerk catching up with us."

Bill replied, "I got myself into a mess, Wendy. I trusted Teddy too much. Now, I'm going to die and go to Hell."

Wendy responded, "I told you he was no good. You didn't want to believe me."

Bill continued, "You don't know the half of it, Wendy. Teddy is pure evil. He's possessed by some kind of demon. I saw him in his natural figure. He's hideous. Not to mention that thing I was with!" He paused for minute to catch his breath. He continued, "Wendy, Teddy...Teddy killed your friends, Barbara and Shan. I'm sorry."

Wendy's hand covered her mouth. She started to cry. Bill took her in his arms. He said, "I'm truly sorry Wendy."

Wendy replied, "It's not your fault." She silently prayed for their souls. She looked up and continued, "Bill, you are loved by God. You can still repent."

317

Bill was shaking his head and said, "I don't think so, Wendy. You see I…" The sound of a shot echoed in their ears, and just missed hitting Wendy in the head. They both ran to the first alley they could find, as more shots nearly hit them.

Bill and Wendy went into a building, and closed the door behind them. They ran up the stairs and ducked into a room. Wendy heard the door to the building open and close. Whoever was shooting at them was now in the building with them. Wendy was scared. She quietly said a prayer, asking God to intervene.

She looked at Bill and saw fear, real fear, in his eyes. Wendy heard a sound outside the door. Then the door swung open and a shadowy figure looked in. Wendy and Bill stayed put and remained quiet. The figure closed the door and left. Wendy was relieved. She whispered, "What now?"

Bill answered, "I don't know. I'm not a soldier." She watched as Bill quietly walked to the door and listened, than slowly peeked out. He motioned for Wendy to come over to him. Wendy quietly got up and eased over to Bill.

Bill whispered, "I don't see anyone. Let's go back the way we came. If we get separated, you have to get to the Living Word. Do you know where it is?"
Wendy whispered her response, "I think so. Is it on Baker?"

Bill said, "Yeah. The best way is to go down Watson to Calish. Take a right there, than go to First. Once you get to First, cut across the park, and you'll come out on Baker. The church is down the block on the right.

Wendy responded, "Okay, but let's not get separated."

Bill replied, "It doesn't hurt to have a backup plan."

Wendy said, "Agreed."

Bill eased out of the room with Wendy behind him. She felt him reach for her hand. She gave her hand to him. She was thinking there was some hope for them after all. Maybe this incident would make Bill see the light, and they could be together. But they had to get away from the person shooting at them.

She suspected it was Jump. She hoped it was Jump. If it wasn't, then someone new was after her, and she didn't know how much more she could take.

Wendy remembered the woman telling her it wouldn't be easy, but she never suspected it would be this hard. She didn't know why Jump was bent on raping her, and killing them. *What did he mean by 'Master'?*

They ran down the hall and to the stairwell. Once they got to the bottom of the stairwell, they went to the door. As Bill stepped out, he was struck by a blow to the face.

It was Jump. Wendy stepped back in shock.

Bill went down to one knee, but quickly struck back at Jump, with a blow to Jump's stomach. Jump grabbed Bill, and they wrestled to the ground. The two of them got up, Jump grabbed Bill, and flung him against the wall.

Wendy eased over to where Jump had dropped the gun. She picked it up, but she couldn't pull the trigger. She had never shot a gun before in her life, and now that she was saved, she didn't believe she could kill anyone, even if Bill was in trouble. She stood, waving the weapon and watching the fight. She yelled, "Stop, or I'll shoot."

Jump half turned at her and sneered, like he knew she wouldn't shoot.

Wendy shouted again, "Stop!" She saw Jump's arm move. She couldn't see what he was doing because of the light, and the angle at which she was standing. Jump had Bill pinned against the wall.

Suddenly Bill shouted, "Awwwwwwww! Wennnnndy!" Wendy saw blood, as Jump turned and stared at Wendy. Wendy saw a knife in Jump's hands. It was dripping with blood. Bill slid down the wall and to the ground, leaving a trail of blood on the wall as he went. Wendy started to cry.

She cried out, "Bill!" Jump started toward her. She pulled the gun back up, but Jump didn't stop. She found the strength to squeeze the trigger. The first shot hit Jump in the chest, and the recoil knocked Wendy backward. She tripped, and fell to the ground. Jump staggered, and then continued to come toward Wendy.

Wendy quickly gathered herself. She balanced herself against the ground and fired again and again. She fired until the gun started to click. She had emptied all the rounds into Jump. He fell to his knees, and then to the ground. His face hit first. He didn't move. He was dead.

Wendy felt guilty for being happy he was dead. She got up and ran over to Bill. He was still alive, though barely. He looked up at Wendy with tears in his eyes. Wendy said, "Bill, hang on. I'll get you to a hospital."

Bill reached up and grabbed Wendy's arm. He looked her squarely in her eyes and replied with barely enough strength, "It's too late, Wendy. I really screwed up. You have to make it to the Living Word. You'll be safe there."

Wendy responded, "No Bill, I'm going to get help for you."

Bill said, "Wendy, listen to me. I'm not going to make it. You have to get to the church. Reverend Collins will protect you." He grabbed her collar with both hands and passionately said, "Remember that name...Reverend Collins!"

Wendy responded, "God will protect me, Bill." Bill touched her chin, smiled and said, "I should have believed, like you. Now, I'm going to Hell."

Wendy grabbed him and sternly said, "Bill you're not going to Hell. You can repent your sin, and be saved."

Bill grabbed her and said, "You don't understand. I made a deal with the devil. I traded my soul for life after the asteroid strike. I had to try and make you sin. I couldn't do it. I couldn't go through with it. Wendy, I couldn't rape you. I realized when Jump slapped you just how much I truly love you. I wish I had seen it earlier. Now, I'll never see Heaven. Wendy, I...love...yo..."

He never finished. Both arms dropped to the ground. His head fell to the side, and all the life in him was gone. He died in Wendy arms. Wendy cried out, "Nooooooooooo!" She was shaking his body as though he were asleep. She cried out, "Bill, you can't die, please don't die!" She held his dead body tightly against hers, and cried until her eyes hurt.

IX

Evangelist Jones and Mark got the equipment set up, and were ready to start their broadcast. She looked herself over in an attempt to ensure she was ready to make her statement to the world about her friend, Bishop Carroll. A loud 'bam' at the door startled her. The men had found them.

Evangelist Jones shouted at Mark, "Upload the video to your tablet quickly!"

Mark responded, "What about the broadcast?"

Evangelist Jones answered, "Forget it for now. We need to make sure we get the video out to the people. They'll be able to draw their own conclusions."

Mark asked, "You want me to email it to someone?"

Evangelist Jones pondered for a minute, then she said, "Send it to Reverend Collins at the Living Word Ministries. His email is 'revc@livingword.com'."

Mark responded, "Got it! It's gonna to take a minute."

Evangelist Jones replied, "Hurry, they're getting close."

***

Johnny was sitting with the President, Reverend Collins and Roger, while the ladies were getting ready for the wedding. He was thinking about the first time he married Vanessa. It was the greatest day of his life.

Seeing her come down that aisle in her beautiful white dress was a memory he had forgotten, but now he cherished. She was the most beautiful woman he had ever seen in his life. His mind continued to remind him of the pain he caused her by chasing other women. He had been so consumed with lust and sex, that he had forgotten how special Vanessa was, and how much he loved her.

It became all about the conquest to him. The first time he cheated on Vanessa, he was so excited about being with Linda. His boys egged him on every day. They teased him, and called him names, until he felt he had to prove something to them. Now, he wished he would have proven to them that being a dedicated man was the right path to take. He realized there was truly a difference between love and sex.

For the last ten years, he was having sex trying to find love. It didn't work. Now he knew real love could only be found without sex. The love he had for Vanessa was true, because he found it without having sex. He thanked God for giving him another chance.

Vanessa walked in the room and put her arms around Johnny's neck. He turned and kissed her. They realized that everyone was watching them, smiling. Johnny didn't care at all. He was with the woman he loved so dearly. Things couldn't possibly be better for him.

Johnny said, "Okay guys, cut me a break. I've been through a lot."

Reverend Collins responded, "We're not laughing at you. We're happy for you. There's a difference, my brother."

Johnny said, "Reverend Collins, I thank God for the second chance."

Reverend Collins replied, "Amen to that."

Samantha came in the room and said, "Okay, love birds, the wedding is scheduled for 1:00, so come on V, let's get you ready." Vanessa looked in Johnny's eyes and said, "Bye love."

Johnny replied, "Bye Peaches."

He watched Vanessa smile. He hadn't called her Peaches in years. That was his pet name for her when they were kids. Only Johnny called her Peaches, and that made it special to them both. He was in love with her all over again. He couldn't see it any other way.

***

Tommy and Marcie were running down Manhattan Drive,

when a voice whispered to them, "Hey, in here!"

Tommy turned and saw a young boy who looked no more than eight years old. The boy continued, "Are you running from the gang?"

Tommy replied once they were inside the building, "Yeah, you know about them?"

The boy answered, "Who doesn't? The leader's name is Dogg. He's a convicted murderer, and a rapist."

Tommy asked, "How'd he get out of prison?"

The boy answered, "He was on his way to jail, when the announcements were made. Rumor has it, he killed the cop who was taking him to prison, and escaped. That's bad for all of us. He's mean!"

Marcie asked, "What's your name?"

The boy proudly answered, "Me? I'm Matt." She replied, "Hi Matt, where're your parents?"

Matt embarrassingly answered, "I don't know. Me and my mom were staying with my aunt. Both of them ran off to the Zone last night and left me here. My mom has been strung out on crack for years. She's not coming back. It's been me here, all by myself, since then." Matt boasted, "Dogg and his boys almost caught me one time,but I got away."

326

Tommy stepped in and asked, "Is there a phone around here?"

Matt answered, "Yeah, two blocks over. I can take you to my aunt's house."

Tommy replied, "Okay, lead the way, little man."

Matt responded, "Little?"

***

Teddy stood in front of the mirror in the hotel room relishing over, his victory in the contest. He was ready to have his way with his virgin prize. He saw the smoke beginning to form behind him and he quickly turned to wait for him.

Satan materialized in front of Teddy. Teddy got nervous as his Master looked dauntingly at him. Something was wrong. His team must have failed again.

Satan said to Teddy in a soft, but bone-chilling tone, "You have failed me again."

Teddy went to one knee and quickly responded, "Master, please let me personally handle the situation."

Satan answered, "Go now, and if you fail, you will never see the light of Earth again."

Teddy replied, "Yes, Master. I will not fail you."

The smoke reappeared and engulfed Satan. In seconds he was gone. Teddy signed with relief. He turned and looked in the mirror again. This time he was not happy with himself, or his team.

They had failed him, and made him appear weak to his master. They had to pay. First, he had to find Wendy and make her pay. He turned to his henchmen and instructed them, "Make sure no one comes in this room."

The both nodded. The woman lying on the bed called for Teddy.

She cried out, "Don't go baby." Teddy wanted her, but he knew he had to complete his mission first.

***

Evangelist Jones knew they would not make it out of the generator room alive. She looked at Mark, as the upload of the video was taking longer than expected. The men at the door were getting closer getting through.

She asked Mark, "How much longer?"

Mark answered, "Just a few more minutes. You have to get out of here."

Evangelist Jones replied, "There's no way out."

Mark appeared to have an idea, "Wait, remember when those kids broke in and stole that equipment?"

Evangelist Jones said, "Yes."

Mark continued, "They came in through a vent in this room."

Evangelist Jones said, "That's right."

Mark replied, "We covered it up to prevent that from happening again."

Evangelist Jones smiled, and now she believed they could get out. She said, "Right, it was over here somewhere, I believe."

Mark replied, "Right, but we need something to pry it open. I think I saw some tools earlier." They moved some boxes and other items out of the way, until Mark found a crowbar. He pried the vent open. Another loud bang hit the door. Evangelist Jones turned to see if the door had been opened.

She was getting concerned. The door was still holding, but she didn't know how much longer it would hold. Mark turned to Evangelist Jones and said, "Okay, you guys get
out of here. I'll try and stall them. The upload is

finished."

He typed the email address in and attached the file. He hit send, and handed the tablet to Evangelist Jones. He continued, "Here take the tablet. Get out of here. The email will continue sending while you're escaping."

Evangelist Jones said, "Mark, we can't just leave you here. They'll kill you."

Mark looked at her. He knew the sacrifice. It was in his eyes.

Evangelist Jones said, "Mark, no, I can't let you do this."

He said, "I have to. Someone needs to stay here and slow them down, while you and Sister Carroll escape. I'll cover the vent, and make them think you escaped another way. Now go. Hurry, they're getting closer!"

Evangelist Jones replied, "No, Mark I can't…"

Mark said, "That door won't hold much longer…go!"

Evangelist Jones was in tears. She motioned to Jessica to go. Jessica began crawling into the vent. Evangelist Jones entered once Jessica got a few feet into the vent. After she was in, Mark closed the vent behind them.

Evangelist Jones saw him place something over the vent, blocking it. She looked at the tablet and saw that the email had been sent. As she turned the corner in the vent, she heard gunshots for a few minutes, then nothing. She dropped her head. Mark died trying to protect them.

***

Wendy had made it to the park. All she had to do was cut across it, and then down Baker a block to the church. She was covered in Bill's blood. She looked at herself and cried again, because despite it all, she loved him, and she knew Bill loved her. She could have saved him if she had just a little more time. She failed him.

If I make it to the church, then at least I have done the one thing Bill tried to do for me. She thought about Barbara and Shan. She wished she had gotten through to them. Now it was too late. Teddy had murdered them. Oblivious to any of her surroundings, she ran through the park as fast as she could. She had been to this park before, but never this part. The park was the biggest in the city, and had two running trails through it.

Wendy was in the forest part of the park. After 20 feet, she felt a resounding blow to her face. Her feet whipped in front of her, as her head went backwards. She hit the ground hard and rolled ten feet down a slight incline.

Wendy was stunned and dazed. After a few moments, she looked up and saw Teddy standing over her. She could see the evil within him, and it scared her. She tried to slowly crawl backwards, away from Teddy, but he

331

grabbed her by her ankle and pulled her back, "You have made me lose favor with my Master. You will sin, and be damned to Hell. I will see to it."

This angered Wendy and she proudly said, "I don't care what you do to me; I will never sin.
You hear me, you freak? I will never sin! You murdered my friends, but you won't have my soul!"
Wendy heard Teddy let out a shivering sound that scared her, but she held to her faith. She knew it was all she had left to protect her from this evil.

VIII

Earth was five hours from the impact. The world was set to end, but the atmosphere at the Living Word Ministries was one of joy and excitement. The wedding of Johnny and Vanessa was getting ready to commence. Everyone was excited, sitting in the sanctuary waiting for Vanessa to make her grand entrance.

Johnny stood at the altar with Reverend Collins waiting patiently for Vanessa. He was excited. He felt more excited than the first time he married Vanessa. He heard a loud crash at the front door.

Everyone jumped, turning their heads in that direction. The front glass door shattered. Vanessa and Samantha came running into the sanctuary, screaming. After them, a man walked in waving a gun. The Secret Service agents pulled their weapons out.

Johnny heard one of them shout, "Stop, or we'll shoot."

Without thinking, Johnny ran to Vanessa to protect her. He pulled her behind one of the pews. Shots rang out all around them. Johnny heard a voice shout, "Stop shooting, or she's dead!"

The shooting stopped and the voice shouted again, "V, come out or I'll kill the wench."

Johnny and Vanessa got up and looked in the direction of the shooter. Johnny knew Calvin from church. He suspected he was the kind of man that would go to this level, but he wasn't afraid of him. Nothing was going to stop Johnny from protecting his bride.

Calvin had Lisa by the neck, pointing a gun at her head. Johnny and Vanessa looked at each other. Vanessa was crying, and said through her tears to Johnny, "Johnny, Calvin and I were…"

Johnny cut her off. He really didn't want to hear her say it. He replied, "It's okay, Baby. I'll protect you."

Vanessa responded, "No Johnny, I have to go to him. I can't let him kill Lisa."

Johnny said, "No V, I can't lose you."

Calvin shouted, "Shut up punk! She doesn't want you. She's my woman! You had your chance. V, get over here!"

***

Evangelist Jones and Jessica came out of the sewer about four blocks from the studio. They found an empty cab sitting in front of a coffee shop. They ran into the shop looking for the cab driver. Evangelist Jones was out of breath as she ran into the shop, "Who's driving the cab,

334

out front?"

Everyone seemed to turn at once to look at her. One man answered, "That's my cab but lady but I'm off the clock…forever!"

She responded, "Please, we need someone to take us to the Living Word Ministries."

The man replied while tossing the keys, "Here, take it. In a few hours, I won't need it anymore."

The men broke out in laughter as Evangelist Jones caught the keys. They headed out the door. While running, she turned and said, "Thanks, and God bless you!" She didn't hear what they said but she heard laughter.

Evangelist Jones strutted towards the car. She was confident they would be alright, "Girl, we're gonna be alright. God is in control of this thing."

Jessica just smiled. As they got to the cab, a limousine came tearing around the corner. It was the Bishop's men. She heard Jessica shout, "Let's get out of here! I'll drive."

They jumped in the cab and sped off down the street, hoping and praying to elude the limousine.

***

The clocks in the Eastern Time zone reached 2:00 pm.

The end of the world was now four hours away. Johnny looked at his wife, and knew he wasn't going to allow her to go to that maniac. But like his wife, he couldn't allow Lisa to be killed. He had to do something.

Calvin said, "I don't have time V, get over here, or she's dead. I'm gonna count to ten. If you're not here by then, she's dead."

Vanessa stood up and said, "Don't, Calvin. I'm coming."

Johnny reached to Vanessa and grabbed her by the hand. When his hand touched her arm, it felt like the first time he touched her. It was as smooth as silk. It sent a chill through his entire body. He felt like he was a kid again.

He was so caught up in the beauty of touching his wife again, in the name of love that the pain didn't register immediately in his mind. A few seconds went by before he felt his chest feeling like it was being cut open.

Vanessa shrieked loudly in shock at the sound of the gunshot and the emergence of blood on Johnny's chest. Johnny just looked at her. Vanessa's eyes and mouth were wide open; her hands covered her mouth.
Johnny looked down. Blood was slowing covering his chest. He realized he had been shot. Calvin screamed, "You b..." More bullets filled the air. As Johnny fell to the floor, Johnny saw his beloved crying over him. She was caressing his head, saying something. He couldn't really understand what she was saying, but he loved her,

and he was glad his last minutes were in her arms.

Johnny said to Vanessa, "I'm sorry, Baby. I'm so sorry for not being a good husband to you all these years. Please forgive me."

Vanessa said through her tears, "I love you, Johnny and nothing else matters. You just hang on, we have the ambulance coming. Just hang on, baby."

Johnny slowly replied as the life went out of him, "Peaches…I'll…see you…in Heaven." Then he looked to the top of the ceiling. He saw a beautiful angel smiling, with her hand outstretched. He tried to raise his hand, but he couldn't. The life left his body, and his spirit rose toward the angel. It was over. His physical body on Earth was no longer alive.

***

Vanessa cried out, "Nooooooo! Nooooo! This can't be happening. God, why? Why is he dead?" Samantha and Lisa put their arms around her to console her. Vanessa looked Samantha in the eyes and said, "Why?"

She knew Samantha couldn't tell her why, but she had to ask. She had changed her life, but deep inside, she believed that she didn't deserve anything better. She just continued to cry.

***

Calvin was lying on the floor, almost dead. He looked up and saw Raven standing over him, grinning. Calvin asked, "Why? Why am I dying? I thought you were going to help me kill all of them?"

Raven said laughingly, "I never said that. I said there was going to be death where we're going. There is death. One of them happens to be yours. Too bad that minister repented, but you, my friend, you get an escort to Hell."

Calvin said angrily, "You tricked me!"

Raven laughed and said, "No, I told you what you wanted to hear."

Calvin tried to get up and grab Raven, but he couldn't. The last of his life force slipped out of him and he was dead. Raven transformed from a man into large birdlike creature. For the first time, Calvin was afraid. His spirit tried to run, but the creature grabbed him with a powerful claw that ignited pain in Calvin's spirit that he never experience on Earth.

Raven spread his mighty wings and descended downward. Calvin screamed for help as many others had done before him. He shouted, "No! Don't take me, someone help me! Help me!
Get this thing off of me! Help me!"

VII

Teddy grabbed Wendy and picked her up by the throat, like she was a rag doll. He pulled her close to his face and looked deeply into her eyes. He said, "I had both of your friends. Shan, she was good, so good. Barbara wasn't what I wanted, but I still had her just the same."

He laughed. Wendy couldn't stand the stench of Teddy. She turned her head, hoping she didn't have to see or smell him. She didn't like him before and now it was even worst. She struggled to get free of him.

Teddy said, "Struggle all you want, but you will never be free. I plan to inflict so much pain on you, you will beg me to let you sin."

Wendy replied with clenched teeth, "Nnnever."

Teddy reeled back with his fist and punched Wendy in the jaw, knocking her to the ground. He slowly approached her. He said, "Give yourself to me now, and be done with it. I assure you, you do not want this pain."

Wendy spit the blood from her mouth and answered, "That's the best you got, freak?"

Teddy reached down and grabbed her again. He tried to punch her in the face again, but Wendy put her hand up and grabbed his wrist.

Teddy shouted, "Why do you fight me? You cannot defeat me."

Wendy replied, "I'd rather die than give in to you."

She kicked Teddy between his legs. Teddy let go of his grip on her, and she fell to the ground. While Teddy was bent over, she got up and ran. She could hear Teddy running hard after her. All of sudden, the park seemed bigger; but her will to resist evil had grown to a level she never knew was within her. She kept running as hard as she but she could sense Teddy catching up to her.

Teddy grabbed her by the ankles. She hit the ground face first. Wendy quickly turned over and kicked at Teddy. Teddy easily deflected each kick, and got on top of her. She yelled, "Get off me, you freak!"

Teddy grabbed her throat and slapped her by the face several times, until she was nearly unconscious. Teddy ripped her blouse opened and smiled.

She screamed, "You pervert!"
He was ready to take her for his own. She struggled even harder. Teddy hit her with a force that knocked her unconscious. His master suddenly appeared before him.

Satan commanded, "No! She must willingly sin. You have failed me!"

Teddy replied, "No master, I have not."

Satan answered, "I have grown impatient with your failures."

Teddy replied solemnly, "Yes, Master."

Wendy wasn't completely unconscious like Teddy believed. She could feel herself losing consciousness. Teddy was being lifted into the air as he screamed. The sound was so eerie, it made Wendy cringe.

She was afraid for him, as it appeared his body was being pulled apart piece by piece. She didn't like Teddy, but no one deserved to have such pain inflicted upon them. Teddy screamed and screamed as each part of his body was torn away from him. She prayed for his soul.

Once Teddy was gone, Satan turned to Wendy and said, "Now, I will make you come to me willingly. You will be mine, forever!"

Wendy said, as she fell into a state of unconsciousness, "You will never take me willingly."

***

Everyone was quiet in the church. They had seen so much drama over the past day. None of them believed they could stand much more. Reverend Collins stood there and watched, as Vanessa cried in Samantha's arms.

He remembered when Johnny and Vanessa came to the Living Word Ministries. He thought they were a match made in Heaven. He was so impressed with them and how they carried themselves.

He was glad that Johnny had come to his senses, and repented his sins before death. His heart was saddened because he had to watch Vanessa cry. He looked at his phone to discover an new email.

Reverend Collins didn't think anyone was still sending emails at this time. He opened the email because the subject said it was from Evangelist Jones. There was an attachment to the email. He opened the attachment and watched the video.

Reverend Collins was appalled by what he heard and saw. The video showed Bishop Carroll having an extramarital affair with a man. It also showed Bishop Carroll shooting a man Reverend Collins recognized as Pastor Cecil Williams. In the video, Pastor Williams threatened to tell the world Bishop Carroll was a homosexual.

Reverend Collins sat down in a chair and stared out in amazement. He couldn't believe the video. He was stunned when he felt the touch of a hand against his shoulders. It was the President. President Murphy asked, "What you got there?"

Reverend Collins looked up at him and said, "You wouldn't believe me if I told you. So, I'll just show you." He showed the video to President Murphy. Reverend Collins watched the look of amazement form on his face. After the video concluded, the two of them just looked at each other not saying a word.

President Murphy broke the silence, "Can we get this on the air?"

Reverend Collins replied, "Evangelist Jones emailed it to me. The email said they were in danger."

President Murphy got on the phone and made a phone call.

***

Tommy, Marcie and Matt made it to Matt's aunt's place. Matt opened the door, and directed Tommy to the phone. Tommy dialed his father's number and waited for an answer. The voice at the other end of the phone said, "Hello?"

Tommy answered, "Dad."

President Murphy said, "Tommy! I tried to call you. Where are you son?"

Tommy said, "We're in trouble! We're in the warehouse

district. I was trying to get to the church to see you, but our car was sabotaged. We lost my good friend."

President Murphy shouted, "What? Give me your exact address."

Tommy asked Matt, "What's the address here?" Matt said, "4578 Doppler Place, apartment 'A'." Tommy relayed the address to his father.

President Murphy said, "Son, I'm sending my agents to get you. Stay put."

***

Evangelist Jones was praying that Jessica could lose the limo that was trying hard to catch them. Jessica shouted, "I'm going to hit this left corner hard. As soon as I do, you jump out and run. I'll keep them going long enough for you to escape and get to the church."

Evangelist Jones cried 'No!' as the car screeched around the corner and came to a halt. She was tired of everyone sacrificing themselves for her. Jessica pushed Evangelist Jones, as she screamed, "Jump, now!"
Evangelist Jones jumped out of the vehicle and ran into a doorway. She hid as the limo zoomed past her and out of sight. Evangelist Jones stomped her foot in anger at Jessica.
How could she do that? Why, did she do that?

She hoped and prayed Bishop Carroll would not harm his wife and her friend. In the meantime, she had to get to the church, and somehow get that video on the air. She felt that if she could do that, she might save her friend's life.

VI

Wendy's vision returned as she regained her consciousness. She tried to move, but her body reeked with pain. She grabbed her forehead and felt around her face, hoping there wasn't much bruising. She remembered what Teddy had done to her, and what happened to him.

Wendy struggled to get to her feet, but lost her balance. As she started to fall backwards, a hand grabbed her arm. She immediately looked up to see who it was. Shock engulfed her from head to toe. She couldn't count how many times she had been shocked in the last 24 hours, but this one took the cake. She asked, "Mom?"

The familiar woman smiled, happy to see her. Wendy couldn't believe her mom was standing in front of her now. *How could this be? My mother died years ago. Is this a trick?* Wendy's mom said, "I know you're shocked, baby but it's really me. That man was trying to hurt you, and I came to help you. While you were unconscious, I fought him, beat him, and sent him on his way."

Wendy said, "But mom, you're dead. I saw you die years ago."

Her mom replied, "I did die years ago, and I've been in a better place since then. This place, baby, you wouldn't believe how wonderful it is to be here."

Wendy responded, "Mom, are you talking about Heaven?"

Her mom answered, "No, baby. You see, there is no Heaven or Hell. It's just a new life on another plain of existence. This life begins when your life here on Earth ends."

Wendy sternly replied, "Mom, that's not true. There is a Heaven. I know it in my heart and mind. God is real"

Her mom answered, "Baby, God is real, but He doesn't want you to be bound to these things that book has taught you. You have been deceived by those so-called pastors and preachers. God had nothing to do with the Bible. Those preachers just want you to put money in the collection plate."

Wendy said, "I don't believe you!" She got up and tried to walk away, but her mom grabbed her by the arm.

She said, "Wait, I'm sorry. Wendy, the world I live in is the greatest. You're wasting your time trying to live by the Bible. Live your life the way you want to live it, then come and be with God, and your mom."

"You can have all the sex, drugs, and alcohol you wish. There's nothing wrong with it. Man's interpretation has steered many down the wrong path. I kick myself when I think about all the fun I could have had on Earth. But, I am making up for it now."

Wendy just stood there looking perplexed. Her mom continued, "I wasted so much time trying to be right in this world, when I could have partied, and enjoyed life to its fullest.
When I died, I found out the truth. That is, there is no Heaven or Hell. You don't have to make the same mistake I made. Enjoy your life. They are having so much fun in the Zone, and you're missing it. I cry every time I see you missing it. Go over there, enjoy it."

Wendy started to think about what her mother, was saying. She started questioning her new found beliefs. She stood there and looked at her mother and wondered.

***

Tommy peeped out of the window, to see if he could see any of the gang members around the apartment. He hoped his father's agents would get to them in time to save them. He watched as Marcie talked with Matt. He was afraid for Marcie, but Marcie didn't seem to be frightened by anything. She seemed much stronger than Tommy.

Suddenly, the door blasted off its hinges and down to the floor. Marcie grabbed Matt, and they ran over to Tommy. Tommy saw Dogg and his men standing at the door smiling.

He strutted into the room and said intently, "Did you think you could escape me? I know this neighborhood better than anyone, especially this little boy."

Matt shouted, "I'm not little!"

Marcie covered his mouth.

Dogg reared back, laughing, "He's got spunk!"

Tommy replied, "Why don't you leave us alone? The world is ending in a few hours. Just let us be."

Dogg answered sarcastically, "Naw, don't think so. The fact that the world is ending is all the more reason to have some fun with you. Now, let's go." Dogg's men guided them out of the apartment and down the street. Tommy didn't know where they were being taken. He had to try and create a diversion, so his sister could escape.

***

Evangelist Jones looked at her watch. It was near 3 o'clock, three hours from impact. She was out of breath as she got her bearings, and tried to figure out the best route to take to the Living Word Ministries.

She had to stay off the main streets, so she wouldn't be caught by the Bishop's men. She decided to continue through a series of back allies, praying as she went. These

349

allies were not the best places to be, and she knew only the Lord could protect her now.

As she started through the allies, she heard a scream come from the park. It was a scream of fear and horror. Someone needed help. She questioned if she had time to help anyone else right now. She started to continue her journey, than stopped. Evangelist Jones couldn't turn her back on someone who needed help. If she didn't help, she would be no better than the Bishop.

***

Tommy, Marcie and Matt were walking ahead of Dogg and his henchmen, when Tommy heard a gunshot ring out behind them. He grabbed Marcie by the arm and ran. Marcie had a hold of Matt's hand as they were running.

The gun shots continued behind them. Tommy stopped at a storefront, and looked back. Dogg and his men where shooting at someone. Tommy didn't know who he had to thank for the diversion, but he was glad he got another chance to get away.

The three of them went into the store. Tommy locked the door behind them. He had to find somewhere to go, where Dogg and his men couldn't find them. He looked around for a back door. As he was going out the door, he heard another gunshot. This one was loud. They all stopped and looked at the door.

Marcie shouted, "Jack!" Tommy smiled and ran over to his friend. Jack had a bandage around his head and blood on his shirt, but he appeared to be okay.

Jack asked, "You guys okay?"

Tommy said, "Yeah buddy, we're good. What happened? We thought you were killed by that maniac."

Jack answered, "No, he got the best of me for a minute, but these guys saved me."

Jack turned and pointed at his new friends.

Tommy responded, "They're kids."

Jack replied, "Yeah, but they're a tough bunch. After Dogg left, these guys broke me out of the place they were holding me. Most of them don't know where they parents are, and have been fending for themselves since the announcement."

Tommy smiled again and hugged his friend, "I'm just glad you're okay, dude."

Tommy turned and looked at Marcie. Marcie walked over to Jack and kissed him on the cheek. Jack's face had a big smile on it. Tommy smiled. He couldn't think of anyone better for his sister, than his best friend.

***

Jessica thought she had eluded the limo. She was speeding down the street. She decided it was safe to head to the church. From out of nowhere, the limo struck Jessica's vehicle, spinning it in a circle.

Jessica's head hit the steering wheel, and she was dazed. She could hardly see anything. She could make out someone approaching her vehicle. She tried to start it, but it wouldn't start. A tall burly man ordered Jessica, "Open the door!"

Jessica wouldn't open it. She feared for her life. The man took the butt of his gun and smashed it against her window, breaking the glass. He then tried to open the door but Jessica was fighting him as much as she could; it was pointless. The man got the door opened and grabbed Jessica.

He shouted, "Where's Evangelist Jones?"

Jessica yelled back, "I'll never tell you!"

The man slapped her across the face and dragged her to the limo. Another man opened the door, and the burly man threw her inside like she was a rag doll.

Once inside, Jessica saw her husband sitting there, smugly sipping on Champaign, "If you tell me what I want to know, I will allow you to return home to your family. If not, then I can't control what they do to you."

Jessica sneered at him and said, "Go to Hell."

Bishop Carroll replied, "Such language for a Christian woman. I thought you were saved."

Jessica responded, "I am. Hell isn't a curse word. It's a real place, where you will be going."

Bishop Carroll laughed and said, "I don't think so, my dear. You see, I have known for a long time that this existence is all there is. Once you die, well, you simply go to another plane of existence. A good friend of mine taught me that lesson years ago. You're a fool for believing all that Bible junk. For me, all you Christian fools just made me rich…filthy rich."

Jessica replied, "I guess we'll see in three hours. You and your money will be burning in Hell."

Bishop Carroll continued to laugh and responded, "If you don't tell me what I want to know, you'll see Hell sooner than that."

V

Wendy chastised herself for her momentary lack of faith. She could not believe she was about to fall for this trick. She knew the truth and the woman in her apartment told her to keep her faith.

She had to be an angel, and this person, this impersonator of her mother, had to be a deceiver. She turned to her mother and said with force and strength, "You're a deceiver. You're not my mother, and Heaven is real. I will not sin against my Lord and Savior, Jesus Christ!"

Her mother responded, "Why do you say this me? I saved your life five years ago, and now you call me a deceiver. I love you, and I would never hurt you."

Wendy stood paralyzed, not knowing what to say. Her mother fell to her knees and started crying. Wendy felt sick to her stomach as she tried to comfort her mother. Surprisingly, her mother pushed her away and ran, startling Wendy. She gathered herself and started after her mother but she couldn't find her.

Now she was truly depressed. She turned, and fear captivated her body. Before her eyes was a tall evil looking figure. His hair was long and curly. His body was bronze and muscular. Scars of evil were etched across his face. She tried to run but quickly fell to the ground. Satan said with a forceful voice, "You should have listened to your mother. You will sin, I promise you!"

Wendy shouted, "No, I will never sin!"
Satan struck her in the face, knocking her to the ground. She tried to run again, but he grabbed her by the leg. From out of the woods, Wendy heard a voice. The voice said, "Stop! I rebuke you in the name of the Lord, Jesus Christ!"

Satan shouted, "Who dares challenge the King of the Underworld?"

The voice yelled, "Evangelist Mattie Jones, a servant of the Lord, challenges you!" She swung a two by four and hit Satan in the head, knocking him down. She then grabbed Wendy by the arm and shouted, "Girl, let's get outta here!"

Satan shouted, "Noooooooooooo! You can't escape me!"

The two women ran as fast as they could. Wendy felt she was running faster than she ever ran in her life. She could hear sounds behind her. They were horrible sounds and they were getting closer. When they reached the edge of the park, Satan landed hard on the ground in front of them. The landing was so hard; it knocked them to the ground. Wendy and Evangelist Jones got up slowly. Wendy was behind Evangelist Jones. Evangelist Jones was holding her back with one arm. Evangelist Jones said, "You won't have this girl. I'll fight you to my death."

Satan said, "I will be glad to oblige."

Evangelist Jones said, "Bring it on Buddy."

Wendy yelled, "That makes two of us. Bring it. I'm not scared anymore!" She began rolling up her sleeves, ready to fight.

Evangelist Jones added, "That's my girl!"

Satan then said, "But Wendy, why would you hurt me?"

Wendy was stunned and mumbled, "Denise? But how…"

Evangelist Jones grabbed Wendy by the arm and said, "Don't fall for it! It's a trick."

Satan said, "You let me die. Why didn't you help me?"

Wendy started crying, "But I tried…"

Satan shouted sternly, "No you didn't! You should have died with me. Why did you let me die alone?"

Wendy began crying profusely. Evangelist Jones tried to shake her out of it. She shouted, "It's a trick, don't believe it girl."

Satan said, "Wendy, you have to help me. I'm in Hell. They said I could leave, if you took my place. Wendy, you owe me! You let me die."

Wendy through her tears said, "Denise, I can't, I can't take your place

Satan shouted, "You're not my friend! You let me die and now you still won't save me? Please Wendy, don't let me suffer anymore. The pain, the gnashing of teeth… It's soooo hot. Wendy…it's so awful here!"

Evangelist Jones couldn't hear what was being said but she knew it wasn't good. She got in front of Wendy, grabbed her face and sternly told her, "Don't listen, he's trying to trick you into submission."

Wendy moved around Evangelist Jones. She reached out her hands and said softly, "Denise…"

Evangelist Jones shouted, "Noooo, I won't let you!"

While still appearing as Denise to Wendy he said, "Come with me Wendy. Save me."

Wendy fell to her knees sobbing, in despair. She didn't know what to do. Her friend appeared in front of her crying and suffering, and it was her fault. If she had moved quickly that day, she might have saved Denise. Now, she should take her place in Hell.

Satan said, "Take my hand, Wendy. Come down here and take my place, so I can enjoy the last few hours on Earth. Pleasssssseee Wendy. Don't let me suffer anymore."

Wendy stood up and looked at Evangelist Jones. She then looked back at Satan, appearing as Denise.

***

The warehouse was cold and drafty. Jessica was barely conscious after being beaten repeatedly by the Bishop's men. Blood covered her face, but she was a strong person, and refused to give up. She heard her husband say, "Jessica, why do you continue this foolishness? Give in, and we will let you go. You still have time to be with your family."

Jessica responded, "They're your family, too!"

Bishop Carroll said, "No my dear, they're not my family anymore. I have a new family and it doesn't include you or them."

She barely replied, "I can't believe I married you."

Bishop Carroll laughed and responded, "You were just as enamored with me as everyone else. I gave you the chance to be my wife. Any one of 1000 women would have killed to be in your position. You were just a fool not to appreciate it."

Jessica just stared coldly at him. She couldn't believe she married this man. She had loved him so much; she would have done almost anything for him. Now, this person who looks like her husband, makes her stomach hurt. Through it all, she still managed to say, "God bless you and help you to see the light, before it's too late."

Bishop Carroll snickered and blew her off. One of Bishop Carroll's men came in the room and whispered to the Bishop. He started to smile. She feared for her friend and silently prayed that they had not been successful at catching her.

Bishop Carroll shouted, "Load up. We know where she is now."

A voice asked, "What about her?"

Bishop Carroll answered after pondering the question, "Bring her. She might be useful when we get there."

IV

Tommy and his new gang started walking toward the church. They didn't have to worry about Dogg anymore. Now, Tommy just wanted to get them all to the church. He couldn't believe that Jack and Marcie were falling for each other. I guess it took Jack saving them to make Marcie see him differently. Inside, he really didn't mind because Jack was a standup guy.

After they walked for about two miles, they saw two cars pull up behind them. The kids got their weapons out and ready. Tommy thought they would make to the church without having to fight again. Now he was afraid again.

***

Wendy fell to her knees and asked, "Father in Heaven I ask you, please guide me. Please give me what I need!" She couldn't stop crying.

Evangelist Jones said, "Fight it, girl! Don't let him beat you!"

Wendy looked at her, then at the illusion of Denise.

Satan said, "Don't listen to her Wendy, she's deceiving you."

Wendy said, "I wanted to save you Denise, but I

couldn't."

Satan responded, "Liar! You didn't care then, and you don't care now! No one cared. You were just like the others. It just took me dying to see it! You were the only reason I was there!"

Wendy looked down and defeated. Denise was right. She didn't save her because she was scared to move. She let her best friend die. She was sobbing profusely as she said, "You're right, I didn't try because I was scared! I'm sorry Denise, I'm so sorry." She started to walk toward Satan. He smiled.

Evangelist Jones yelled, "Wait!" She ran in front of Wendy and put the palm of her hands firmly on Wendy's shoulders. She said sternly, "I'm not going to let you do this! He's deceiving you!"

Satan angrily grabbed Evangelist Jones and threw her to the side. Wendy stepped back. She looked over at Evangelist Jones. She was lying motionless on the ground. She took a couple of more steps back and said, "You're not Denise. Leave me, Satan. I will not submit to you, or your tricks!" She ran over to Evangelist Jones.

Satan shouted, "Nooooooo!"

Wendy was startled by a loud thunderous voice, "Enough! You have failed. Leave them be!"
Satan fell to his knees, and was devoured into the ground,

"Noooooooooooooooooooo…."

Wendy took Evangelist Jones into her arms and tried to wake her up. She tapped Evangelist Jones on each side of the face, trying to wake her up. Evangelist Jones started to recover.
She asked, "What happened?"

Wendy answered, "That thing threw you over here. You were unconscious for a minute. I realized it was deceiving me. Then this voice, a loud voice that sounded like thunder, told it to leave us alone. After that, it disappeared into the ground."

Evangelist Jones said, "Honey, that 'thing' had to be Satan, himself, and you beat him. You should be proud. Oh my body aches. I'm getting old."

Wendy said curiously, "Satan? Why did he want me so bad?"

Evangelist Jones replied, "Honey, I don't know, but you beat him." She looked at Wendy proudly, "You must be really special."

Wendy said, "I didn't realize these things actually happen."

Evangelist Jones responded, "They do girl, most people don't see or believe it, but if they trusted in God like we do, they would see it. There's a spiritual war going on, and we have to fight, every minute of every day. I must say this; Satan doesn't show himself in his natural form often so he must have really wanted you."

Wendy asked, "What do we do now?"

Evangelist Jones said, "We go to the Living Word Ministries. I have to finish what I started. And after what I've just seen, I need to finish it now more than ever!"

Wendy said, "That's where I was headed."

Evangelist Jones said, "Amen, the Holy Spirit is at work today!"

***

The door to one of the cars opened, a man approached Tommy and asked, "Sir, are you okay?"

Tommy smiled and answered, "I am, now. We all are."

Tommy turned to the kids and said, "Put your weapons down, gang. These are the good guys."

The man got on the radio and said, "Mister President, we have both of them and several others. Most of them are children. We're on our way back." The man then said, "Okay, let's load up and get back to the church."

Matt smiled at Tommy and Marcie. He said, "Cool."

363

***

It was just after 4 pm, when Wendy and Evangelist Jones arrived at the Living Word Ministries. Wendy couldn't believe that the Lord granted her favor to make it. She was so thankful.

She regretted Bill wasn't with her and the thought of him dying in her arms kept repeating in her mind. It was one of the saddest things that had ever happened to her. She was happy she had a new friend who was a devout Christian, even if it is for only a couple of hours. If the Earth wasn't ending, she could learn a lot from Evangelist Jones.

Evangelist Jones went up to the door of the church and knocked loudly. Wendy prayed that there would be no more surprises. A man appeared at the door and was happy to see Evangelist Jones. He was so happy; he was having trouble opening the door.

Once the door was opened he shouted, "Evangelist! It is good to see you. The President was sending someone out to look for you."

Evangelist Jones responded, "The President?"

The man replied, "Yes, President Murphy is here with us. Who is this, and what happened to you both?"

364

Evangelist Jones answered, "Reverend, let me introduce you to my new friend, Wendy. She's a new Christian, and she must be special, because Satan has been hard after her for the last 24 hours. We saw him in the flesh and she beat his butt. Hallelujah, and praise the Lord! There's a lot going on with this last day, but God granted us strength to beat down the enemy. Hallelujah!"

Reverend Collins said joyfully, "Well, welcome to you both! It is good to have new and victorious Christians with us."

Wendy asked cautiously, "Are you Bill's pastor?"

Reverend Collins answered, "Yes. You know him?"

Wendy replied sadly, "Yes, he died saving me. I tried to get him to turn back to the Lord, but for some reason, I couldn't. He kept listening to that friend of his, and it cost him his life." She felt tears forming in her eyes.

Reverend Collins put his arms around her and said, "All we can do is pray for his soul. All we can do is pray for all the lost souls out there."

Evangelist Jones added, "Amen Rev, Amen."

Reverend Collins solemnly said, "Come on in, both of you." Reverend Collins brought both of them into the church and then to the sanctuary. Everyone was standing around talking and watching the clock, as the final hours were ticking away.

Reverend Collins introduced everyone to Evangelist Jones and Wendy. Wendy was so happy she couldn't believe it. Everyone came over to her, and welcomed her to the fold. When Samantha came up to Wendy she stood by her staring. Wendy just stared back at her. She hadn't met this woman before, so she didn't know why she was staring at her. Wendy asked softly, "Is something wrong?"

Samantha appeared to be startled, than responded, "Nothing, it's just your face; I know I've seen it before."

Wendy said, "I don't think we have ever met."

Samantha said, "No we haven't, but I've seen your face before, somewhere."

Lisa interrupted them and said, as she hugged Wendy, "Welcome! I'm a new Christian, too."

Wendy hugged her back and said, "Thank you. I'm so happy to be here. I've been through so much lately. It's just refreshing to be here with people who believe as I do."

Martha came over and asked, "Girl, looks like you've been fighting for your life! Can we get some ice and fresh clothes for this woman?"

Wendy said, "I have been. Thank you. I think I could use something. My body is aching all over."

Brittney said, "I'll get it, Momma!"

***

President Murphy ran to the door shouting, "They're here!" Everyone was behind him. He didn't even wait for his Secret Service men to ensure it was safe to leave the building. Once outside, one of the car doors flung open, and Marcie jumped out and hugged her dad.

Tommy stepped out, along with Jack, and all the children. The ladies from the church came over and hugged the children. The women took the children into the church.

President Murphy stepped over to his son and grabbed him by the shoulders and said, "Son, I know we didn't agree on this issue and it caused..."

Tommy interrupted, "Dad, there's no time for that now. Let's just be happy we get this time together."

President Murphy smiled and hugged his son. He was glad that he had the opportunity to be with his older kids one more time, before the world ended.

Elizabeth walked up to President Murphy, Tommy and Marcie and said, "Guys look, I'm sorry for all the confusion I caused. I think I got a little jealous, and that's not Christ-like. Please forgive me."

President Murphy was glad to hear those words. There were only a couple hours before the world was to end, but he was glad his family had buried the hatchet.

Tommy said, "Forgive me for all the problems I caused. I was a little jealous as well."

Marcie added, "Yeah, let's just all forgive each other and start over."

They all embraced each other as President Murphy said, "Praise God for forgiveness."

***

Samantha shouted, "That's it!" Everyone looked at her. They were all startled by her outbreak. She continued, "My great grandmother told us an old wives tale that involved Satan and Eve. Before he was cast out of Heaven, he fell in love with an Angel. She was remarkably beautiful."

"He could not convince this angel to join him when he was casted out of Heaven. Her image was used to make the first woman, Eve. Eve's image has been made over in every generation since the beginning of time."

"You look like Eve, the first woman. My great grandmother had old portraits that were thought to be of the woman, and you look exactly like her."

Evangelist Jones said, "I heard that story before. It was told to me a long, long time ago. I never saw a picture, but it would explain why Satan is after you girl. When Satan couldn't have the angel, he went after Eve. That is why he enticed her with the apple in the garden."

Wendy stood there in shock, not knowing what to say over all of this new information. She could not believe that she could be modeled after the first woman. *Why me?*

***

Evangelist Jones excitedly asked, "Rev, did you get the video?"

Reverend Collins answered, "Yes! I can't believe what I saw. It's no wonder he made the announcement he did."

Evangelist Jones replied, "Amen, but we need to make a broadcast, and get it out to the people. I know it's late in the game, but if we can save one, well that's good for me."

Reverend Collins responded, "Right, but how do we do that?"

Evangelist Jones said, "We can use the video camera on your computer. We can make a video, and upload it to the Internet. Hopefully, we can reach millions."

Reverend Collins replied, "Let's get started."

III

Colonel Nick Thomas was one of the few remaining people at NASA headquarters tracking the arrival of the asteroid nicknamed Doomsday. He was sitting in his office looking at the picture of his wife, whom he lost to cancer five years ago.

He wondered if she was the lucky one in all of this. She didn't have to deal with the challenge of their Christian beliefs. She didn't have to wonder if God was real. Nick never gave into the talk that the Bible was wrong and made fools of those who believed. Instead, he knew that God has something for all of those who continue to have faith in Him.

Nick didn't know what that reward would be, but he thought it would be much better than finding some worldly party, and partying the last day away. His thoughts were interrupted by his deputy, Major Conrad Williams.

Major Williams didn't believe in Christ. He didn't believe in any benevolent being. He laughed at Colonel Thomas when the news broke, but he stopped because he saw that the Colonel was still holding on to his beliefs.

Colonel Thomas didn't let Major Williams' laughter ruin their friendship. He respected Major Williams and counted on him through this time. Major Williams said, "Sir, the asteroid is picking up speed. We're estimating it will strike at 5:45 now."

Colonel Thomas looked at his watch. It was a few minutes after four. He thought it was almost over now. He responded, "Thank you, Major. All we can do is continue to wait. If you want to leave, I will understand."

Major Williams replied, "No sir. I'm here until the end."

Colonel Thomas nodded his head and turned back to the picture of his wife.

***

Evangelist Jones and Reverend Collins scrambled to make a report on the Bishop Carroll story. Brittney was helping them with the story because she was good with computers.
Evangelist Jones said, "Okay, I want to finish the story with this scripture. Hang on a second and let me get ready."

Brittney was running the camera and said, "Ready?"

Evangelist Jones replied, "Okay, go ahead."

Brittney said, "On three; one, two, three."

Evangelist Jones said, "And let me conclude by quoting

372

first John chapter 4 verse number 5."

"And it says, '*They that are from the world and therefore speak from the viewpoint of the world, and the world listens to them. We are from God, and whoever knows God listens to us; but whoever is not from God does not listen to us. This is how we recognize the Spirit of truth and the spirit of falsehood.*'"

She continued, "The Bible is clear that there will be deceivers amongst us. You have to watch and listen, then decide for yourself. The video tape of the exploits of Bishop Carroll shows he was not of God, and that he was of the world. Now you decide."

After thirty minutes, they had a good tape of the story and they were ready to upload it to the Internet. Brittney found a news site that was accepting stories about the end of the world, and they all agreed that this was the place to put it.

Evangelist Jones said, "Well, this is the story that will probably save the lives of many. But that's only if they see it, and believe they have been deceived. Before Brittney could upload the video, they all heard a loud voice shouting from in front of the building.

Reverend Collins asked, "What now?"

Evangelist Jones looked out the window and answered, "Oh my God!"

II

Evangelist Jones was shocked when she saw Jessica on her knees with her hands tied behind her back. Her hair was disheveled, her face a mutilated mess. She looked as though she had endured a severe beating.

She couldn't blame her for telling the Bishop where she was, but now the Bishop just stood there, smug, pointing a gun to his wife's head. Evangelist Jones heard the Bishop shouting, "If you upload that video, I will kill her. Don't test me, because if you watched the video, you know I'm capable."

Evangelist Jones turned and said, "Don't send it. He has a gun to Jessica's head."

Brittney asked, "Why does he care? The world is going to end in an hour or so. Why does he care so much?"

Evangelist Jones answered, "He is severely vain. He doesn't want any negative press about himself, and obviously he doesn't even care that the world is ending. He's so arrogant; he probably believes he'll survive the impact."

Brittney asked, "And you worked closely with someone like that?"

Reverend Collins interrupted, "Britt, don't…"

Evangelist Jones cut him off, "No Reverend, she's right.
I should have seen it years ago, but I was caught up in the
fire this man portrayed for the Lord. I thought he was
the greatest minister of the gospel, ever. I was fooled."

She continued after a brief pause, "I have to go out there
and talk to him."

Reverend Collins said, "No, that maniac might kill you."

Evangelist Jones replied, "No, he won't. There're too
many witnesses here for him to kill us all."

The President came in the room and asked, "What's
going on now?"

Reverend Collins answered, "That's Bishop Carroll out
there, and he wants the video."

Evangelist Jones joined in, "I'm going out there to stop
him from killing Jessica."

President Murphy asked, "Isn't that his wife?"

Evangelist Jones answered, "Yes, but he's that crazy; trust
me."

President Murphy said, "Oh I do. I saw the video."

They all turned as Bishop Carroll yelled, "Somebody better tell me something, or she's dead!"

Evangelist Jones shouted back at him, "I'm coming out!"

She then turned to everyone in the room, saying, "Pray for me."

She calmly walked out of the room and toward the main entrance to the church. She was nervous, but she believed God had her back. She could hear people whispering as she readied herself to walk through the door.

She smiled as she heard Wendy say, "She's a true warrior for God. I totally respect that woman."

Vanessa yelled, "We're praying for you, Evangelist."

Evangelist Jones turned to them and smiled. She looked at each of their faces and saw every emotion from fear to love. She turned and proceeded through the door. As soon as she walked out, she saw Jessica shaking her head 'no'.

She didn't know why, but she wasn't about to let Jessica die. As she came out and looked to her left and then her right, she saw why Jessica was shaking her head.

I

It was 5:15, and the asteroid was entering Earth's atmosphere. Colonel Thomas knew that most of the population of the world didn't know, and didn't care that it was going to strike earlier than first anticipated. Major Williams called him into the situation room.

Major Williams hurriedly said to Colonel Thomas, "Sir, you've got to see this!"

Colonel Thomas ran into the room and asked, "What am I looking at?"

Major Williams answered, "Sir, it's the asteroid."

Colonel Thomas said with a puzzled look, "It looks different."

Major Williams continued, "That's because it's losing density. You see, we have been trying to destroy the asteroid with our nukes. We've been trying to blow it up. But it appears Earth's atmosphere is doing the job for us."

"Instead of blowing it up, the atmosphere is melting it. As it goes through the atmosphere, it's getting smaller. If my calculations are correct the impact won't destroy the world! It'll cause some damage, but Earth will survive!"

Colonel Thomas stood perplexed, and didn't know what he should do. He wondered if he should track down the President, or let the world see as it happens.

***

Reverend Collins shouted at Brittney, "What are you doing?"

Brittney proudly replied, "I uploaded the file."

Reverend Collins said, "Why? He's going to kill both of them now."

Brittney answered, "He's going to kill us all anyway."

***

Evangelist Jones stood there as she saw two men, one on each side of her ready to shoot her, and enter the building. Bishop Carroll had deceived them again. He was going to kill her and storm the church.

Evangelist Jones just stood and prayed. She said to Bishop Carroll, "You're truly a deceiver."

Bishop Carroll smiled and said, "Evangelist, I'm tired of you. You need to die. Goodbye, my friend."

Evangelist Jones slowly closed her eyes. She could swear

she heard music playing softly; she knew her life was now over. Quietly she whispered, "Jesus, I give my all to you." Suddenly the sound of two guns firing filled the air.

*****

Bishop Carroll could not believe his eyes. Both of his men were lying on the ground. Each one was shot to death by the other one. Nothing was left of Evangelist Jones and Jessica, except their clothes. The Bishop looked at the two piles of clothes and then at his men. He shouted, "Nooooooooo!"

He ran in the church and saw no one inside. There was nothing there but piles of clothes everywhere. He ran to the cafeteria, then to the study rooms, then to the offices. No one was there. Everyone inside the church was gone. He ran back to the sanctuary and fell to his knees. Bishop Carroll cried out, "Father what have I done!"

Through his tears he thought he saw a figure standing in front of him. He pleaded, "Father, please don't leave me. I repent. Father I repent all of my sins!"

He heard the figure say, "I know you not." The figure turned and walked away. With each step, it faded slowly into the distance. Bishop Carroll was lying on the floor as he continued to sob.

*****

In the situation room, the remaining officers were standing around wondering what happened to Colonel Thomas. In the wink of an eye, Major Williams saw his friend disappear, leaving nothing but a pile of clothes. He stood there in disbelief, staring at the uniform once worn by the Colonel. Major Williams said out loud, "You were right all along, my friend. Congratulations!"

***

In the Zone, the party was still going strong when someone pointed to the sky. The asteroid could be seen from their vantage point, but it wasn't as big as first reported. Linda stood on the street watching it. She had her day of sex, drugs, and alcohol, and now she watched as she thought it was about to end. She started to cry.

On the big screen television behind her, a news reporter was on the air saying, "Something has happened! Millions of people all over the world have disappeared and nothing was left but their clothes!"

Linda turned quickly from the asteroid after hearing the report. She stared at the television in disbelief. Her friend was right, and now she was left behind. Vanessa had turned her life around and spent the last day in church, while Linda spent her last day in the Zone. As she stood there, she could see some of the people looking at her.

Their faces had changed from normal faces to demonic looking faces. They were pointing and laughing at her.

One woman yelled to her, "Hey, you're one of us now!"

Reports of Earth's survival poured into news outlets all over the world. Linda's eyes continued to fill with tears. Everyone else in the Zone continued to party like nothing ever changed.

She heard DJ Fever shout, "If you're still here, ya missed the boat! So, Linda, you might as well parrrrrrrrrrrty!" She heard him let out a laugh that curled her skin. Linda stood up, turned, and slowly walked down the street. She didn't know where she was going, but she wanted to get away from the Zone. She wanted to get away from the one distraction that cost her salvation.

Epilog

I'm sitting here at the desk of my good friend. A week ago, his faith proved to be right. Now me and millions of others are left behind.

I found his letter and decided to finish it. The world realized shortly after the asteroid stuck, that most of it melted in Earth's atmosphere, and the strike didn't destroy the world like first reported. Many lost their lives, but it was not the Extinction Level Event we first imagined it would be.

My friend, President Murphy, and millions like him, kept their faith in God, and their reward, we can only assume, is that they are in Heaven rejoicing. Those of us who have been left behind face a struggle.

We will face many obstacles, but if we keep our faith, it is said that we can also make it to Heaven. I reflect on the final 27 hours before the asteroid strike, and now I can clearly see how the devil fooled many of us, myself included.

He sent a prominent man of the cloth to us to tell us that the Bible was filled with fairy tales…that was a lie.

He set up a place for thousands in each city to do drugs, have sex, drink alcohol, and commit any sin they wished…that was temptation.

He told us that the world was going to be destroyed, and it wasn't in accordance with the Word of God…that was a test of our faith.

We had others who stood tall in their beliefs. We had the Gospel Today Show and Evangelist Mattie Jones…we didn't listen.

We had other prominent men of the cloth come out and retort what Bishop Carroll said…we still didn't listen.

Most of all, we were all told of Jesus and his Word…and again…we didn't listen.

I sit here now reading Romans 14:11. It says "As surely as I live,' says the Lord, 'every knee will bow before me; every tongue will confess to God.'" A tear falls from my face as I realize now that this scripture is and was always true. I should have kept my faith.

Signed,
Joe W. Simpson,
Acting President of the United States of America.

Somewhere in Syria…

Anas Sultan was speaking to his assistant Yesoph Barkat, "It has happened. The church has been raptured and now my reign shall begin." Yesoph replied, "What need I do master?" Anas answered, "Now is time to negotiate a peace with Israel thus fulfilling the prophecy." Yesoph asked, "But master the prophecy also says you will lose to the Christ." Anas looked at him coldly and responded, "I will change the outcome!"

Continued in "The Rise of Evil" coming in 2015!"

Bible Lesson

Hebrews 11:1 says, "Now faith is the substance of things hoped for, the evidence of things not seen."
27 Hours is a Christian faith based story. The story shows the struggle and test of those who believed that the Word of God is correct and will not change. They also believed that God would take care of them and protect them in their trials of life.

The woman who visited Wendy is a dramatic illustration of the Holy Spirit helping us along our journey. We don't know the Holy Spirit is protecting and guiding us all the time, but as Christians, we trust the Spirit.

The Holy Spirit does not appear as a person all the time. Sometimes things that appear as obstacles or barriers in our life are there to prevent us from making a mistake, or to protect us from evil or harm.

For instance, I was stopped at a stop light in Washington, DC one day. The light changed to green, but no one on either side moved. If you live in Washington, DC, you know this is a rare occurrence.

I can't speak for the others that day, but I felt a strange resistance that didn't allow me to hit the gas pedal. There was no music playing in the car, and I didn't hear anything. After a few moments, a car came roaring through the intersection at about 90 miles per hour.

Behind the car, three police cars, traveling at the same speed, was attempting to catch the driver.

I believe that resistance I felt was the Holy Spirit protecting me from harm that day. If anyone had entered that intersection that day, they probably would have suffered serious injury or worst, died.

Even when I was unsaved, I believed the Holy Spirit protected me from harm or danger. Once, before I accepted Jesus Christ as my Lord and Savior, I was riding down the interstate in California with a good friend of mine. We'd both been drinking at the time, and consequently we both fell asleep. That wasn't good.

However, we both woke up at the same time, and my friend was able to pull the car back onto the road. The car was an inch away from striking the railing. Although again not in physical form, the Holy Spirit saved me and my friend that night by waking us up just in time for my friend to pull the car back onto the road.

Keeping one's faith is a test in and of itself. The trials of life will certainly come upon you and test your faith. Vanessa clearly saw that she needed to change her life, but the trials of her past life continued to try and bring her down. She decided to keep her faith and not give in to those trials.

The best thing she did was go to a place where she was surrounded with people who believed as she did. The others at the Living Word kept her pointed in the right direction through every trial.

In our lives, going to church, not just on Sunday, but throughout the week, is what keeps us strong. We have to be surrounded by like minds, so when the trials of life come upon us, we have a support system that can help us stand against them. Vanessa kept her faith in the midst of everything, and God forgave her and she was saved.

27 Hours is an example of life in a microcosm. It shows examples of people staying faithful to what they believe in, and others who changed for the better, or for the worst.

The scenes with Satan and his henchmen using their demonic illusions to entice believers to change are evident all over the world. Although not so dramatic in our day to day life, there are forces attacking us as we go through our journey.

In my life, I came to Christ and it seemed everything started coming against me. I have many good Christian brothers and sisters surrounding me, helping me keep my faith as strong as possible. It is virtually impossible to remain faithful in God and be surrounded by nothing but nonbelievers.

The greatest example of faith I have for myself is the time when doctors told me there was little chance I would ever have a child. Now I say unto you, I have a little boy who my wife gave birth to in 2005. She was so faithful, God delivered unto us a child, and that made my faith stronger.

Bless All Who Read This book!

Gerald C. Anderson, Sr.
Author, 27 Hours

Made in the USA
San Bernardino, CA
13 July 2014